LATIN AMERICA

Enlarged Edition

LATIN AMERICA

A Sociocultural
Interpretation

Enlarged Edition

Julius Rivera
The University of Texas at El Paso

WITHDRAWN

IRVINGTON PUBLISHERS, INC.

New York

Halsted Press Division
JOHN WILEY & SONS, Inc.
New York London Toronto Sydney

Copyright © 1978 by
IRVINGTON PUBLISHERS, INC.

Copyright © 1971 by
MEREDITH CORPORATION

Distributed by HALSTED PRESS
A division of JOHN WILEY & SONS, Inc. New York

Library of Congress Cataloging in Publication Data

Rivera, Julius.
    Latin America : a sociocultural interpretation.

    Includes bibliographies and index.
    1. Latin America—Social conditions—1945- 2. Latin America—Civilization. 3. Latin America—Politics and government—1948- I. Title.
HN110.5.A8R54   1978   309.1'8'003   77-27271
ISBN 0-470-99391-X
ISBN 0-470-99392-8 pbk.

PRINTED IN THE UNITED STATES OF AMERICA

In Memoriam

Custodio Rivera Bermeo
Marcelina Orozco Esterlin de Rivera

To

My sister, Nelly Rivera Orozco

Linda
Lisa Carol, Julian Lynn
Marcos Gerard

Preface to
the Enlarged Edition

Since the first edition of this book was published in 1971, materials on Latin America have flooded from publishing houses. The quality of the materials has improved dramatically. Latin America as a civilization has developed a more differentiated identity and, at least on the surface, businesses are run more independently and more efficiently. Under these conditions, arriving at an intelligent synthesis and a meaningful interpretation has become easier. There are today better analyses of the Latin American scene, and both data collection and theoretical views are more integrated. This is not to say that the book needs to be rewritten. On the contrary, I believe that the fundamental premises enunciated in it are as solid as ever and that the direction indicated in 1971 for Latin American development at all levels is still sound today.

For this reason, what I have done in this Postscript is to discuss some areas that were neither fully analyzed nor introduced in the original work. One of course wishes to have more time and space to extend the discussion. As circumstances are now, I hope that the synthesis offered is not only useful but also original. For example, as far as I know, the discussion of trade areas has not been presented in this form by other writers. This is also true of the typification and theoretical integration of the multinationals. I think that this contribution, although short, is significant.

The selection of points to be emphasized is naturally arbitrary. There is no "objective" criterion on which the choice can be based and there should not be one. It is time that honest investigators stop claiming objectivity as if their efforts to be accurate and correct needed apologies. In fact, what must be realized is that in studying human affairs, objectivity has to be transcended. The interpretation presented here is intended to read the Latin American realities as they evolve and as they could be altered for the benefit of all, not as an exercise in intellectual narcissism. In other words, my interpretation is definitely committed and unalienated.

All of this means that the volume is still intended as a contribution to the betterment of human understanding. In this vein I wish to express my appreciation to my brother Carlos Enrique and my cousin Marco Tulio Sterling for recent information, and to my new editor Ronald Cohen for his skillful guidance.

Julius Rivera
El Paso, Texas
January 1978

Contents

Acknowledgments

Intellectual debts are perhaps impossible to pay. Therefore, my teachers (especially W. H. Form and C. P. Loomis) and classmates at Michigan State (1953–1956), my colleagues and students at Texas Tech, the University of Chile and the *Católica* of Chile in Santiago, California State College at Hayward, and the University of Houston certainly deserve some form of recognition. Challenge has always forced my rethinking. The University of Houston provided for some financial assistance through the Office of Research and the Binational Fulbright Commission helped me likewise, especially by granting me, through Mr. Joaquin Barcelo, the Executive Secretary, almost complete freedom of movement while teaching two courses in Chile. It was a most rewarding intellectual experience. My editor, Dr. Arthur Vidich, has been generous in his guiding, and so has been my wife, Linda, in her expecting. I would not like to apologize for my errors, or anticipate praise for my achievements. I have just written candidly.

J. R.

Introduction

Whoever becomes acquainted with Latin America soon comes to realize the tremendous complexity of the continent. To the geographic intricacy, one has to add the ethnic variety, the cultural heterogeneity, the political scramble, the religious mixture, the linguistic plurality, the multiplicity of nations, the institutional mosaic, the social class criss-cross, and the economic puzzle; all in ferment. And this list is not exhaustive. The present work does not intend to explain this complexity. It only intends to pull some threads so as to make visible the basic patterns of the amazing and elusive fabric. In brief, what I intend to do is to interpret Latin America for the interested American student.

My claim to the right to play this role is based not on my having been born, raised, and partly educated in that continent, nor on my having studied, lived and taught in the United States for sixteen years, or being a sociologist with a special interest in Latin America; rather, my claim lies in the fact that without a choice on my part I have been placed at the crossroads of two main cultural streams. I have been confronted with two contrasting solutions to the same fundamental human equation and feel that this has given me a special viewpoint from which to write this book.

I have studied the United States and Latin America for many years, and I have studied them with passion. In other words, I have made every effort to understand them both intellectually and emotionally by placing them against each other in order to perceive the differences and the common denominators. As a consequence, I have found myself, a true marginal man, somewhat alienated from both of them. The "good" Americans will not understand this; neither will the "good" Latin Americans.

My readings of material on Latin America published in the United States have been extensive and my thinking intensive. As may be expected, I have not ignored Latin American writers. Objective information on Latin America is scarce. Many books have been published, of course, but most of them are quilts of colorful but unintegrated information. Is it that there is no common denominator to Latin America? I think so.

There are plenty of recent works on Mexico, Brazil, and Argentina; some on Colombia, Chile, and Venezuela; and fewer on the remaining countries, except perhaps Cuba which has suddenly become so important. However, good attempts at interpretation of Latin America are lacking. I realize that social scientists are busy gathering facts and that interpretations are not fashionable. Should one wait until all the facts are in? In the meantime those who have to vote and those who have to make decisions in America will continue to be guided by disconnected and often dislocated facts.

In selecting topics for any work one has to be arbitrary to a great extent. One's limitations originate in the field of specialization, in the amount of reliable information available, in the time allotted to the task, and even in one's preferences and prejudices. Some authors have with great wisdom limited themselves to a country or two, and/or to one or two topics. T. Lynn Smith, Charles Wagley, R. J. Alexander, K. H. Silvert, Edwin Lieuwen, I. L. Horowitz, J. J. Johnson, are the names in this group that first come to mind. Many others have been even more specific in their concerns. The bibliographies at the ends of each chapter list them.

Latin American sociologists seem to have followed the same course of action. They are too busy trying to find answers to the problems they face, anxious to grasp a reality that seems to escape them, even though it exists right under their noses in their native lands. Some well known names may be mentioned, such as that of Mendieta y Nuñez in Mexico, George Hill (an American) in Venezuela, Fals-Borda in Colombia, McClean-Estenos in Peru, Germani and di Tella in Argentina, and Gilberto Freyre in Brazil.

Perhaps other disciplines such as Political Science and Anthro-

pology can claim better knowledge of Latin America. In Political
Science four names have already been listed, Alexander, Silvert,
Lieuwen, Johnson. In Anthropology to Wagley three others may
be added: John P. Gillin, Ralph Beals and Richard Adams. Julian
Stewart and Sol Tax have been interested primarily in Latin
American Indians, as many other students of Latin America have
been; Melville Herskovitz has been interested in Negroes and
Mulattoes. No well known economist has been interested in Latin
America except in an indirect way. The ones who have written
about Latin America have been trying to construct models that
would fit "underdeveloped" countries. In fact, all they have done
is remodel frames previously applied to the American economy.
Thus, they have ignored the idiosyncrasies that may lie at the
sources of change in the continent. Rostow, Berle, and Galbraith
are good examples. Incidentally, these three have been Presidential
Advisors. Others come to mind also: Hagen, Hoselitz, Hirshman.

Some Latin American economists are internationally known,
such as Raul Prebish, Felipe Herrera, Celso Furtado, Anibal Pinto,
Victor Urquidi, and Jacques Chonchol. As might be expected, they
often have clashed with the American economists.

The view of Latin America in the present work is a social and
cultural one. The emphasis will be on social relationships and the
values and norms guiding these relationships. Since the scope has
to be limited as suggested above, only the most basic sociocultural
phenomena will be treated, and some only very indirectly. For
example, the response of the people to the physical conditions of
the various areas of the continent has been almost entirely ignored
and only passing remarks are made on the economy.

The thread running through the network of the sociocultural
configuration presented is the Latin American search for prestige.
It is my contention that this characteristic constitutes the thrust
that is felt throughout the whole Latin American scene, although
I do not offer it as an explanation of every event. This thread, however, will not be completely visible until the very end of the book.

The Latin Americans inherited the dismembered elements
still pulsating, of two great traditions rooted in the autochthonous
distant past: the Inca and the Aztec (the former in the South, the
latter in the North), plus the truncated bodies of hundreds of

smaller subcultures dispersed the length and the width of the land from New Mexico to Tierra del Fuego and from the Pacific to the Atlantic. The two monolithic societies just mentioned were only the largest pyramids of power that had crystallized. The whole continent was boiling and every crest of power was also a summit of prestige.

When the Iberians arrived, they brought with themselves two new status layers to become the top and the bottom of whatever society would result. Then, after three centuries of scrambling, the Latin Americans inherited from the Iberians parallel status systems topped with aristocratic pretensions, some real, some fictitious, but all split and all hungry for prestige. And the prestige rush has never stopped since.

Sex and the family are mechanisms of prestige accretion, and so are experience, knowledge, and education, joining the clergy and the military and participating in full armor in the political joust. In fact, wealth is often just a step to power, which is in turn the quickest path to prestige. Every Latin American is a Quixote, and I have the feeling that he wants to remain one.

This, in synthesis, is the content of this work. At least, this has been the intended meaning. There is only one final note to be added. It is a note of appreciation to my Destiny that has placed me at the crossroads of two great traditions: Saxon America has set my feet on the ground; Latin America continues seeding my dreams.

Capitals and Major Cities

Latin American Population Statistics

Country	Area in Sq. Mi.	Pop. Mid 1967	Est. Pop. 1980	G.N.P. 1965
Argentina	1,072,068	23,031	27,580	17,526
Bolivia	424,163	3,801	4,554	524
Brazil	3,286,473	85,655	122,992	21,420
Chile	286,400	8,925	12,912	4,730
Cuba	44,278	7,200	9,100	2,751
Colombia	439,513	19,215	28,289	3,947
Costa Rica	19,563	1,594	2,728	537
Dominican Rep.	18,703	3,889	6,174	700
Ecuador	104,506	5,508	8,473	1,053
El Salvador	8,083	3,149	4,910	800
Guatamela	42,040	4,717	7,191	1,349
Haiti	10,714	4,577	6,919	280
Honduras	43,277	2,455	3,771	500
Mexico	759,530	45,671	72,392	19,128
Nicaragua	53,668	1,783	2,824	506
Panama	29,208	1,329	1,987	548
Paraguay	157,047	2,161	3,361	400
Peru	494,293	12,385	18,527	2,816
Trinidad-Tobago	1,980	1,027	1,551	628
Uruguay	72,172	2,783	3,255	1,325
Venezuela	347,029	9,352	14,848	7,465

COUNTRY	% OF TOTAL GOVT. EXPENDITURE			% OF LITERACY	% OF URBAN POP.	LIFE EXPECTANCY AT BIRTH	INFANT DEATH RATE	DEATH RATE
	Public Health	Military	Education					
Argentina	5.4	12.0	15.3	91.4	73.7	67.0	59.3	8.2
Bolivia	2.8	11.0	27.5	32.1	35.0	50.0	106.5	14.1
Brazil	3.3	21.0	7.4	61.0	46.3	56.0	105.0	13.0
Chile	10.1	10.0	18.3	83.6	68.2	59.0	101.9	10.0
Cuba	5.0		20.0		55.0	66.0	37.7	6.5
Colombia	4.0	24.4	12.4	72.9	52.0	59.3	79.0	9.4
Costa Rica	6.9	1.0	25.8	84.4	34.5	66.0	69.9	7.7
Dominican Rep.	9.1	14.1	13.5	64.5	30.3	52.0	81.1	7.1
Ecuador	2.8	15.5	13.5	67.5	36.0	54.0	93.0	11.7
El Salvador	11.4	10.1	22.9	49.0	38.5	52.0	61.7	9.9
Guatemala	8.2	11.0	14.5	37.9	33.6	47.0	91.5	16.6
Haiti	12.0	25.7	12.6	10.5	12.2	45.0	17.2	22.8
Honduras	6.0	8.0	23.0	45.0	23.2	49.0	41.2	8.6
Mexico	7.7	10.0	14.3	65.4	50.7	63.2	62.9	9.6
Nicaragua	5.8	15.4	16.5	49.8	40.9	69.0	51.6	7.3
Panama	12.8		24.3	76.6	41.5	61.0	44.7	7.4
Paraguay	4.4	23.1	15.4	74.3	35.4	59.4	84.3	10.6
Peru	5.4	19.1	29.7	61.1	47.4	54.0	109.9	16.7
Trinidad-Tobago	7.5		13.3	88.7	40.0	64.0	35.3	6.9
Uruguay	8.5	8.5	22.0	90.3	62.5	66.0	46.6	6.8
Venezuela	8.5	10.1	12.8	76.2	80.0	71.0	42.5	9.0

Adapted from Inter-American Development Bank, Social Trust Fund, Seventh Annual Report, passim, *United Nations Yearbook, 1967, 1968* and *World Mark Encyclopedia of the Nations.*

1

The Latin American
World View

Two historical and cultural currents remain distinguishable in Latin
America in spite of all efforts to produce a synthesis: the European
and the Indian. Even the *mestizo** groups that have resulted from
the miscegenation of the Iberian and the Indian remain culturally
ambivalent, appearing sometimes European, sometimes Indian. In
the pages that follow, I hope to elucidate the extent of this
ambivalence.

For the Iberian and for the Indian of the 15th and 16th
centuries, the physical universe was neither changing nor changeable. It could only be manipulated. The Peninsulares manipulated
it through faith, prayer, and organizations; the Indian through
sacrifices, rituals, and submission..

Neither was the social universe changeable. Man just moved
in it as a spider on the cobweb. Social mobility was not really
sought; it occurred, however, through the established mechanisms,
the military, the clergy, or suddenly-acquired wealth and mystic
revelation. The status network remained stable and the mobile
individual acquired the characteristics of people of his new status,
forgetting his past and expecting other people to forget it also.

As with the rest of the universe, man's worth was in *being*
not in *becoming.* Even his *becoming,* when it happened, was understood as a series of *beings.* The best expression of his being was

---

* Foreign words in italics are defined in the Glossary.

1

his *palabra*,* its shield was his honor, its crowning his pride in the
mask of a gentleman's behavior *(caballerosidad)*.[14]

La palabra was for the Spaniard, and still is for the Latin
American, the beginning of all things.

> In principio erat verbum
> et verbum erat apud deum
> et verbum erat deus.

La palabra was God, or at least it was God's expression. It
was a divine gift to be able to talk and talk for hours, as if possessed by a deity. To be a leader one had to be a speaker. It is not
what one does that counts, but what one says, especially if it is well
said. This is a special Latin American characteristic. A Latin
American's *honor* is his *palabra*.[14] Therefore, his deeds neither
add to nor detract from what a man has said. They may, or may
not, follow. By the same token, his *orgullo* (pride) was—and still
is—in his *palabra*. You are not supposed to remind him today of
what he said yesterday. Remember that his being is a series of beings: he may not be today what he was yesterday. Thus, a man
is true to himself not if he says today what he said yesterday, but
only if what he says today reflects his today's being.

A man has to speak as often as possible, even to himself if
he does not have an audience, and when he speaks to himself he
does so as to an audience.

His speech is not merely a communication of ideas; it is giving
of a part of himself because a man's ideas are his self. Thus, for
the Latin American, speaking is not just an exchange, but an
attempt to convince, to proselytize and also not to be convinced.
This is one of the reasons why in Latin America religious and
political ideas have brought about bloodshed. If a man cannot convince another, a gun might.

Ideas and emotions are not separated. They never have been.
Your self is a totality. Thus deep feelings tie together whatever a
man may be.

---

* *La palabra* (the word) is often also the distinguishing characteristic
of a man versus a woman as expressed in this proverb: "El hombre por la
lengua y la mujer por la pierna"; a man's worth is in his tongue, a woman's
in her legs.

A man's soul *(el alma)* is all this plus his cultural heritage: values, symbol-meanings, beliefs. However, each man views them from a different perspective; consensus, therefore, is not to be expected. What is good for one person is not meant to be good for everyone else. Symbol-meanings convey varying ideas to various men. Beliefs are subject to the interpretations required by the individual's life situation.

Each man is two personalities. He shares his inner, private personality with his family and his very intimate friends; he shares his outer personality with everyone else. These two personalities not only are frequently at odds, but they are not supposed to coincide. *La dignidad de la persona* (the dignity of the person) that Latin Americans cherish so much does not rest on consistency.[2] Moreover, an insult is nothing more than the expression of that discovery. What is said on stage may contradict what is said backstage, but no one is expected to make explicit this contradiction.

Lest this be interpreted as a form of hypocrisy, it should be kept in mind that a man's personalities correspond to the two worlds in which he lives. For the Latin American, his inner world ends with his relatives and friends; the outer world begins afterwards. These two worlds do not speak the same language, are not made of the same stuff, do not share the same symbols, do not reflect the same realities, and are not governed by the same laws. Perhaps this explains the alleged Latin American disregard for the law. *Se obedece pero no se cumple* (laws are accepted but not fulfilled); moreover, a law does not apply to the lawmaker, and a lawmaker is not just himself. He is himself plus the members of his inner world. Thus, laws should be interpreted accordingly.

The physical universe is not a part of a man's outer world. Man is in communion with the universe. Sunrise and sunset, mountains and streams, flowers and birds live in his inner world. Even time is man. It is not to be measured, because there is no measure for man. This is the other meaning of *la dignidad*. Do not speed because you are running man. Moreover, space is where a man is, not what lies between two men. Thus communication, being an exchange of roles, implies for the Latin American physical proximity. When speaking he will move closer and closer to you; he will move where you are with the hope that his ideas (his self)

4 Latin America: A Sociocultural Interpretation

will be where yours are also. This is particularly true of the intimacies between man and woman (see Chapter 3).

If a man's *palabra* coincides with another man's ideas, they embrace each other as if to draw each other into their inner worlds. If others join in, then a *caudillo* has arisen and the future will be a struggle between two inner worlds, but not between two *caudillos** as it has been assumed. The same analysis could apply to the Latin American's *personalismo*. There is, however, something more to it. To use *personalismo* in the common meaning of the term, as an explanation for Latin America's political and religious upheavals, is to ignore how easily Latin Americans shift loyalties as they adopt new ideas or experience new moods or are faced with new combinations of ideas and moods. When they follow, Latin Americans are following themselves; if they do not see themselves in the movement they abandon it. This is what makes change in Latin America so unpredictable. It is true that in every struggle there is a principle involved. Principles, nonetheless, are not eternal; only man is, man as a species; humanity, that is; and beyond that, being, existence. In the final analysis, the Latin American zest for life is the only enduring thing.[24]

What, then, is death? Death is the beginning of a new cycle. It is not much different from birth. They are just two expressions of the same phenomenon. The two are adjacent links in an unknown chain. Death is as much a mystery as life. Whatever difference there is (*¿quién sabe?*) between life and death is a matter of awareness; it is, in a way, accidental. "¿Qué es morir? Cerrar los ojos y no volverlos a abrir." (What is to die? To close your eyes never to open them again.)[23]

Ultimately, what is significant about life for the Latin American is not how one lives, but living. By contrast, what is significant about death is not dying, but how one dies. Dying is significant because a man's last words are the last sentences of a life-long speech. This seems to be the traditional meaning of a *testamento:* gathering the members of your inner world around your death bed to seal the communion of the living and the dead with words that

* Since the configuration of the *caudillo's* group is so similar to the configuration of the family and the community, this point will not be clear until the Latin American family and community have been discussed.

will not be forgotten. This characteristic is not Indian at all. An Indian dies alone, in silence. His group is not expected to express sorrow but endurance and joy, both mixed in the music played at the wake. For the Indian, death is not a departure, but a return.

Dying is also meaningful when accompanied by bloodshed. It does not matter whose blood. Blood is the symbol of ultimate dedication; it is something sacramental. You give your blood to your progeny, to your loved ones, to your faith, to your fatherland. Bloodshed is the closest expression of your animal past, and is second only to sex. As a matter of fact, sexual intercourse is a transmission of blood. It is an act of death and life.

Seen from this perspective, the Latin American emphasis on sex and warfare makes perfect sense. It may be sad to realize this phenomenon, especially if one is fighting for a "better" world. Nevertheless, this perspective helps in understanding the Latin American love for tragedy—which is a tragedy. The Latin American seems to move on the edge of life and death and does not seem to care which way he falls. But when nothing bridges the shores of the inner and the outer world, what can one expect? Let it be remembered that the physical universe belongs to a man's inner world (an Indian heritage) and that death might be just a return.

Living, therefore, (and dying) is a gamble. It is a matter of destiny. Man's destiny has been designed in advance; not necessarily by God but by forces hidden in nature—physical nature, man's nature. Man has no control. Destiny—with a capital D—is also an all-penetrating force, the source and genesis of all individual destinies. At this point Christian and Indian cosmologies meet.

A *macho* gambles with Destiny, ready to win or to lose. He gambles with Death, he gambles with God. A burning love affair is a victory over Destiny; a revolution a victory over Death; sin a victory over God. When the three come together, man has completed his fulfillment. This is the essential meaning of *machismo*. It is not just to be tough, to take risks, to threat, to drink, to flirt, or to dispute.[11]

Now one can understand why the Latin American has been called idealistic. It is not that he does not care about profits and money. He certainly does. He cherishes quick profits and quick money so he can go on gambling with Destiny, Death, and God. His is a subtle materialism often centered around the flesh *(la carne)*. In every instance what counts most is the human contact. This is the cementing element in his inner world. Babies are held and hugged; friends are embraced, patted on their shoulders, and touched; lovers are bonded together. It used to be quite customary to unfold paper ribbons *(serpentinas)* into the air on fiesta days toward the admired or the loved ones.

The preceding also explains why the Latin American is not thrifty. Why should he be? Deprivation today in order to have something tomorrow does not make any sense. "A cada día le basta su propio afán"; each day unto itself. In the Latin American world view, certainly man is being, but being today weakens his probability of being tomorrow. In his mind he has already had his share.

To the Latin American, man's destiny is full of sorrow *(tristeza)*, which is often indistinguishable from suffering *(dolor)*. This is also his Indian heritage. Hope—and happiness—is just a veil over sorrow. Chocano has put this beautifully: "Sobre el fango se tiende la verdura, como sobre un dolor una esperanza." In this vein, uncertainty is man's lot also. Not only the morrow is unpredictable, but everything significant: nature, rain, harvesting, birth, loyalty, and love. Ultimately, one cannot trust anything. However, a man can sing his sorrows away into the night, over the hills, walking alone through the forest, or walking along with other pilgrims toward the sacred shrine where the unpredictable may happen.

Sorrow, suffering, and uncertainty are not the only ghosts haunting the Latin American mind. There is one more to which frequent reference is made in folklore; it is oblivion, *el olvido*. Latin Americans fear oblivion and defy death; they even welcome death but refuse to be forgotten. They constantly ask you to remember, not to forget them. It may be that fear of oblivion is a search for immortality. Certainly oblivion is a form of destruction of identity. It must be related to the century-old threat to the Indian heritage about which Latin Americans have been terribly ambivalent. The main source of this ambivalence is of course *el mestizaje.*[1] As it will be shown in the next chapter, more than one third of the Latin American population is *mestizo* by blood, and many more by identification. From this characteristic many Latin Americans derive at the same time inferiority and superiority. When they look at their Indian present, they feel inferior. When they look at their Indian past, in depth, they feel superior. The memories of the Peninsula are mostly ignored. Latin American societies have moved from revolutions to submission with most surprising regularity and have not found their synthesis. Even as individuals, Latin Americans have shown this pendulum-like behavior. One would like to exempt Uruguay, Argentina, and Chile, where there is little trace of *mestizaje.* The complex is expressed here in an olympic arrogance, often mixed with bitterness, resulting from another source also found in the United States of America. It is the youth of their traditions and the fresh memories of an adventurer's past not purified yet by history that tinges their behavior. Overdeveloped teenagers, they are aware of their strength and still conscious of their immaturity. As will be shown later, the ethnic variations have produced in some Latin American countries a quasi-caste system from which parallel social classes have resulted, adding to the confusion and complexities of the societies. Thus, Latin America appears split both vertically and horizontally: vertically, by unredeemed ethnic differences of which people do not dare to be proud; horizontally, by a fermenting class system too fluid to be thought acceptable.

References and Selected Bibliography

1. Adams, Richard N. "Cultural Components of Central America." *American Anthropologist.* Vol. 58, No. 5, 1956.
2. Adams, Richard N., et al. *Social Change in Latin America Today.* (Harper & Row, New York). 1960.
3. Alba, Victor. *Las Ideas sociales contemporáneas en Mexico.* (First Edition). (Fondo de Cultura Económica, Mexico). 1960.
4. Alba, Victor. *The Mexicans: The Making of a Nation.* (Frederick A. Praeger, New York). 1967.
5. Albornoz, Orlando. *Valores sociales en la educación venezolana: Una investigación sociológica.* (La Imprenta Universitaria, Caracas, Venezuela). 1962.

8   *Latin America: A Sociocultural Interpretation*

6. Almoina, José. *Rumbes Heterodoxos en Mexico.* (Universidad de Santo Domingo). 1947.
7. Altamira, Rafael. *Los Elementos de la Civilización y del Carácter Españoles.* (Losada, Buenos Aires). 1950.
8. Alvarado García, Ernesto. "El significado de la cultura Hispano-americana." *Avales, Sociedad de Geografía e Historia de Guatemala.* (Guatemala). Vol. 24, pp. 257–61.
9. Arciniegas, German. *El Continente de Siete Colores.* (Editorial Sudamericana, Buenos Aires). 1965.
10. Bailey, Helen M., and A. Nasatir. *Latin America, The Development of its Civilization.* (Prentice Hall, Englewood Cliffs, New Jersey). 1960.
11. Beals, Ralph L. "Culture Patterns of Mexican American Life." *Proceedings of the Fifth Annual Conference, Southwestern Conference on the Education of Spanish-Speaking People.* (Los Angeles). January 18–20, 1951.
12. Bernal Jiménez, Rafael. "La cultura de contrastes en Colombia y países afines." *Boletín del Instituto de Sociología,* Colombia. Vol. XI, No. 8, 1953, pp. 15–34.
13. Biesanz, John B. and Mavis Biesanz. *Costa Rican Life.* (Columbia University Press, New York). 1944.
14. Castro, Américo. *Aspectos del vivir hispanico.* (Editorial Cruz de Sur, Santiago). 1947.
15. Castro, Américo. *España en su historia: cristianos, moros y judíos.* (Editorial Losada, Buenos Aires). 1948.
16. Cuneo, Roberto Fabregat. *Carácteres Sudamericanos.* (Universidad Nacional, Mexico). 1950.
17. Davis, Harold Eugene. *Latin American Social Thought: The History of its Development since Independence, With Selected Readings.* (1st American Edition). (University Press of Washington, D.C., Washington). 1904.
18. Fillol, Tomas R. *Social Factors in Economic Development (The Argentine Case).* (M.I.T. Press, Cambridge, Massachusetts). 1961.
19. Form, William H., and Julius Rivera. "Work Contacts and International Evaluations: The Case of a Mexican Border Village." *Social Forces.* Vol. 37, No. 4, 1959.
20. Foster, George M. "Culture and Conquest (America's Spanish Heritage)" *Viking Fund Publications in Anthropology.* (Quadrangle). No. 27, 1960.
21. Foster, George M. "What is Folk Culture?" *American Anthropologist.* No. 55, 1953, pp. 159–73.
22. Fuentes, Carlos. *Cantar de Ciegos.* (Joaquín Mortez, Mexico). 1964.
23. Fuentes, Carlos. *La Muerte de Artemio Cruz.* (Fondo de Cultura Económica, Mexico). 1962.
24. Fuentes, Carlos. *La Region Transparente.* (Fondo de Cultura Económica, Mexico). 1958.
25. Gillin, John. "Ethos and Cultural Aspects of Personality." In *Heritage of Conquest,* ed. by Sol Tax (Free Press). 1952, pp. 193–212.
26. Gillin, John. "Modern Latin American Culture." *Social Forces.* Vol. 25, No. 3, 1947, pp. 243–48.
27. Gillin, John. "Ethos Components in Modern Latin American Culture."

American Anthropologist. Vol. 57, No. 3, Part 1, June, 1955, pp. 488–500.

28. González, Natalicio. *Proceso y Formación de la Cultura Paraguaya.* (Buenos Aires). 1938.

29. González Palencia, Angel. *La España del Siglo de Oro.* (Oxford University Press, New York). 1939.

30. Heath, Dwight B., and R. N. Adams. *Contemporary Cultures and Societies of Latin America.* (Random House, New York). 1965.

31. Jiménez Rueda, Julio. *Historia de la cultura en Mexico, el virreinato.* (Editorial Cultura, Mexico). 1950.

32. Kluckhohn, C. "Comparison of Value-Emphases in Different Cultures." *The State of the Social Sciences,* edited by Leonard D. White. (The University of Chicago Press, Chicago). 1956.

33. Kluckhohn, Florence R. "Variations in the Basic Values of Family Systems." *Social Casework.* Vol. 39, No. 2–3, February-March, 1958, pp. 63–72.

34. Kluckhohn, Florence R., and Fred L. Strodtbeck. *Variations in Value Orientations.* (Harper & Row, Evanston, Illinois). 1961.

35. Marquez, Gabriel García. *Cién Años de Soledad.* (Editorial Sudamericana, Buenos Aires). 1967.

36. Mijares, Augusto. *La interpretación pesimista de la sociología hispanoamericana.* (Second Edition). (Afrodisio Aguado, Madrid). 1952.

37. Paz, Octavio. *El Laberinto de la Soledad.* (Cuadernos Americanos, Mexico). 1947.

38. Picon-Salas, Mariano. *A Cultural History of Spanish America: From Conquest to Independence,* translated by Irving A. Leonard. (University of California Press, Berkeley). 1962.

39. Pineda, F. Gonzalez. *El Mexicano, Su dinámica psicosocial.* (Editorial Pax Mexico, Mexico). 1959.

40. Prescott, W. H. *History of the Reign of Ferdinand and Isabella the Catholic.* (Lippincott, Philadelphia). Vol. I, 1887.

41. Ramírez, Santiago. *El Mexicano, Psicología de sus Motivaciones.* (Editorial Pax-Mexico, Mexico). 1959.

42. Ramos, Samuel. *Profile of Man and Culture in Mexico,* translated by Peter G. Earle. (The University of Texas Press, Austin). 1962.

43. Redfield, Robert. *The Little Community, Viewpoints for a Study of a Human Whole.* (The University of Chicago Press, Chicago). 1955, pp. 4, 34, 40–41, 44.

44. Roura-Parella, Juan. *Tema y Variaciones de la Personalidad.* (Institute of IS of UNAM, Mexico). 1961.

45. Saunders, Lyle. *Cultural Differences and Medical Care.* (Russell Sage Foundation, New York). 1954.

46. Tannenbaum, F. "Discussion of acculturation studies in Latin America: more needs and problems." *American Anthropologist.* Vol. 45, 1943, pp. 205–6.

47. Tigerino, Julio Ycaza. *Hacia Una Sociología Hispanoamericana.* (Ediciones Cultura Hispánica, Madrid). 1958.

48. *Tipología socioeconomica de los paises latinoamericanos.* Union Panamericana, Secretaria General. (Organización de los Estados Americanos, Washington, D.C.). Vol. II, 1963.

49. UNESCO. *The Old and the New World* (*Their Cultural and Moral Relations*). (*International Forums of Sao Paulo and Geneva. 1954*). (UNESCO, Paris). 1956.
50. Venturino, Agustín. "Sociología General Americana." (estudio experimental hecho en 15 países). (E. Cervantes, Barcelona). 1931.
51. Wilgus, A. Curtis, and Raul D'Eca. *Latin American History*. (Fifth Edition). (Barnes & Noble, New York). 1963.
52. Wolf, Eric R. "Types of Latin American Peasantry: A Preliminary Discussion." *American Anthropologist*, June, 1955, Vol. 57, No. 3, Part 1, pp. 452–71.
53. Worcester, Donald E., and Wendell G. Schaeffer. *The Growth and Culture of Latin America*. (Oxford University Press, New York). 1956. p. 823.

The Un-melting Pot

It has been customary to classify Latin American populations into four major groups (the last called by various names in different countries): Negroes and Europeans, Indians and *mestizos.* Not all of these are mutually exclusive categories. Some others are often either forgotten or confused, such as the *criollo,* the Orientals, and the immigrants from the Middle East, frequently called *Turcos.*

Estimates of the total population of Latin America range from 215 to 250 million for 1966,[46, 76] of which total roughly 45 percent are *criollo,* 35 percent are *mestizo,* 10 percent Indian, 7 percent of European and other origin, and 3 percent are either Negro or mulatto. Exact figures are impossible to gather: censuses are very unreliable, the judgments of experts are contradictory, and the measures of ethnic variation too elastic. Thus, one has to approach the subject with great care.

Even where there is concern with one of these ethnic groups, no generalizations can be made. To wit, the Europeans in Chile, for example, did not all come from one country in Europe (an ethnically complex continent), and many of them did not even come from Europe; they are European in origin only. *Mutatis mutandis,* similar statements may be made about the Indians. Those in Mexico, for example, may be so different from each other physically and culturally that the only common characteristics are common descent from truly American ancestors. *Mestizos,* in turn, are found in all shades of color: Negroid, Indian, white, or mixed. The same applies to Negroes and Orientals. This is not to imply that Latin America is unique in the matter of race and color. The world is not that simple even when our minds might be. With regard to ethnicity, there is no common cultural characteristic in Latin America. The dream of *la raza* or *la raza cósmica* which from time to time has been voiced is just that, a dream. The proclaimed advent of a new olive-skinned human type mixed of white, black, and bronze and proud heir of ancient Indian and Iberian traditions has been an ideal to be attained and nothing more. *La raza* has come to imply a cultural unity centered around established Iberian values such as Catholicism (the Latin variety), the Castilian or Portuguese languages, some recognition of umbilical linkages with "the mother land" (Spain or Portugal), a romantic and mystic view of man, and messianic overtones in the form of typical Latin American contributions to the "ultimate values" of mankind, whatever they may be. The ideal has never reached deep into the masses, and in certain areas it has been redefined to express something very different from the original meaning. Around the Rio Grande, for example, it may mean just a group of Mexicans or Mexican-Americans brought together to have a good time. *La raza* was mainly a creation of some Hispano-American intellectuals of the ante-war era. Little of it remains even among the educated.[63]

Neither has Spanish become a unifying language throughout Latin America. First, it is not spoken everywhere. Moreover, there are a great variety of Latin American versions of the Spanish language. Each one of these versions has been affected by either local tongues older than Spanish (as in Southern Mexico, Guatemala, Ecuador, Peru, and Bolivia), or by the imported languages of immigrants from Italy, Germany, Lebanon, Catalonia in Spain, etc., as in Argentina, Chile and Uruguay.[34] Within the same country one may find a rich variety of Spanish forms. In Colombia, for example, the Castilian spoken in Antioquia is very unlike the language spoken in Huila, in Cauca, in Santander, or in the Caribbean cities of Bolívar, Atlántico, and Magdalena. Add to this the language variations associated with social class position (which are not peculiar to Latin America).

Roman Catholicism is not a unifying institution either. To

put it bluntly, there are as many interpretations of Catholicism as
there are countries, or as many interpretations as there are bishops,
priests, and faithful.

The remaining part of this chapter will show in some detail
the ethnic mosaic which is Latin America. Then it may be seen
more clearly why the pot is not really melting.

The Indians

No agreement exists among the experts regarding the date of
arrival of the very first inhabitants of Latin America. Counts run
from 10 to 30 thousand years. Experts do not agree either with
regard to the route followed by the original immigrants (though
immigrants they were): some experts suggest the Bering Strait,
some other postulate a submerged continent, still others suggest
rafts floating across the Pacific.[109] On one thing they all agree:
Adam was not made of Latin American mud. That seems certain.

Nor does agreement exist about the number of tribes. There
is even controversy concerning the idea of tribe.[109] A hint may be
derived from the number of languages so far classified. According
to McQuown, records of 1,820 languages have been gathered, and
dialects are innumerable. About half of the classified languages
are still spoken. Thus, there would be innumerable tribes if
languages and dialects were used as a criterion. In the immediate
vicinity of the Isthmus of Tehuantepec in Mexico, more languages
are spoken than in the Old Continent. A similar situation exists in
the Andean countries, Ecuador, Peru and Bolivia, although
Quechuas and Aymaras predominate here.[18] (See map.)

The aboriginal population of the whole hemisphere has been
estimated at the time of the Conquest to have been between 8.4
million and 75.0 million. For what is today Latin America, estimates range from between 4.5 to over 50.0 million (if the Andes
alone could have had 32.0 million).[109]

The wars waged against the Spaniards brought many Indian
groups close to destruction. The conquerors broke the native
communities quite systematically by massive population relocations

U.S.

MEXICO
27.9%

HONDURAS
9.5%

GUATEMALA 55.4%
EL SALVADOR 20%

NICARAGUA 23.9%

COSTA RICA .6%

PANAMA 10.3%

COLOMBIA 1.6%

VENEZUELA
2.8%

EQUADOR 40%

PERU 46.2%

BRAZIL 2.7%

BOLIVIA 50%

PARAGUAY 4.2%

CHILE 2.6%

ARGENTINA .4%

URUGUAY

Latin America: Distribution of Indians, 1940

across the Aztec and Inca domains. Diseases brought by the invaders corroded mercilessly the structures of the growing societies. The bitter odyssey and the gradual crumbling of the Indian sense of identity had just begun. It was to continue, as a slow leprosy, during the colonial period and early decades of the independent republics; with the twentieth century, the *mestizo,* finally risen to the top in several countries, began to look after his half-brother whom he himself had abused.[63] Programs for Indian rehabilitation started to emerge in Mexico, Brazil, and Peru, and some political parties, like APRA in Peru, made the Indian cause a battle cry.[61] In most cases, however, the Indians did not respond, partly because they could not trust the self-proclaimed redeemer and partly

Table 1 Indian Population in Sixteen Latin American Countries, Circa 1941

	INDIAN POPULATION	POPULATION PREDOMINANTLY INDIAN		POPULATION TOTALLY INDIAN	
		Number	*Percent*	*Number*	*Percent*
Argentina	188,425	150,000	79.6	38,425	20.4
Bolivia	2,800,000	. . .	–	. . .	–
Brasil	3,277,265	2,027,265	61.9	1,250,000	38.1
Colombia	2,212,750	1,962,750	88.7	250,000	11.3
Costa Rica	5,854	2,661	45.5	3,193	54.5
Chile	654,519	553,401	84.6	101,118	15.4
Ecuador	1,600,000	. . .	–	. . .	–
El Salvador	790,685	503,163	63.6	287,522	36.4
Guatemala	1,624,908	324,981	20.0	1,299,927	80.0
Honduras	467,568	295,616	63.2	171,952	36.8
Mexico	8,661,476	4,040,590	46.7	4,620,886	53.3
Nicaragua	372,235	159,529	42.9	212,706	57.1
Panama	167,688	124,791	74.4	42,897	25.6
Paraguay	442,519	300,000	67.8	142,519	32.2
Peru	6,500,000	1,500,000	23.1	5,000,000	76.9
Venezuela	538,147	402,000	74.7	136,147	25.3

SOURCE: United States Senate, Executive Report No. 7, 77th Congress, 1st Session, according to Poblaciones Indigenas, Geneva, International Labor Office, 1953.
Reprinted from *Estudio Económico y Social de América Latina, 1961,* p. 262, by permission of the Pan American Union, General Secretariat of the Organization of American States.

because the governmental policies were ambivalent as to how to proceed. The pendulum oscillated from policies of enforced assimilation to policies of well-meaning but badly-executed cultural preservation. And the Indians were caught on a seesaw.

For four hundred years, the Indian's flight to mountains and jungles never stopped. In his periodic exodus, only the Church followed him. But even here he did not feel secure. First, his "pagan" beliefs did not quite fit into the rigid theology he was supposed to learn in a catechism he could not understand. Second, in return for the "divine" gift of his faith and for his sharing in colorful religious rituals and pilgrimages, he had to contribute regularly to the ever-expanding land ownership of the Church.*[98] And this Holy Master was often severe. Thus he had to undertake a last psychological flight into narcotics and alcohol. By 1941 the total Indian population for sixteen continental Latin American countries was only about 30.3 million. This number is about half what it had been at the time of the Conquest. In the meantime, the other Latin American population had increased by leaps and bounds. Of the countries listed in Table 1, Peru has the highest number (5.0 million) of pure Indians, Mexico next (4.6), then Guatemala (1.3), followed by Brazil (1.2+). It is probable that the majority in the figures given for Bolivia and Ecuador are also pure Indians (2.8 and 1.6 respectively). The tremendous variety of Indian languages, family-kinship systems, primitive technologies, folkways, mores, and values has built a barrier almost insurmountable to united action.[76, 109] Consider in addition the intricately rugged terrain that isolates group from group, the long experience of frustrated attempts for liberation from the burdens of their past, and, at the same time, the attachment to traditions they do not dare to betray and their unspoken hope of a cosmic intervention.

---

* For what was happening in Brazil the following may be illustrative: ". . . the priests of this order (the Society of Jesus) wished to found a holy republic of 'Indians domesticated by Jesus', like those in Paraguay: seraphic *caboclos* obedient only to the ministers of the Lord and laboring only in his gardens and plantations, with no individuality and without any autonomy, the chief being clad in garments that resembled an infant's nightgown in an orphan-asylum or boarding-school, with the men indistinguishable, so far as their raiment was concerned, from the women and children."[35]

With these insights, one gets a hint of understanding of the Latin American Indians.

Concerted action has nonetheless taken place here and there. The Bolivian revolution of the fifties is probably both the most recent and the most successful act of Indian self-assertion.[27] Nothing like it has occurred anywhere in the hemisphere. The Mexican revolution was mainly a *mestizo* revolution and the repeated rebellions of the Motilones in Colombia have been vain skirmishes leading nowhere. The governments of all countries have taken measures, desperate at times, to rescue the last shreds of Indian cultures. For some, the time may have elapsed. Missionaries of all faiths have also contributed to the rescue, and archaeologists and cultural anthropologists are rushing in all directions with similar intents. Thus the Indian tragedy may become a beautiful drama after all.

The Mestizos

To assert that Latin America is a *mestizo* continent developing a *mestizo* civilization is not only an oversimplification of reality but an error. How this error has crept into even highly respected scholarly publications is hard to explain. One reason may be the elasticity of the definitions of *mestizo,* which range from "mixture," through procreation of members of any distinctive ethnic groups or races, to the more limited but most common meaning which refers only to progeny of a European and an Indian. If the broader definition were to be used then not only Latin America but the whole world would be *mestizo* also. If the latter meaning is adopted, then Latin America is not *mestizo* at all. Of course, the greater problem lies in the fact that to establish clear boundaries between races has been proven to be impossible. The majority of the works on Latin America do give *mestizo* the meaning herein adopted: the offspring of a European and an Indian.[96]

Two other reasons for the confusion may be added. One is the mental and physical proximity of the United States to the

Table 2 Population Distribution According to Ethnic Groups in Latin American Countries, 1940

	Total Population		Indians		Mestizos		Negroes & Mulattoes	
	Absolute	Relative	Absolute	Relative	Absolute	Relative	Absolute	Relative
Argentina	13,129,723	100.0	50,000	0.4	1,312,972	10.0	15,000	0.1
Bolivia	3,300,000	100.0	1,650,000	50.0	990,000	30.0	12,800	0.4
Brasil	41,356,605	100.0	1,117,132	2.7	4,135,660	10.0	1,066,245	2.6
Colombia	9,206,283	100.0	147,300	1.6	4,234,890	46.0	2,610,458	28.0
Costa Rica	656,129	100.0	4,200	0.6	65,612	10.0	46,900	7.1
Chile	5,023,539	100.0	130,000	2.6	3,014,123	60.0	4,000	0.0
Ecuador	2,500,000	100.0	1,000,000	40.0	900,000	36.0	200,000	8.0
El Salvador	1,744,535	100.0	348,907	20.0	1,308,401	75.0	200	0.0
Guatemala	3,284,269	100.0	1,820,872	55.4	985,280	30.0	6,011	0.2
Honduras	1,107,859	100.0	105,732	9.5	775,501	70.0	65,275	5.9
Mexico	19,446,065	100.0	5,427,396	27.9	10,619,496	54.6	120,000	0.6
Nicaragua	1,380,287	100.0	330,000	23.9	828,172	60.0	130,000	9.4
Panama	631,549	100.0	64,960	10.3	135,604	21.5	354,079	56.0
Paraguay	960,000	100.0	40,000	4.2	672,000	70.0	10,000	1.0
Peru	7,023,111	100.0	3,247,196	46.2	2,247,395	32.0	109,054	15.5
Uruguay	2,145,545	100.0	—		100,000	4.7	60,000	2.8
Venezuela	3,580,000	100.0	100,000	2.8	2,000,000	55.9	1,100,000	30.7

Source: Angel Rosenblat, *La Población Indígena de America desde 1492 hasta la Actualidad*, Buenos Aires, Institución Cultural Española, 1945, according to Poblaciones Indígenas, Geneva, International Labor Office, 1953. Reprinted from *Estudio Económico y Social de América Latina, 1961*, p. 262, by permission of the Pan American Union, General Secretariat of the Organization of American States.

definitely *mestizo* areas of Mexico and Central America (exempting Costa Rica, a *criollo* country, and Guatemala, a predominantly Indian country; see Table 2). The population of these areas constitutes about one fifth of the total Latin American population. The second reason may be the attention given to the ascension of the *mestizo* in the history of the hemisphere, particularly after the wars of independence when the *mestizos* shared with the *criollos* both status and power in the emerging nations. Writers began to exalt the virtues of the olive-skinned mixture that became socially visible at this time.

Two countries in South America seem to be definitely *mestizo*. They are Paraguay and Peru. However, the types that have resulted are very different from each other, owing primarily to the different Indian elements involved. Ecuador and Bolivia are for the most part Indian. Venezuela, Panama, Colombia, and Chile are characterized by decreasing proportions of *mestizos,* but these groups do not seem to constitute the majority of the population (no matter what Table 2 says about Chile). As a matter of fact the *criollos* have dominated in these countries both numerically and politically in inverse proportions; the higher the number of *criollos* the lower the number of *mestizos,* and in reverse order: Chile, Colombia, Panama, and Venezuela. Moreover, there is ample evidence that Chile ought to be listed with Brazil, Argentina, and Uruguay as predominantly *criollo,* that is, as inhabited mainly by descendants of Europeans.

In terms of the genetic pool characteristic of various Latin American countries there is something more important than physical appearance. The *mestizos* of Latin America—roughly around 35 percent of its population—do possess socioculturally differentiating characteristics.

Socially, the visibility of the *mestizos* has increased throughout the years. In Latin America, like everywhere in the West, there has been a constant relationship between the color of one's skin and the prestige ladder in the stratification system. However, power and wealth have opened a breach in every society, and in those societies in which the *mestizos* are the majority, they are the dispensers of wealth, power, and prestige. The best example of this is Mexico.

The *mestizo* is power hungry. For him political power has been the shortest way to the prestige summit and eventually to wealth. Wealth is not yet the path to power in Latin America, as it is in the United States of America. The *mestizo* has found that entering a university will place him on the track of a political career that sooner or later will open the doors for him of the *criollo* aristocratic castle. Thus, aggressiveness is his most distinguishing characteristic. This aggressiveness is shown in the *machismo* (on its way out) of the lower classes and in the competitive attitude which often twists basic values in politics and business. In contrast, the Indian has withdrawn, and the *criollo* has kept on the defensive, except, of course, in those countries in which he is in the majority.

The *mestizo* is tense and vibrant, like the guitars he plays. For him, more than for any other group, *romerías* and *fiestas* are safety valves—fully opened. He celebrates noisily and often destructively. He celebrates by singing loud in the night throughout the streets and will even break his guitar—strings and all—at the end. The *criollo* drinks to get to know the other, the *mestizo* to let himself be known, and the Indian to lock himself from the world. The *criollo* drinks to put himself to sleep, the *mestizo* drinks to be able to shout and scream, and the Indian drinks to get drunk. But the *mestizo* is genuinely gay.

To be sure, the *mestizo* has shared some of the *tristeza* of the Indian. But this sadness is only a technique to squeeze joy out of everything in life—as you step on the grapes to make wine. To him, sadness always erupts into joy. The Indian, on the other hand, is genuinely sad.

A commonly held stereotype of Latin Americans is the attributed tendency to be lazy. Neither the *criollo,* a man of leisure, nor the *mestizo,* in love with life, can possibly be called lazy with any degree of accuracy. How then can the aggressiveness be explained? As for the Indians, they are just frustrated. They have learned this by hitting walls with their heads for four hundred years. The so-called *mañana* attitude is a cross-cultural misreading, and a very superficial one at that. For the Latin American man is in communion, almost in identity, with time. As stated above, time as man cannot be measured. There is no measure for time as there is no measure for man. At his best, man is the measure of time. Therefore, the Latin American thinks that only those things that cannot be left for tomorrow should be done today, because each day unto itself—"a cada día le basta su propio afán." Things that should be done tomorrow will be done tomorrow; there is no need to bring them to today.

Some scholars have found the Latin Americans irresponsible.* And they have found explanation for this irresponsibility in some Spanish expressions. A Latin would not say, they argue, "I dropped it"; instead, he says "se me cayó," it fell out of my hands. He would not say "I am late," but "se me hizo tarde," it became late on me. Thus he is transferring the blame on to some extraneous element. What they fail to do is to bring these and other very similar expressions together into a pattern that would point to deeper meanings in the culture. A Spanish-speaking person would not say, "I like it"; he says instead, "me gusta," it likes me, so to speak. From a friend returning from a trip he would ask, "Como le fue?" how did it turn out for you? And his friend would reply: "Me fue bien, fue un exito," it turned out to be a success. There seems to be something deeper in all these expressions than the simple denial of responsibilities. For the Latin American, as suggested earlier, only he and the universe make a totality. By contrast—and arguing *ad hominem*—some English expressions seem to make the individual more responsible than he may really be and to claim a credit that he does not really deserve. The former may be illustrated by the housewife who says upon breaking a dish, "I dropped it," confessing perhaps a guilt that in truth she must share with her nagging husband, her screaming child, and even with the hot water running over her fingers from the faucet. And to illustrate the second point—claiming more credit than one deserves—remember *My Fair Lady*. Professor Higgins claims, "I did it, I did it . . ." and Colonel Pickering agrees, "You did it, You did it. . . ." Apparently Miss Doolittle had no part in the joint undertaking. However, could this be better understood in conjunction with other linguistic expressions and in the larger cultural context? In fact, "it is done," "it is finished," "it was a success"

---

* For example, Frank Tannenbaum.

are also very common English expressions that may point to a deeper meaning in the culture; perhaps to a mastery of the universe rather than to a communion with it. In any case, Latin Americans —whether *mestizo* or Negro or Indian or *criollo*—are not irresponsible, although there are irresponsible Latin Americans.

Of course the theme of irresponsibility has been advanced as an explanation for the alleged instability of Latin America, under

Figure 1   A Comparison of the Age-Sex Pyramid
for the Population of Brazil in 1950
with that of the United States in 1850

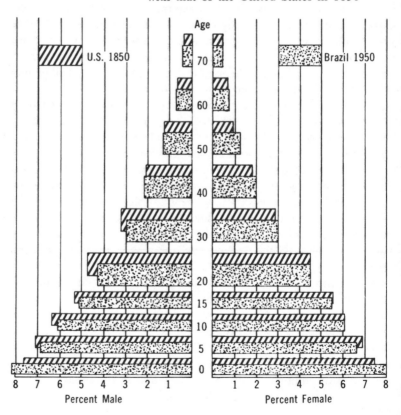

From T. Lynn Smith, *Latin American Population Studies*, Gainesville: University of Florida Press, 1961, p. 15. With permission.

the assumption of a *mestizo* civilization. The issue of instability will be taken up later. For the present, suffice it to say that the Latin American population pyramids available (See Fig. 1) are wide at the bottom and very narrow at the top, indicating the abundance of youth and the scarcity of old people. It may be significant to note that of the nine countries given in Table 3, only Argentina has a relatively small proportion (39 percent) of people under 20. In all the others (excluding Chile) the people under 20 make more than 50 percent of the total population; and in Costa Rica and Honduras considerably more (57 and 58 percent respectively). By contrast the people over 60 make 11.3 percent in Argentina and about half of that figure in the remaining countries given. Longevity likewise has hardly reached 70 in Argentina and 65 in Mexico; for most Latin American countries, longevity falls in the forties and fifties. And most Latin American leaders are young—if presidents are leaders. In fact, only the dictators of Brazil and Paraguay are in their sixties.

A final characteristic of the *mestizo* to be mentioned here is his incapacity for concerted action. If the Latin American in general is taught to be different, the *mestizo* in particular is taught to be rebellious. The sole evidence to the contrary could be the relatively small number of political parties in each country. However, there is very little political participation. If the Indians do not agree with each other, it is in part because they can hardly communicate with each other. By contrast, the *mestizos* seem to communicate in order to disagree.

The Criollo

More than the *mestizo,* the *criollo* (often called white) is right in the middle of the Latin American ethnic (perhaps semantic) scramble.[95] There is, however, ample evidence that there is such a group. Its members cannot be considered European (although they have been so considered), because they are not born in Europe, or *mestizo,* because their ancestry is supposed to be clearly European; if in doubt, any amount of Indian blood that has sur-

Table 3 Total Population by Age Groups According to Recent Censuses in Nine Latin American Countries

Age Group	Argentina (1960) Thousands	Percent	Chile (1960) Thousands	Percent	Peru (1961) Thousands	Percent	Venezuela (1961) Thousands	Percent	Panama (1960) Thousands	Percent
0–4	4,214.0	21.0	1,115.6	15.1	1,639.8	16.8	1,340.9	17.8	169.2	16.7
5–9			985.2	13.3	1,459.4	15.0	1,132.5	15.0	145.5	14.3
10–14	3,610.1	18.1	833.6	11.3	1,144.0	11.7	879.3	11.9	122.9	12.1
15–19			729.1	10.0	955.7	9.8	710.5	9.4	101.6	10.0
20–24	3,039.6	15.2	599.1	8.1	807.5	8.2	617.5	8.2	85.0	8.4
25–29			524.4	7.1	720.7	7.4	554.4	7.3	70.4	7.0
30–34	3,009.4	15.0	473.7	6.4	611.5	6.3	507.2	6.7	61.8	6.1
35–39			390.2	5.3	525.1	5.4	405.1	5.4	55.6	5.5
40–44	2,385.7	11.9	393.3	5.3	412.1	4.2	332.3	4.4	48.2	4.7
45–49			346.6	4.6	361.1	3.7	294.0	3.9	41.7	4.1
50–54	1,877.4	9.4	275.9	3.7	296.6	3.0	217.6	2.9	30.7	3.0
55–59			212.0	2.8	223.3	2.3	169.8	2.2	23.6	2.3
60–64	1,785.6	8.9	182.6	2.4	213.9	2.2	136.9	1.8	20.3	2.0
65+			313.9	4.2	371.3	3.8	208.0	2.7	36.7	3.6
Unknown	49.5	2.4	—		5.0	.5	—		—	
Total	19,971.3	100.0	7,375.2	100.0	9,747.0	100.0	7,524.0	100.0	1,013.4	100.0

Age Group	Costa Rica (1963) Thousands	Percent	El Salvador (1961) Thousands	Percent	Honduras (1961) Thousands	Percent	Mexico (1963) Thousands	Percent
0–4	248.3	18.6	432.8	17.2	354.2	19.0	5,776.7	16.5
5–9	216.7	16.2	383.6	15.3	308.6	16.5	5,317.0	15.2
10–14	169.5	12.7	309.1	12.3	233.9	12.5	4,358.3	12.5
15–19	126.3	9.5	238.7	9.5	184.3	9.9	3,535.3	10.1
20–24	107.6	8.1	210.7	8.4	152.6	8.2	2,947.1	8.4
25–29	84.9	6.3	175.6	7.0	127.6	6.8	2,504.9	7.2
30–34	77.5	5.8	153.4	6.1	108.9	5.8	2,051.6	5.8
35–39	66.5	5.0	139.2	5.5	94.9	5.1	1,920.7	5.5
40–44	52.2	3.9	112.6	4.5	72.3	3.9	1,361.3	3.9
45–49	45.9	3.4	89.5	3.6	61.4	3.3	1,233.6	3.5
50–54	42.3	3.2	76.2	3.0	50.2	2.7	1,063.4	3.0
55–59	26.1	1.9	50.9	2.0	33.7	1.8	799.9	2.3
60–64	25.8	1.9	57.0	2.2	34.8	1.8	744.7	2.1
65+	42.6	3.2	81.3	3.2	48.4	2.6	1,195.0	3.4
Unknown	1.3	.1	0.7	.2	0.8	.1	113.5	.3
Total	1,333.4	100.0	2,511.3	100.0	1,866.4	100.0	34,923.1	100.0

Adapted from United Nations Economic Commission for Latin America, *Statistical Bulletin for Latin America* Vol. 1, No. 1, March, 1964 (Sales No.: 64.II.G.9). New York: United Nations, 1964, p. 19.

reptitiously been transfused into the sap of the genealogical tree has not changed the color of the "blue" blood.* As defined here, a *criollo* is a Latin American born of European parents. This group was easily recognizable and recognized soon after the Conquest. Many *conquistadores* did go back to the Peninsula to bring legitimate wives to oversee the illegitimate ones and their offspring, and obviously to procreate "legitimately." This latter group was to be the origin of the *criollo*. Moreover, as the bureaucracy of the Colonial administration spread throughout the continent and grew large in the succeeding centuries, the families who immigrated with the new waves of administrators contributed generously to the numbers of *criollos*. By the end of the colonial period, they had become bitter about their second class citizenship; many joined the forces of independence and in some instances led them through the early years of the republics. Thus, when Latin America gained full control of its own political destiny, the *criollos,* heirs of the Spanish wealth and prestige, moved easily to the top of the power structure. In Brazil, the process was somewhat different, but the end result very similar. Close behind them moved the *mestizos,* and the Indians remained "indios."[116] In the countries where the Indian population had been large, the *criollos* soon had to face the threat of the climbing *mestizos* and eventually lost all control of the political wheels. They were never rejected from the prestige circles, though, so that the successful *mestizo* still had to buy his way into traditional *criollo* respectability through marriage. Neither group has ever forgotten the bargain. As in the political structure, the *criollos* climbed also in the ranks of the clergy and the military, as will be shown later. This is the social picture.

Culturally, they have advanced more than their ancestors and this is true even for the Colonial period.[95] Soon they were almost the exclusive manipulators of all sorts of cultural symbols, from sciences, art, and literature to native folklore, music, and languages. Their knowledge, however, never meant assimilation. It has taken civil wars and revolutions to throw doubt on their pedigrees. The *mestizo* intelligence that was never trusted by the

---

* It is said that people of blue blood are white, called so because when rolling the sleeves up, the skin appears blue over the lines of their veins.

Spaniard has never been trusted by the *criollo* either. Of course, the *mestizo* has contributed to the other side of the equation.

Paradoxically, the *criollo* is the most insecure of all Latin American types. He has no roots. Oriented toward the Peninsula by language and blood, he nevertheless found, if he ever visited his "motherland," his status highly superior to that of his ancestors. At the same time, regardless of how high his status has been in Latin America, it has never been so recognized by his counterparts in the Peninsula—an irritating source of embarrassment. Never loved and often feared by the Indian and the *mestizo,* he has tried to exploit them both and to live in Paris. If this longing turns out to be unattainable, he either moves back and forth across the ocean to retain some form of identity or withdraws into a romantic isolation among "his" Indians. But he remains unrooted. This tragedy has been understood by very few and ignored by most. In fact, contrary to all expectations, practically no Latin American considers himself *criollo,* although some speak of the *criollo* culture. To escape the label, (hardly used in Brazil, for example, and then with a variant meaning), not fitting any other ethnic classification, he proclaims himself Argentinian or Chilean or Brazilian or whatnot. Upon further questioning, however, he jumps the Atlantic. This could never happen to the *mestizo* or to the Indian. Thus, you have here a partial explanation of a point to be developed later, to wit, that practically all Latin American countries are states but not nations.

The Europeans

As an ethnic group, Europeans are the most easily classifiable. This is so not only because they are characterized by rather clear physical traits, but because they either speak different languages or a different form of Spanish and Portuguese. The most distinguishing characteristic seems, however, to be the relentless efforts they appear to make to retain their European identity. A very extreme case which may be used as illustration is that of the

Table 4 Latin America: Percent Foreign Born and Born in Europe According to Various Censuses

Country	Year	Percent Foreign Born	Percent Born in Europe
Argentina	1869	12.1	...
	1895	25.5	25.4
	1914	30.3	27.2
	1947	15.3	12.7
Brazil	1872	3.8	...
	1890	2.5	...
	1900	6.2	...
	1920	5.1	4.7
	1940	3.4	2.8
	1950	2.3	1.9
Chile	1854	1.4	0.5
	1865	1.2	0.6
	1875	1.2	0.8
	1885	3.5	1.0
	1895	2.9	1.6
	1907	4.2	2.2
	1920	3.2	1.9
	1930	2.4	1.6
	1952	1.8	1.1
Colombia	1912	0.4	...
	1951	0.4	0.1
Costa Rica	1927	9.4	1.4
	1950	4.2	0.4
Cuba	1899	11.3	8.7
	1907	11.2	9.3
	1919	10.7	9.5
	1939	11.8	6.9
	1943	5.2	3.6
	1953	4.0	...
El Salvador	1930	0.9	0.1
	1950	1.0	0.0
Guatemala	1940	0.8	0.2
	1950	1.1	0.0
Mexico	1900	0.4	...
	1910	0.8	...
	1921	0.7	...
	1930	1.0	...
	1950	0.7	...
Panama	1911	11.6	...
	1930	10.1	...
	1940	8.1	0.8
	1950	6.2	0.6
Uruguay	1908	18.1	12.8
Venezuela	1926	11.3	0.3
	1936	13.5	0.7
	1941	12.2	...
	1950	4.2	2.4

SOURCE: Census of each country. Reprinted from *Revista Interamericana de Ciencias Sociales*, Vol. 2, número especial: Tipología socio-económica de los países latinoamericanos, by permission of the Pan American Union, General Secretariat of the Organization of American States.

Germans in Brazil, who have resisted assimilation to the point of having sizeable communities where German is spoken to the nearly total exclusion of Portuguese, the official language.[100]

European migration to Latin America did not attain significance until the second half of the nineteenth century (and then without any sort of uniformity or with very little planning). Brazil and Argentina were the main migration targets, but primarily for Italians, Portuguese, and Spaniards.[100] However, Chile, Paraguay, and Uruguay shared somewhat in these successive waves of migration from Europe, as did, to some extent, Cuba and Costa Rica. Venezuela and Colombia did not feel the impact until the second quarter of the twentieth century.*

At no one given time or in any given country have the Europeans ever constituted a majority of the population. Their influence has always been either flagrant, as in the southernmost countries of South America, or quasi-overt, as in Central America, excluding Costa Rica.[77] In all countries they have been the pace-

---

* Meaningful and reliable statistics for intercontinental migrations to the various Latin American states are impossible to obtain. Some countries list entries without indicating the point of departure and departures without giving the point of destination. Even those sources surrounded with a halo of respectability furnish volumes filled with confusing, unsystematic, and contradictory statistics. No matter how bad, however, they do show certain trends.

The United Nations 1957, 1959, and 1966 Demographic year books suggest, for example, that Brazil continues to appeal primarily to immigrants from Portugal (109,000), Spain (44,000), Italy (35,000), and to a lesser degree to people from Japan, the United States, Lebanon, and even less to Germans and Frenchmen, at least during the 1953-1958 period. Mexico, the second largest country in the Latin American continent, attracted Spaniards (2,500) and North Americans (4,000 ?) (The majority of the 120,000 residing in Mexico are not immigrants.) Very few migrate to Mexico from extra-continental countries. Argentina, the third largest, continued to attract Italians (99,000), Spaniards (over 41,000) and lesser numbers of Germans, French, Japanese, and Chinese during the same period (1953-1958). Similarly, Colombia, the fourth largest, attracted mostly Spaniards (over 2,500), Germans (over 1,700), Italians (1,500), French (over 800), very few Japanese and Chinese, and a rather sizeable number of North Americans (over 6,000), but the figures relate to 1956, 1957, and 1958. All these "statistics" assume that most long-term entries to the countries are immigrants; which, needless to say, is not a legitimate assumption. Nevertheless, all countries continue to appeal from the point of view of national origins, to approximately the same type of extra-continental immigrants.

setters for life styles. It is not that the great majority of Europeans have moved upward automatically in the new social scene. Whether they have moved up or not in the social scale, they have all kept the memories and some of the realities of the old world culture alive in the new environment. And of course their children have become the new *criollos,* as unrooted as the old ones and as their parents.

Two errors in perspective have eroded the prospects of the European migrant to Latin America. The first, most serious, and of greatest consequences for themselves and for the new nations has been the painful and often sudden realization that the new land was not the promised land of which they had dreamed before their departure. They found everything unpredictable: the soil, the rainfall, the people, and the economy. Soon these peasants found themselves jamming the metropolis and becoming proletarians. Thus, Buenos Aires and Montivedeo, São Paolo and Rio de Janeiro on the Atlantic seashore, and Santiago on the Pacific, swelled with immigrants and vibrated with transplanted ideologies, mimicked organizational techniques and duplicated political maneuvers. As a consequence, the Latin American one would be a carbon copy—not very faithful at that—of the European labor movement. And all this was happening in a lapse of a few decades around the nineteen hundreds. Of course, the growth of these cities has not stopped; but the new immigrant is more urban than rural. The dream of vast expanses of land intensively cultivated by skillful European farmers remains almost totally unfulfilled. Here and there, as in Chile, some pockets of relatively mechanized agriculture did develop. Brazil and Argentina, and to a certain extent Uruguay, Paraguay, and Chile, were to remain the countries of the large plantations and *estancias* where the early comers left no land to be taken by the late arrivals. True, the Europeans brought skills, know-how, and entrepreneurship; and this leads to the second error in perspective. Not finding the land hospitable, many tried to crack the established social structure or make enough to return comfortably to the womb of mother Europe by the route of the "quick fortune." A few settled modestly in the countryside, and still fewer have faded away in the process of miscegenation. In summary, the early comer from Europe brought tragedy to the new world and the late comer has in a sense become a tragedy: the countries they founded or that they have adopted are still searching for identity.

The Orientals

The chapter of Oriental experience in the history of Latin America has not been written, and when it is written it is not going to be flattering to the continent. Latin Americans claim to be free of prejudice, but they forget the Orientals. Even Brazil—the country of open arms—cannot exhibit a clean record when it comes to this ethnic and racial group. And the record—not yet forty years old —of Mexico is not clean at all.

The Orientals in Brazil originated predominantly from Japan, and those still in Mexico from China.[36, 87, 100] There are of course scattered numbers of Orientals throughout all of Latin America. The Chinese migration to Mexico anteceded the starting (1908) of the Japanese migration to Brazil by a few decades.[36] The Chinese (nobody knows how many) in Mexico engaged first in agriculture and then in many other business undertakings in addition. The clash of the two cultures was most striking; the clash did not last very long and eventually developed into a tragedy for the immigrants. The incompatibility of the two cultures deserves an analysis that cannot be undertaken here. Suffice it to say that the complex constitution of the family, the tight solidarity of the group, the magnificent mastery of the soil, the sharp shrewdness in business, and the keen achievement motivation framed in the extreme acceptance of deprivation unthinkable to a Mexican, all contributed to the rise and fall of the Chinese in Mexico. When the Revolution erupted in 1910, Sonora, for example, was blooming with orchards and vegetable gardens across her arid land and her towns had almost suddenly become exciting trade centers. Soon the Mexicans found themselves displaced from every economic activity in their own territory; they had only kept command of the government bureaucracies. After the Revolution, the reconstruction of the country demanded first concern. But the misunderstandings that had brewed for decades finally led, in 1929, to the exile of any Chinese not married to a Mexican. As a result, the orchards wilted soon thereafter, and vegetable gardening was abandoned. The country turned once more to United States farms for pinto beans. In the process the Chinese could hardly save their skins. There was a time when the head of a Chinese was worth five dollars, thirteen times less than a Yaqui Indian head was worth during the Porfirio Diaz regime.[63]

Nothing of this kind happened to the Orientals in Brazil (well over 400,000), or in any other Latin American country for that matter. But the myth has been fertilized by the experiences of World War II and more recently by China's entering the nuclear club. Thus the miscegenation characteristic of Latin countries, especially Brazil, has not proceeded as rapidly with Orientals as with other groups. There are other reasons, some of which have been mentioned, such as the complexity of the Oriental family and the tight solidarity of the Oriental group. From the economic point of view, the Orientals have been relatively successful in almost every place they have lived. Socially and politically, they have for the most part remained marginal.

The Negroes

Writings on the Latin American Negroes abound;[23, 35, 81] by contrast, statistics are wanting, particularly for those who inhabit the continent.[25] Not counting the islands of the Caribbean, the largest numbers are found in Brazil (over six million) and Colombia (around four hundred thousand). The figures for Venezuela and Panama are much smaller, and still smaller are those for Mexico, Peru, Ecuador and the rest of the countries.

It is well known that slavery was introduced in Latin America, under the blessings of the Church and the Crown, soon after the so-called discovery of America in 1492. With the Inquisition and the exploitation of the Indians, the Negro slave trade makes up a trinity of unsurpassed cruelty. In all of this, Portugal competed successfully with Spain, and the Portuguese in Brazil accomplished the dubious achievement of hunting Indians with dogs to make slaves of them also.[100] The belated efforts during successive decades at least to alleviate if not to stop the inhuman trade could hardly be an apology for Church and Crown. Neither the penance for his error of the Dominican Las Casas nor the sacrifices of Pedro Claver could cleanse the record. The ideal of brotherhood of man under God could never have been more negated. No wonder that often the first targets of both Indian and Negro uprisings were the missionaries and their missions. Paradoxically, the Aztecs, "pagan" as they were, did not debase themselves so deeply in the treatment of their *tlacotli.*[105]

It is true that legal segregation has never existed in any Latin American country. But it is also true that prejudice, while it has been subtle, has not been less effective. No Negro (nor Indian for that matter) has ever reached the top in either the clergy or the military; and in the political sphere, none has ever climbed the pyramid of power even though several Negroes and Mulattoes have obtained high positions. A very Latin American characteristic seems to be that, in contrast to the United States, the relationship between prejudice and socioeconomic status is direct; that is, the higher is the socioeconomic status, the greater is the prejudice. This may have been mediated in Latin America by the spread of free marital unions and illegitimacy, typical of the low income groups. Prejudice is not so obvious in the areas of regular social intercourse as it is in the "expected" patterns of marriage and highly visible political positions. On the other hand, in the educational and economic spheres, there is very little discrimination, if any.

The influence of the Negro subculture in the larger Latin American culture has not been as penetrating as it has in the United States. As a matter of fact, excluding again the Caribbean islands, only Brazil, Colombia, and Venezuela, and to an extent Panama have felt any significant impact from the African cultures introduced into the continent by the Negro. The main channels for this influence have been music, religious beliefs, and poetry. Colombia, Venezuela, and Panama are, of course, part of the Circumcaribbean cultural area flavored so heavily with Negro value-orientations and institutions. *Mutatis mutandis,* the statement applies with equal validity to Mexico and Central America. Brazil is somewhat unique not only because the original streams of forced migration from Africa were at variance with the rest of the continent, but because, as in the United States South, the plantation brought together slave and master in a close cultural contact, and, unlike in the United States South, the tropical sexual freedom between master and slave extended almost beyond all limits to all levels of society, excepting no group, not even the clergy.[35] This is not to imply that Spanish Americans did not mix with the Negroes sexually. They just lacked the same opportunities. The same color shades found in Brazil can be found anywhere else in Latin America, but in smaller proportions.

As in the United States, the Negroes have settled on the eastern sea shore and have only gradually moved inland. Their move to the South American Pacific has been relatively recent. In Colombia, they followed the Cauca river upstream, panning gold for their masters, and the Pacific coast from Buenaventura to Tumaco. It should be remembered that many Negroes were taken to the hinterland of Colombia, Ecuador, and Peru to exploit gold and silver mines during the Colonial period and that many had to fight the wars of independence with Bolívar and San Martín in Ecuador and Peru respectively. Thus, the beginning of Negro settlements in these countries dates to those centuries. The freedom for which they fought hardly changed their destiny. Their new masters were more unpredictable but not less exacting.

Enduring his lot, the Negro learned to endure distress and live on very little. Small signs of reciprocity turned his service into loyalty. The Negro woman became cook and governess and mistress. Eventually she reached the heart of her master; however, this was the time when technology made the labors of her race uneconomical. By the end of the 19th century (Brazil, 1888), the emancipation of the Negroes had at last been completed. Final freedom meant some form of geographical mobility but their social mobility remained crippled. Only after World War II, when Latin America had to turn toward some sort of industrialization, did the Negro find room in the fluid social structure. The course no doubt, has been uncertain, but at least it has been challenging. Today, the Negro is found everywhere except in the high clergy, the top military, and the aristocracy: the Sancta Sanctorum of the *criollo* and the *mestizo*.

The Scattered Melting Pots

A widespread myth concerning Latin American societies is their assumed tendencies to erase ethnic boundaries. Like all myths, this one is based on segmental views of complex realities. There is no doubt that a great deal of miscegenation has occurred, but this has most often occurred in the three types of melting pots scattered and disconnected throughout the continent, to wit, the *hacienda,* the plantation, and the metropolis.[33, 35, 50, 51, 67, 100, 110]

The *hacienda* is the tail-end of the *encomienda* introduced by the conquistadores in Spanish America. The latter was originally a grant of land deeded to a loyal vassal by the Crown in recognition of his services. The Indians came with the land and were assigned to his responsibility, as children of God, to be taught catechism. In return for the divine gift of Christian faith they were to work for the *patrón* in the land of the *encomienda.* The exchange could not be more profitable to the Indian, and for as long as his faith remained unbroken he could not be any happier. In turn, the *encomendero* could not be any happier either. For him the *encomienda,* soaked in Indian sweat and blood, soon became a cornucopia of earthly goods.[98, 116]

Independence from Spain did not bring automatic freedom for the Indian in the *hacienda.* He was permitted to stay, but he had to pay rent either in labor or in goods, or both. Moreover, whatever cash he earned he had to spend—by the force of circumstances if not under pressure—in the store of the *hacienda.* Too often he had to borrow money from the *hacendado* to care for the ill, to get married, or to bury the dead. At his death, his debts would be passed on to his sons, making the knot between the tenants and the *hacienda* so tight through generations that it could only be broken with revolutionary dynamite. Shooting the *mayordomo* or the *patrón* was not always enough.[118]

From the point of view of economics, the *hacienda* was relatively self-sufficient, producing enough to keep the owner absent. He would live in the capital or abroad most of the year. The *hacienda,* however, was not market oriented except in beef and milk, and in mules and horses, but the periphery of its market never went beyond the village or the county seat. Modernization has painfully arrived to many *haciendas,* it is true, but only under the threat of expropriation. The enlightened *hacendado* is seldom found.

From the political perspective the *hacienda* has continually exerted a centrifugal pressure on the forces working for political integration in all countries. The *hacendado* has been often the *caudillo* or the *cacique*; he controls local politics and its pork barrel; he manipulates elections; he refuses to be taxed. His interests in public affairs do not stop here, however. He contributes heavily to road opening and conservation, to some school construction, to the organization of county fairs, and he is always present in the welcoming receptions of high dignitaries.

The preceding is only the background of the presently considered function of the *hacienda*. It has been the stage for the meeting of races. Firstly, the *patrón* and his sons have never unduly restrained their impulses in contributing generously to the process of miscegenation, and have not always been strongly resisted by the young maidens scattered in the hacienda. Often they were brought to the big house as maids and eventually as mating partners of the *patroncitos* in an effort to protect the latter from the syphilis of the houses of prostitution. Secondly, the definitions of morality of the peasants and the standards set for them by the dominant groups have seldom jibed. Moreover, the short life span of men coupled with a low sex ratio and a high male migration rate to urban areas have all been factors in the relatively free sexual mixing of the races in the *hacienda*. It is also said that low education, economic necessity, and frequent desertion have made children assets to a woman. In addition, in many rural areas, a woman has not reached self-fulfillment unless she has borne many children and her man has not fulfilled *her* measure of *machismo* unless he gets her pregnant often.

The emphasis so far has been on the "deviant" aspects of behavior because in fact they are not deviant; they are the norm in most of the rural areas of Latin America. Nevertheless, marriage in some areas does bind the majority of the couples including those of mixed races, the ones at the center of our present consideration.

Although characteristic of Brazil, the plantation is found here and there in all Latin American countries. The functions discussed in connection with the *hacienda* are to be found in the plantation, but sizeably enlarged. The main difference between the two systems may be that the plantation is oriented toward national and international markets and consequently weighs heavily in the shaping of the foreign policies of governments. As a melting pot, the plantation brought together blacks and whites more than *criollos* and Indians or *mestizos*. The results have been so striking that the history of Brazil could be said to be centered around the miscegenation that took place in the plantation throughout the Colonial period to the present.

This function was most efficiently performed by masters and slaves not only on account of the mores of the times to which even priests had to succumb, but with the help of the very physical layout of the plantation quarters that kept together the *casa grande* and the *zenzala*.[35] In this regard, the *hacienda* was less centralized than the plantation. In thinking of the *hacienda* and the plantation, it must be kept in mind that great mountains frequently separated *haciendas* from *haciendas* and great land expanses separated plantation from plantation. In all cases communications were difficult. This may not fully apply to the third type of melting pot, the metropolis, usually connected with each other at least within the confines of the same country.

Latin America is not as yet an urban continent. Only six countries, (Uruguay, 80 percent; Argentina, 74 percent; Chile, 68 percent; Venezuela, 62 percent; Colombia, 52 percent; and Mexico, 51 percent) had registered as urban countries by 1964. Some countries are very far from being urban, such as Haiti, 12 percent; Honduras, 23 percent; and the Dominican Republic, 30 percent. Often, however, each Latin American country is dominated by a major city. Argentina (22 million) is dominated by Buenos Aires (7 million); Uruguay (2 million) by Montevideo (1.2 million); Chile (8.5 million) by Santiago (2.3 million);

Paraguay (1.9 million) by Asunción (305 thousand); Peru (11.5 million) by Lima-Callao (1.7 million); Bolivia (4 million) by La Paz (380 thousand); Ecuador (5.5 million) by Guayaquil (750 thousand) and Quito (550 thousand); Venezuela (9 million) by Caracas-LaGuaira (2 million); Panama (1.3 million) by Panama City (300 thousand); Costa Rica (1.5 million) by San Jose (350 thousand); El Salvador (2.9 million) by San Salvador (300 thousand); Nicaragua (1.7 million) by Managua (300 thousand); Honduras (2.3 million) by Tegucigalpa (200 thousand); and Guatemala (4.5 million) by Guatemala City (600 thousand). The other three remaining countries of continental Latin America are dominated by very few major cities: Brazil (85 million) is dominated by Sao Paulo (3.9 million), Rio de Janeiro (3.4 million), Recife (1 million), Salvador and Belo Horizonte (700 thousand each) and Fortaleza (600 thousand).

Likewise Colombia (18.5 million) is dominated by four major cities: Bogotá (1.8 million), Medellín and Cali (750 thousand each) and Barranquilla (450 thousand).

Finally Mexico (42 million) is dominated by Mexico City (5 million), Guadalajara (700 thousand) and Monterrey (550 thousand). Two other Mexican cities may be mentioned, both located along the United States border: Cuidad Juárez and Tijuana, each with about 350 thousand people.

For the purposes of the present discussion, not all of the cities listed are considered to be racial and ethnic melting pots of great significance unless they are strategically located at the crossroads of culturally different groups. Guatemala City and La Paz are small indeed when compared with Mexico City or Buenos Aires, but they are meeting points of Indians, *criollos*, and *ladinos* and of Aymara and Quechua Indians with *criollos* and *mestizos* in their respective countries. By contrast with the remaining cities of the continent, Tegucigalpa, Managua, and San José in Central America and Asunción in South America could hardly be considered important in the miscegenation of the area.

Although the urbanization of Spanish America and the urbanization of Portuguese America have followed varying courses, one thing is clear from the records kept by historians: urbanization in Latin America cannot be explained by industrialization.[46] Industrialization has neither been a primary factor, nor even a significant factor until very recently. The agrarian structure of Latin America is most responsible for its urbanization,[101] followed by the growth of the central government and earthquaking political unrest in Spanish America, by the influence of merchants and plantation owners in Brazil, by the immigration waves sweeping the shores of Brazil, Uruguay, Argentina, and Chile, and very late Venezuela, and by the unparalleled population explosion on the whole continent. The impact of industrialization did not noticeably affect Latin America until the late forties and early fifties and it has not as yet touched many countries.

In any case, the urban centers of Latin America are the most boiling of all the melting pots. The melting effect does not appear even across the layers of the social structure. There seems to be a positive correlation between urbanization and the ratios of legitimacy to illegitimacy, and between the consolidation of stratification blocks and class endogamy. Therefore, assuming that the preceding considerations are correct, the melting effect is felt more obviously toward the bottom than toward the top of the social pyramid. Add to this that, in contrast to the United States, the Latin American socioeconomic pyramid is narrow at the top and very broad at the bottom. This fact will be taken up in more detail later. One more thing should be kept in mind presently: the pyramid is not entirely solid; there are cracks in it, both vertical and horizontal. It is in these cracks that change is taking place.

From the viewpoint under scrutiny here, migrations from other continents to Latin America are extremely significant, as they have been significant in the rural-urban flow of people, those primarily pushed away from the countryside by an unpromising agrarian system. As already indicated, heading the list of countries affected by international (primarily extra-continental) migrations comes Brazil, followed by Argentina, Uruguay, Chile, Mexico, Venezuela, Colombia, and Panama; North American immigrants prevail in Central America, and the remaining countries have token numbers of people from abroad. And most immigrants settle in the cities. The cities are, therefore, the centers where practically all streams meet.

It has been shown previously that class and color—interchangeable in Latin America—are the major barriers to miscegenation. It has been suggested also that the Latin American socio-economic pyramid is narrow at the top and broad at the bottom, meaning that the great bulk of Latin Americans are poor. Then one can expect that whatever melting is occurring must be found in the slums and quasi-slums of the urban centers. The melting mechanism will be taken up in the succeeding chapter.

References and Selected Bibliography

1. Adams, Richard N. *A Community in the Andes: Problems and Progress in Muquiyauyo.* (University of Washington Press, Seattle). 1959.
2. Adams, Richard N. *Encuesta sobre la cultura de los ladinos en Guatemala.* (Versión Castellano de Joaquin Noval). (Editorial del Ministerio de Educación Publica, Guatemala). 1956.
3. Bailey, Helen Miller. *Santa Cruz of the Etla Hills.* (University of Florida Press, Gainesville). 1958.
4. Bancroft, Hubert Howe. *The Early American Chroniclers.* (A. L. Bancroft and Company, San Francisco). 1883, pp. 33–34.
5. Bandelier, Adolf. "The Social Organization and Mode of Government of the Ancient Mexicans" in Harvard University Peabody Museum of American Anthropology and Ethnology, Cambridge. (Salem Press, Salem). 1876.
6. Barber, R. K. *Indian Labor in the Spanish Colonies.* (University of New Mexico Press, Albuquerque). 1932.
7. Baudin, Louis. *A Socialist Empire: The Incas of Peru.* (Van Nostrand Company, Princeton, New Jersey). 1961.
8. Bazzanella, W. *Problemas de urbanizacao na America latina: Fontes bibliograficas.* ("Publications of the Latin American Center for Research in the Social Sciences," No. 2). (Centro-Americano de Pesquisas em Ciencias Socias, Rio de Janeiro). 1960.
9. Beals, Ralph L. *Cheran: A Sierra Tarascan Village.* (Government Printing Office, Washington, D.C.). 1946, p. 91.
10. Beals, Ralph L. "The History of Acculturation in Mexico." *Homenaje al Dr. Alfonso Caso.* (Imprento Nuevo Mundo, Mexico). 1951, pp. 73–82.
11. Bennett, Wendell C., and Junius Bird. *Andean Culture History.* (American Museum of Natural History, Handbook Series, Second Revised Edition). (Doubleday, New York). No. 15, 1964, p. 319.
12. Beyer, G. H., editor. *The Urban Explosion in Latin America (A Continent in Process of Modernization).* (Cornell University Press, Ithaca, New York). 1967.

The Un-melting Pot 41

13. Biesanz, John B., and Mavis Biesanz. *The People of Panama*. (Columbia University Press, New York). 1955.
14. Blomberg, Rolf. *The Naked Aucas: An Account of the Indians of Ecuador*. Translated by F. H. Lyon. (Essential Books, Fair Lawn, New Jersey). 1957.
15. Boltshauser, Joao. *Nocoes de evolucao urbana nas Americas. (2a parte)*. (Minas Gerais, Brazil). 1960.
16. Boxer, C. R. *Portuguese Society in the Tropics (The Municipal Councils of Goa, Macao, Bahia, and Luanda, 1510-1800)*. (University of Wisconsin Press, Madison). 1965.
17. Caplow, Theodore, Sheldon Stryker and Samuel E. Wallace. *The Urban Ambience: A Study of San Juan, Puerto Rico*. (Bedminster Press, Totowa, New Jersey). 1964.
18. Carter, William E. *Aymara Communities and the Bolivian Agrarian Reform*. (University of Florida Press, Gainesville). 1965.
19. Castro, Américo. *Ibero-América su historia y su cultura*. (Dryden, New York). 1954.
20. Chevalier, Francois. *La Formation des grands domaines aux Mexique. Terre et Société aux XVI-XVII Siècles*. (Travaux et Mémoires de L'Institut D'Ethnologie, LVI, Paris). 1952.
21. Cordoza y Aragón, Luis. *Guatemala, las líneas de su mano*. (First Edition). (Fondo de Cultura Económica, Mexico). 1955.
22. Covarrubias, Miguel. *Mexico South: The Isthmus of Tehuantepec*. (A. A. Knopf, New York). 1946.
23. Eduardo, Octavio da Costa. *The Negro in Northern Brazil: a study in acculturation*. (University of Washington Press). 1948.
24. Davis, Kingsley. "La Causas y Efectos del Fenómeno de Primacía Urbana Con Referencia Especial a América Latina." *Institute of International Studies*. (University of California, Berkeley). 1962.
25. Debuyst, Federico. *La Población en América Latina*. (Centro de Investigaciones Socio-Religiosas, Brussels). 1961.
26. Del Castillo, Bernal Díaz. *The Discovery and Conquest of Mexico*. (Farrar, Straus & Cudahy, New York). 1956.
27. Di Natale, Remo. *Revolución agraria en Bolivia*. (Imprenta Universitaria, Cochabamba, Bolivia). 1953.
28. Dorselaer, Jaime, and Alfonso Gregory. *La Urbanización en América Latina*. (Sues de Rivadeneira, Madrid). 1962.
29. Dorsinnfang Smets, A. "Contacts de cultures et problemes d'acculturation en Amerique du Sud." *Revue del Institute de Sociologie*. (Bruselas, Belgica). No. 3, 1954, pp. 647-666.
30. Espino, Esperanza, et al. *Algunos Aspectos Demonáficos y Económicos de Panamá*. (Dirección de Estadística y Censo, Panama). 1964.
31. *Etnografía de Mexico*. Síntesis Monográficas, Instituto de Investigaciones (Universidad Nacimal Autonems de Mexico, Mexico). 1957.
32. Ferguson, J. Halcro. *Latin America: The Balance of Race Redressed*. (Oxford University Press, London). 1961.
33. Ford, Thomas R. *Man and Land in Peru*. (University of Florida Press, Gainesville). 1955.
34. Foster, George M. "The Significance to Anthropological Studies of the

Places of Origin of Spanish Emigrants to the New World." *Acculturation in the Americas.* (Proceedings and Selected Papers of the 29th International Congress of Americanists, ed. Sol Tax). (The University of Chicago Press, Chicago). 1952, pp. 292–298.
35. Freyre, Gilberto. *The Masters and the Slaves.* (Second Edition). (A. A. Knopf, New York). 1956, p. 23.
36. Fuju, Yukio, and T. Lynn Smith. *The Acculturation of the Japanese Immigrants in Brazil.* (University of Florida Press, Gainesville). 1959.
37. Galvao, Eduardo, and Charles Wagley. *The Tenehara Indians of Brazil: A Culture in Transition.* (Columbia University Press, New York). 1949.
38. Gamio, Manuel. *Consideraciones sobre el problema indigenista.* (Instituto Indegenista Interamericano, Mexico, D.F.). 1948.
39. Gillin, John. *The Culture of Security in San Carlos: a study of a Guatemalan community of Indians and Ladinos.* (Middle American Research Institute, Tulane University, New Orleans). No. 16, 1951.
40. Gillin, John P. *Moche, A Peruvian Coastal Town.* (Government Printing Office, Washington, D.C.). 1947.
41. Goldman, Irving.* *The Cubeo: Indians of the Northwest Amazon. Illinois Studies in Anthropology,* No. 2). (University of Illinois Press, Urbana). 1962.
42. Gordon, B. LeRoy. *Human Geography and Ecology in the Sinu Country of Colombia.* (University of California Press, Berkeley). 1957.
43. Gourou, Pierre, and E. D. Laborde. *The Tropical World.* (Fourth Edition). (Longmans, Green & Company, London). 1961.
44. Griffen, William B. *Notes on Seri Indian Culture, Sonora, Mexico, 1959.* (A series sponsored by the School of Inter-American Affairs, University of Florida). (University of Florida Press, Gainesville) 1959.
45. Harris, Marvin. *Town and Country in Brazil.* (Columbia University Press, New York). 1956.
46. Hauser, Philip M. (editor). *Urbanization in Latin America.* (Columbia University Press, New York). 1961.
47. Herrick, Bruce H. *Urban Migration and Economic Development in Chile.* (M.I.T. Press, Cambridge). 1966.
48. Herskovits, Melville J. *Life in a Haitian Village.* (A. A. Knopf, New York). 1937.
49. Hohnberg, Allan R. *Nomads of the Long Bow: The Siriono of Eastern Bolivia.* (Government Printing Office, Washington, D.C.). 1950.
50. Hoyt, E. "El trabajo indígena en las fincas cafetaleras de Guatemala." *Ciencias Sociales.* (Pan American Union, Washington, D.C.). Vol. VI, No. 35, 1955.
51. Hutchinson, Harry W. *Village and Plantation Life in Northeastern Brazil.* (University of Washington Press, Seattle). 1957.
52. Infield, Henrik F., and Koka Freier. *People in Ejidos: A Visit to the Cooperative Farms of Mexico.* (Frederick A. Praeger, New York). 1954.
53. Iturriaga, José E. *La Estructura Social y Cultural de Mexico.* (Fondo de Cultural Económica, Mexico City). 1951.

54. Jijon y Caamano, Jacinto. *Antropología prehispánica del Ecuador: Resumen—1945.* (Quito, Ecuador). 1952.
55. Keeler, Clyde E. *Apples of Immortality from the Cuna Tree of Life (The study of a most ancient ceremonial and a belief that survived 10,000 years).* (Exposition Press, New York). 1961.
56. Kelsey, Vera, and Lilly de Jongh Osborne. *Four Keys to Guatemala.* (Revised Edition). (Funk and Wagnalls, New York). 1961.
57. Kirchhoff, Paul. "Mesoamerica: Its Geographic Limits, Ethnic Composition and Cultural Characteristics." *Heritage of Conquest,* by Sol Tax, et al. (Free Press, Glencoe, Illinois). 1952, pp. 17–30.
58. Lannoy, Juan, and Gustavo Perez. *Estructuras demográficas y sociales de Colombia.* (Centro de Investigaciones Sociales, Bogotá). 1961.
59. Levi-Strauss, Claude. "Les structures sociales dans le Brasil central et oriental." *Indian Tribes of Aboriginal America.* (Selected Papers of the 29th International Congress of Americanists, ed. Sol Tax). (The University of Chicago Press, Chicago). 1952, pp. 302–10.
60. Levi-Strauss, Claude. *Tristes Tropiques.* (Criterion Books, New York). 1961.
61. McClean-Estenos, Roberto. *La Presencia del Indio en América.* (Instituto of IS of UNAM, Mexico). 1961.
62. McClean-Estenos, Roberto. *Negros en el nuevo mundo.* (Editorial P.T.C.M., Lima). 1948.
63. Martinez-Estrada, Ezequiel. *Diferencias y Semejangas entre los Paises de la América Latina.* (Escuela Nacional de Ciencias Políticas y Sociales, Mexico). 1962.
64. Mattelart, Armand. *Manual de Análisis Demográfico.* (Centro de Investigaciones Sociológicas, Universidad Católica de Chile, Santiago). 1964.
65. Mejia Fernández, Miguel. *El Problema del Trabajo Forzado en América Latina.* (Institute of IS of UNAM, Mexico). 1961.
66. Montesino Samperio, José V. *La Población del area Metropolitana de Carácas: Factores de Crecimiento y Tendencia futura.* (Quadernos de Información Económica, Caracas). 1956.
67. Morner, Magnus. "The history of race relations in Latin America: Some comments on the state of research." *Latin America Research Review.* Vol. I, No. 3, Summer 1966, pp. 17–44.
68. Morse, Richard M. *From Community to Metropolis: A Biography of Sao Paulo, Brazil.* (University of Florida Press, Gainesville). 1958.
69. Munizaga, Carlos. *La situación de contacto de las sociedades nacionales con sus grupos atrasados: Nota preliminar sobre los Araucanos de Chile.* (Escuela Latinoamericana de Sociología, Santiago, FLACSO). 1959.
70. Murdock, George P. *Outline of South American Cultures.* (Behavior Science Outlines, Vol. II, Human Relations Area Files, Inc., New Haven). 1951.
71. Nash, Manning. *Machine Age Maya: The Industrialization of a Guatemala Community.* (Free Press, Glencoe, Illinois). 1958.
72. Netto, Antonio Jordao, and Santa Helena Bosco. *O Imigrante espanhol em São Paulo.* (Departamento de Imigracao e Colonizacao, São Paulo, Brazil). 1963.

73. Nunley, Robert E. *The Distribution of Population in Costa Rica.* (National Academy of Sciences, National Research Council, Washington). 1960.
74. Ochoa, Julio Duran. *Población.* (Fondo de Cultura Económica, Mexico). 1955, p. 185.
75. Pan American Union. *Middle American Anthropology.* Vol. 2. (Pan American Union, Washington, D.C.). 1960.
76. Pan American Union. *Tipología Socioeconomica de los Paises Latinoamericanos.* (Vol. 2, Numero Especial de la *Revista Interamericana de Ciencias Sociales*). (Pan American Union, Washington, D.C.). 1963.
77. Parker, Franklin D. *The Central American Republic.* (Oxford University Press, London). 1964.
78. Parsons, James J. *Antioquia colonization in Western Colombia.* (University of California Press, Berkeley). 1949.
79. Pendle, George. *The Lands and Peoples of Paraguay and Uruguay.* (Macmillan, New York). 1959.
80. Pierson, Donald. *Cruz dos Almas: a Brazilian Village.* (Smithsonian Institution, Institute of Social Anthropology 12). (Government Printing Office, Washington, D.C.). 1951.
81. Ramos, Arthur. *As Culturas negras no novo mundo.* (Editora Civilizacao Brasileira, Rio de Janeiro). 1937.
82. Redfield, Robert. *Yucatan, una cultura de transición.* (Fondo de Cultura Económica, Mexico). 1944.
83. Redfield, Robert. *A Village that Chose Progress: Chan Kom Revisited.* (The University of Chicago Press, Chicago). 1962.
84. Redfield, Robert, and Alfonso Villa Rojas. *Chan Kom: A Mayan Village.* (Abridged Edition). (The University of Chicago Press, Chicago). 1962.
85. Reichel-Dolmatoff, Gerardo and Alicia. *The People of Aritama: The Cultural Personality of a Colombian Mestizo Village.* (The University of Chicago Press, Chicago). 1961.
86. Rowe, John Howland. "Colonial Portraits of Inca Nobles." *The Civilizations of Ancient America.* (Selected Papers of the 29th International Congress of Americanists, ed. Sol Tax). (The University of Chicago Press, Chicago). 1951, pp. 258–268.
87. Saito, Hiroshi. *O Japones no Brasil.* (Fundacao Escola de Sociologia e Politica de São Paulo, São Paulo). 1961.
88. Saunders, John Van Dyke. *The People of Ecuador: a Demographic Analysis.* (University of Florida Press, Gainesville). 1961.
89. Saunders, John Van Dyke. *Differential Fertility in Brazil.* (University of Florida Press, Gainesville). 1958.
90. Schulman, Sam. "The Colono System in Latin America." *Rural Sociology.* Vol. 20, No. 1, 1955 (March), pp. 34–40.
91. Schwalbach, Luis. "O problema de emigracao humana no quadro contemporaneo." *Boletim Paulista de Geografia.* (São Paulo, Brazil). Vol. 18, October 1954, pp. 3–14.
92. Seminario de Integración Social Guatemalteca. *Cultura indígena de Guatemala: Ensayos de antropología social.* (Editorial del Ministerio de Educación Pública, Guatemala). 1956.

93. Service, Elman R., and Heles S. Tobati. *Paraguayan Town.* (The University of Chicago Press, Chicago). 1954.
94. Service, Elman R. "The Encomienda in Paraguay." *The Hispanic American Historical Review.* Vol. 31, 1951, pp. 230–52.
95. Service, Elman R. "Indian-European Relations in Colonial Latin America." *American Anthropologist.* Vol. 57, No. 3, Part 1, June 1955, pp. 411–425.
96. Simmons, Ozzie G. "The Criollo Outlook in the Mestizo Culture of Coastal Peru." *American Anthropologist.* Vol. 57, 1955, pp. 107–117.
97. Simmons, Ozzie G. "Lo 'criollo' en la cultura peruana." *Ciencias Sociales.* (Pan American Union, Washington, D.C.). VI, 32, 1955. Pp. 87–97.
98. Simpson, Eyler N. *The Ejido.* (The University of North Carolina Press, Chapel Hill). 1937.
99. Smith, T. Lynn, et al. *Tabio: a study in rural social organization.* (Office of Foreign Agricultural Relations, U.S. Department of Agriculture, Washington, D.C.). 1945.
100. Smith, T. Lynn. *Brazil: People and Institutions.* (Revised Edition). (Louisiana State University Press, Baton Rouge). 1963.
101. Smith, T. Lynn. *Current Social Trends and Problems in Latin America.* (A series sponsored by the School of Inter-American Studies, University of Florida, Gainesville, edited by A. Curtis Wilgus). No. 1, September 1957. (University of Florida Press, Gainesville). 1957.
102. Smith, T. Lynn. *Migration from One Latin American Country to Another.* (International Population Conference, Vienna). 1959.
103. Smith, T. Lynn. "Un Análisis Comparativo de la Migración Rural-Urbana en Latino-América." *Estadística,* Washington, D.C. 1958.
104. Soustelle, Jacques. *Mexico.* (Translated by James Hogarth). (World Publishing Company, Cleveland and New York). 1967.
105. Soustelle, Jacques. *La Vida Cotidiana de los Aztecas.* (Fondo de Cultura Económica, Mexico). 1955.
106. Spinden, H. J. *Ancient Civilization of Mexico and Central America.* (Handbook Series, American Museum of Natural History, No. 3, Third Edition, New York). 1928.
107. Stycos, J. Mayone. "Problemas demográficos de América Latina." *Revista Latinoamericana de Sociología.* Vol. II, No. 1, 1966, p. 20.
108. Steward, Julian H. *Irrigation Civilizations: A Comparative Study.* (Pan American Union, Washington, D.C.). 1955.
109. Steward, Julian H., and Louis C. Faron. *Native Peoples of South America.* (McGraw-Hill, New York). 1959.
110. Taylor, Carl C. *Rural Life in Argentina.* (Louisiana State University Press, Baton Rouge). 1948.
111. Vidart, Daniel D. *La vida rural uruguayo.* (Ministerio de Ganadería y Agricultura, República Oriental del Uruguay, Montevideo). 1955.
112. Von Hagen, Victor W. *The Ancient Sun Kingdoms.* (World Publishing Company, New York). 1961.
113. Wagley, Charles. "Regionalism and Cultural Unity in Brazil." *Social Forces.* Vol. 26, 1948, pp. 457–64.
114. Wagley, Charles, and Marvin Harris. "A Typology of Latin American

Subcultures." *American Anthropologist.* Vol. 57, No. 3, Part 1, June 1955, pp. 428–451.

115. Wagley, Charles. *An Introduction to Brazil.* (Columbia University Press, New York). 1963.

116. Whetten, Nathan L. *Rural Mexico.* (The University of Chicago Press, Chicago). 1948, pp. 144–151.

117. Whetten, Nathan L. *Guatemala, the Land and the People.* (Yale University Press, New Haven). 1961.

118. Willems, Emilio. *A aculturacao dos alemaes no Brasil.* (Editora Nacional, São Paulo). 1946.

119. Willems, Emilio. "Caboclo Cultures of Southern Brazil." *Acculturation in the Americas.* (Proceedings and Selected Papers of the 29th International Congress of Americanists, ed. Sol Tax). (The University of Chicago Press, Chicago). 1952, pp. 243–281.

120. Willems, Emilio. "El Problema Rural Brasileño desde el punto de vista antropológico." *Jurnadas.* (Colegio de Mexico, Centas de Estudios Sociales, Mexico D.F.). No. 33, 1945.

121. Willems, Emilio. "Some aspects of cultural conflict and acculturation in southern rural Brazil." *Rural Sociology.* Vol. 7, 1947, pp. 374–84.

122. Willey, S. R. "The Interrelated Rise of the Native Cultures of Middle and South America." *New Interpretations of Aboriginal American Culture History.* (75th Anniversary Volume of the Anthropological Society of Washington, D.C.). 1955, pp. 28–45.

123. Ycaza-Tijerino, Julio. *Monografía Sociológica de Nicaragua.* (Institute of IS of UNAM, Mexico). 1961.

124. Zimmerman, Ben. "Race relations in the arid sertao." *Race and Class in Rural Brazil,* edited by Charles Wagley. (UNESCO, Paris). 1952.

3

The Sexual
Melting Pot

A popular misconception regarding the Latin American family, spread originally from some anthropological sources, is the belief that the extended family is characteristic of Latin America. An extended family is understood to be composed of parents and children living together with some grandparents or uncles or aunts or other relatives. There is another origin of this misconception. It is the typical close relationships that tie-in Latin America family members with various branches of the kinship system. This extended bond of preference and deference gives the impression of an extended family structure. However, this is contrary to fact. Latin America is a society or group of societies made of nuclei of interrelated conjugal families. A conjugal—or nuclear—family is composed of parents and children living together as a unit. This is not to say that there are no extended families in Latin America. Of course there are many of them. Although statistics are misleading, a fair estimate would say that they constitute about 15–20 percent of all families. The nuclear family predominates everywhere. Even in the *barriadas* of Lima and in the *favelas* of Rio, nuclear families make the majority.[46] In any event, the Latin American family is different from the American one in the *kind* of relationships that are woven into its configuration. However, it seems that a discussion of the family should be introduced by a view of the general context of sex and sex-role definitions in which the family is set.

The Meaning of Sex

It is characteristic of Latin America, when contrasted with the United States, to see sex as an adventure rather than a sin. When it is a sin it can be forgiven. There are important differences, however, between the male and the female view of sex. To begin with, women see sex as a privilege to be granted, men as a right to be claimed. This view fits the Latin American definition of the sexes.

Sex-Role Definitions

A female is to be home-bound, untouched, submissive, religious, apolitical and self-effacing. The Latin American home is definitely woman-centered. It is not only that the place of a woman is at home; it is that she is the pillar on which a home is built. Whether she is a wife or a mother or a sister or a fiancée, she is not only the symbol of family unity and security but the very foundation of both.

As a wife she supports, shields, and stimulates her husband. In organizing the household she plans the activities around his schedule of work and leisure so that his family does not become a barrier to his success, be it social, political, or economic. He knows that she is always psychologically firm and that when he comes home she is always there, waiting for him, no matter when he comes.

She erects bridges of understanding between her husband and the outer world and between her husband and other members of his inner world. She explains his behavior to others, be they relatives or strangers. Her husband is never wrong, and when he is obviously wrong she will cry but never speak. It is not that she has surrendered her mind, tastes, or feelings. Rather, is that her mind, tastes, and feelings, when they are in conflict with her husband's, are only made known in the intimacy of the family life. The case of a wife who goes around expressing "frankly" what she feels about her husband is found, but is strongly downgraded in Latin American culture. Thus, the Latin American wife is her husband's shield.

In offering her opinion to her husband, the Latin American wife would think it through first and very carefully. It is not out of fear that she takes this course of action, although fear may not be totally absent. It is that the polite behavior so characteristic of the Latin American is also present in the family world. However, the Latin American wife does not stimulate her husband to succeed merely out of finesse. There is a genuine identification with her husband in which the father image may play some part. This will be taken up later. The fact is that the Latin American family is a team and the husband-father its traditional leader. Thus, a wife would renounce a career, property rights, and family pedigrees in order to contribute to her husband's success. There is only one thing that a Latin American female will not accept: it is childlessness. If she is given the choice, she will remain single. That is, the Latin American woman does not get married just because she loves her fiancé; she expects to become a mother also. For her, sex implies reproduction (sterility is a curse), not necessarily pleasure.

As a mother, the Latin American woman is so dedicated to her children that her influence turns sometimes into some form of obsession in their later life. This dedication is a characteristic of the culture and seems to transcend religious, political, or social class boundaries as well as urban-rural differences. The Latin American folklore is full of it; every institution seems to strengthen it; art and literature have idealized it; poetry in particular has made maternal dedication the very essence of motherhood.

Dating has not caught the imagination of Latin American youth. Girls are still closely supervised during courtship. As a matter of fact, a great deal of this supervision is self-imposed. It fits the image of weakness attributed to the Latin American female. Thus sisters help sisters and brothers help sisters in this regard.

The pattern is one of mutual support, not one of rivalry. To be a sister is to be a small mother's replica in terms of dedication to the family, especially to all brothers and younger sisters. Coalitions do develop between siblings. These coalitions are normally very fluid. Only those between sisters separated by age tend to be stable. It could be maintained that the larger the age gap the stronger the coalition, perhaps because this relationship becomes a microcosmic reproduction of the parent-child bondage. The validity of this interpretation may be apparent if the Latin American family is projected against the background of the high value the culture places on biological reproduction.

It has been said that when a Latin American woman falls in love, she blinds herself to all reason. Parents and other older relatives are quite aware of this phenomenon and skillfully draw designs for courtship and marriage. Often, the whole community plays the game so well that the youths concerned would continue to believe that the choice has been entirely their own. There is little evidence that indicates any major inroad of the American ways in the Latin American courtship patterns, certainly not along the United States-Mexican border where the author has conducted studies from time to time. Even Mexican-Americans in the United States are not as free as the Anglo-Americans in this form of premarital behavior.

In the rural areas premarital sexual intercourse is frequent because it is viewed more as natural behavior than in the urban areas. This is also true of the urban poor. However, this cannot be interpreted as a sign of instability in the nuclear family. Neither are common law marriages symptoms of familial instability. In other words, high figures of illegitimate children do not necessarily indicate high instability in the Latin American family. One of the reasons for the occurrence is that the Latin American female is both jealous and loyal. In fact, both jealousy and loyalty blossom at the first signs of emerging love. Perhaps this is also explained by the emphasis the Latin American female places on motherhood and the prestige attached to fecundity. Normally to be a mother implies to be a wife and to be a wife implies to be a mother. Illegitimacy by means of a *casa chica* or a *zenzala* is a trait of bygone centuries.

The Blessed Virgin is still the highest symbol of the Latin American unmarried female and virginity the highest symbol of femininity; to give it away is the highest expression of dedication. Not to be a virgin is an opening to more stubborn male domination (jealousy is retroactive) and an insidious arm in the hands of the husband's rivals. It must be remembered that the Latin American is extreme in both love and hatred.

In contrast with the female, the Latin American male is first a male and then a fiancé or a brother or a father or a husband. To be male means to have a freedom that often borders on irresponsibility.

There is certainly no responsibility about sex, and very little responsibility in related areas. A Latin American male takes as his inherent right the right to have access to all females no matter their age or status and never mind the consequences. This proneness has been explained in terms of *machismo* by those who forget that *machismo* is not a predominant Latin American male characteristic and certainly not a universal one. But the emphasis on sex is. As it has been discussed in Chapter 2, *machismo* is a complex that includes other traits over and above the emphasis on sex experiences.[3]

This emphasis may be explained in various ways. Psychologically, the Latin American is almost completely uninhibited and sexual relations express this lack of inhibition best. The culture stimulates creativity and for the Latin American there is no better form of creativity than procreation. Contraceptives and onanism are inconceivable in the Latin American mind. Moreover, the Latin American cherishes physical contact even in social intercourse. Sexual relations bring this contact to its highest degree of fulfillment. It seems that sex constitutes the most intimate form of identifications. I think that this is the deepest meaning of *simpático*. To stop on the surface by assuming that the Latin American is an actor, a dramatist, is to forget that if the Latin American does not like you, he will not play his role. Moreover, *simpático* is often synonymous with generosity.

Culturally, the emphasis on sex experiences may be linked to the Latin American view of life as existence, almost identical with living. People are envied not for what they have but for not *living* what they have. Thrift makes sense only if it does not interfere with living. Everything is to be used even though it may be worn out in the process. In this context, sex has the advantage of being inexhaustive.

Furthermore, since sex is inconceivable without reproduction, it becomes the most expressive symbol of prestige and also the symbol most accessible to everyone. Again this seems to have been misunderstood by those who look for explanations of this phenomenon in hedonism or epicureanism or *machismos*.

The seemingly exaggerated freedom in sex behavior of the Latin American man appears to spill over into other areas of family relations. As a husband-father, he tends to be a good provider but not a good companion or a good disciplinarian. Wives would go to their mothers or aunts rather than to their husbands to communicate whatever intimate or family problems may arise; or they would go to their father-confessors. In matters of discipline, a father-husband would support his wife with little recourse to physical punishment. It seems that the status distance or the superordination-subordination relationship that is kept in the Latin American definition of father-child patterns of behavior makes the husband-father a last court of appeals who is simultaneously loved and feared. In the traditional family—and most Latin American families fall in this category—the husband-father often has a place, whether at the table or anywhere else, that only he can occupy. Moreover, mothers may often consult with their children; fathers seldom, if at all. However, fathers do listen to the troubles of their children, secure information and tend to make fair decisions. It should be understood that they—the fathers—always make the final decisions.

The preceding description presents the Latin American husband-father in a setting of centralized authority. It is hard to find exceptions. Moreover, his status is normally supported by the mother-wife and children.

It has been observed by many investigators that Latin American societies are characteristically authoritarian at all structural levels. There is no question about it. The family is only one instance of this cultural ethos, which is common to all nodal institutions. And in every one of them this status distance is duplicated.

It would appear that out of his niche, the idol loses his powers.

The authority of the father-husband is extended to the sons in decreasing proportions according to ages. Thus a son takes responsibilities in regard to his mother to the point that she comes to see in him a prolongation of the paternal authority.

This is particularly clear in the relations of a brother with his sisters and younger brothers. However, it must not be forgotten that the position in itself without the personal qualities to lead does not guarantee that the line of authority will remain unbroken. In Latin America, perhaps more than anywhere else, inherited leadership must be sanctioned in action. At least like anywhere else *ponerse a la cabeza* (to lead) implies also personal qualities and personal efforts. The fact that the term *líder* has been borrowed from the English language does not explain, as someone has suggested, that leadership, as a situational power formation, is absent from Latin American societies. Even the familial processes of authority assignments contradict such an explanation.

Finally, the Latin American man projects his image of freedom and power into his premarital love relationships. Even when he dates, in the North American sense, he does all the planning and makes all the decisions. Only the superior power of the family can control him. Thus, during courtship the Latin American female is faced with a difficult dilemma, either chaperons or surrender. It is true that the scene is changing. However, it is at least doubtful that the changes are really welcome by youth itself. Again, my investigations along the United States-Mexico border and discussions with students coming from all Latin American countries confirm this assertion.

Sex: Dreams and Realities

The Latin American dreams about sex but becomes disappointed at the taste of it. However, the reactions of the two sexes follow almost opposite paths. Most women, who have dreamed of giving themselves in a total act of love, find soon after marriage that a variety of expressions of love are more satisfying for them than sexual intercourse. This attitude may be related to the meaning of sex which is traditional in the Roman Catholic Church. Moreover, since sex education has not yet reached the core of the culture, and since she finds that building a psychological shelter for her family against the outer world is expected of her, sex becomes secondary and, not unusually, even burdensome for her. This reaction is frequently aggravated by her realization that she cannot claim her husband all to herself.

By contrast, the Latin American man goes into a frenzy once he has tasted sex, to the point of destroying its meaning as he breaks the shell of his dreams. He makes his sex life outside his home known to all his intimate friends as if to tie closer the friendship network. This is very characteristic of the culture. To keep sex experiences to oneself is to undermine the solidarity of the peer group and eventually to deserve exile from it. Thus, if one does not care much for sexual experiences, one has to construct imaginary ones and share them in the information exchange that cements the monosexual friendship group.

Latin Americans do not discuss sex experiences with members of the opposite sex. It is improper. Not even spouses talk about sex. This is one of the barriers found in disseminating birth-control information. The Puerto Rican case is just an example. Discussion of sex across sex lines would lead to invidious comparisons which is not only very impolite but a threat to the security sought in the family. Moreover, the prestige of a husband would not be maintained if the communication gap with his wife were ever bridged. Thus, even in matters of sex, the Latin American is extremely ambivalent.

The Mother-Child Closeness and the Father-Child Distance

The dedication of the Latin American mother to her children cannot be exaggerated. There are several contributing forces. Some have already been insinuated.

Motherhood is the highest expression both of femininity *and* masculinity. Nevertheless, the various stages of motherhood are not equally valued in all levels of society. Peasant-minded populations (whether rural or urban) tend to glorify pregnancy but define delivery and child rearing as a burden. The more educated, whether traditional or modern, tend to balance the evaluation of motherhood stages by looking at motherhood as an evolving phenomenon, a continuing process. In this view, the unity of mother and child begun in the womb is carried throughout life. The offspring's marriage may extend this bond to a third generation, thus making the grandmother the most comforting psychological shelter. In Latin America no grandmother can ever be a disciplinarian.

The closeness of the relationship between mother and child is best shown in the intimacy of their communication. There are no secrets between daughters and mothers. Sons begin to withdraw from the mother's lap only at mid-adolescence (age 14) when peer group pressures demand participation in heterosexual adventures.[33b]

In a sense, a girl learns to be a mother before she learns to be a wife. She shares motherhood activities in regard to her siblings. By contrast, a boy learns to be a husband before he learns to be a father, excepting, of course, those rural areas where children work during school age. In these instances, the learning of the two roles is coterminous. In daughters and sons, the attachment to mother is normally well instilled by age 14. Mothers have, by then, become enduring symbols of a devotion that almost never fails. The isolated grandmother living alone is never found. She would feel useless, spent. The Latin American culture has not yet made room for her.

Although the closeness of daughters and mothers is striking, the closeness between sons and mothers is even more so. This is precisely what I think is more typical of the Latin American family. A son's adolescence may bring about a break of authority, but not a discontinuity of the mutual bonds of dedication.[33b] A mother knows that the adolescent boy is becoming a man if he arrives home late at night. A son knows that his mother would never waver even if he "errs." Her attitude of expecting him back in her arms sooner or later and his confidence in finding her with open arms upon his return is what has created the Latin American mother-ideal that makes her a synthesis of a martyr and a saint, a sort of priestess of love. Her son would travel long distances to see her. Upon her death he would cover her tomb with flowers every anniversary, and her image would continue guiding his life as a beneficent spirit. In looking for a wife, he would project the new image against his mother's image and would expect a devotion that can no longer be found. This is why the Latin American wife has to be a mother before in fact she is one. Only the arrival of her first baby begins to break her husband's dream world. This also explains further why the Latin American family is woman-centered.

When viewed against this background, the relations between father and child could not be more different. The process begins with the way a man relates to his wife; he is never a companion to her. Moreover, he would never be a mother-surrogate in any task concerning infant care. The physical contact inherent in the mother-child bond is almost totally alien to the father-child relationship. All this explains why I said earlier that the father-child relationship is one of superordination and subordination, of authority and deference. There is love, of course, but without intimacy. And there is awe. The child learns soon that there are clear boundaries between him and his father; that physical boundaries— father's office, *his* place at the table, *his* auto, *his* horse, *his* tools —are symbols of emotional and decisional boundaries not to be trespassed. His father will never be a pal. Obviously this father-child distance makes the mother-child closeness closer still.

A father would never do for his son what a son can do for himself. Beginning early in life, the son is given gradual responsibilities that mothers often tend to alleviate. Here lies a source of family tensions. Fathers always expect too much. In turn, a boy has to perform in order to deserve the trust. In this way, responsibilities are allocated and reallocated according to past performance.

To explain Latin American instability in terms of personal irresponsibility in this light is to ignore simple facts. For the Latin American *la vida es una lucha,* life is a struggle. The struggle begins with life. A girl has to learn to be a mother very early; likewise, a boy has to learn to be a husband. Neither can do it without *lucha.* Victory is the highest source of prestige.

The same principle applies to other segments of society that must contend for the things they want. To expect that social reform would come from the top, as in 19th century England; that the landed aristocracy would gracefully part with its estates; that management would thoughtfully share its profits; that employers would generously raise labor's wages; that political parties and unions would agreeably distribute their power; that the Church would lovingly decentralize her authority—is to forget that the family is the microcosmos of the Latin American universe. This is not just a symbol. In my view there is no other institution that penetrates the Latin American culture so thoroughly. This point will be made more clear as the discussion proceeds. One thing should already be clear. By late adolescence (age 16), boys and girls have contrasting images of what sort of a wife-mother and a husband-father the Latin American culture expects. At marriage, the young wife expects protective authority; the young husband, unwavering dedication. Thus a new cycle begins.

Family Typing:
The Fluid Kinship System

The preceding analysis has shown that fitting Latin American family relations into a mold or into classifying pigeonholes is a very serious task. The reality is so fluid that it may defy classification. As has been already indicated, the nuclear family is a knot in a network of blood relationships. There is, nevertheless, a continuing transformation of the nuclear into the extended family, and vice versa. It is not unusual for members to drop into other nuclear families for extended periods. Relatives circulate from one family to another, back and forth. Sometimes one can find bundles of nuclear families, representing vertically two or three generations and laterally various radii of relationships, hanging together under the same roof or in the very same block. In general, however, (see Fig. 2) relatives circulate throughout a rather limited network extending from grandparents to grandchildren and covering the in-laws, and the first cousin, uncle-nephew, aunt-niece part of the kinship structure. Circulation of other relatives seldom occurs.

Sometimes, especially in the rural areas, cousins are called brothers (or sisters) and aunts are called mothers. This is, of course, not typical of Latin America.

Figure 2   Most Common Boundaries of the Latin American Kinship System

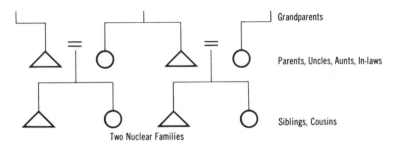

NOTE: Figure 2 makes no justice to the complexities of the typical kinship group since in-laws and *compadres* are not shown in the diagram and the number of uncles and aunts is normally larger than indicated here. Nevertheless, at least three generations appear clear.

The patriarchal family is very seldom found, and to talk about a clan is loose talk, except perhaps among Indian groups, where diversity is still the rule.

Why is it that the Latin American kinship system, so circumscribed and so fluid, is nevertheless characterized by warm face-to-face relationships? Answers to this question cannot make sense outside the context of the value-meaning-norm configuration that cements the Latin American societies in various ways. It was stated in Chapter 1 that the Latin American splits the world in two and builds no bridges between the parts. At one time, I had conceived the blueprint of Latin American social structure as made of concentric levels of varying emotional depth, man being at the center of this design: First his nuclear family, then other relatives, next his *compadres* and other friends, and finally his neighbors; beyond the periphery of this inner world, in the outer world, lay strangers and enemies.[3] In this blueprint, *compadres* and friends bridge the split world. Upon closer study, however, this image of the Latin American's social universe seems quite inaccurate. My present view is somewhat different and seems to make better sense. The Latin American's inner world is still composed of relatives, friends, and *compadres,* but the pattern of relationships in which they move is more intricate than the one just given. Friends often penetrate the nuclear family as a wedge in a degree of intimacy that seems at times to threaten the solidarity of the kin group. In this case, they may be made *compadres.* Some *compadres* also tend to become identified as belonging to the nuclear family. Cousins, especially those of school age, often belong to it too, in such a way as to be considered by both relatives and neighbors equal to the siblings. When related families live close to one another, the flow of communication and the rate of commodity and service exchange grows so complex as to defy description. It is also frequently a source of confusion for anyone not familiar with the exchange. If one adds to this the circulation of grandparents, uncles, aunts, in-laws, nephews, and nieces, especially when the nuclear family has no children, the kaleidoscope cannot be represented in Euclidean geometry.

From the point of view of human ecology, Latin America, with the exception of Brazil and perhaps Argentina, had no West as the United States had. The original settlers arrived by sea, climbed the mountains, went down the mountains, and soon reached the blue horizon of the sea. They could go no farther. Thus, they returned to the top of the mountains whence they had come to orient themselves and to decide where to go from there. In all probability they followed the direction of the great mountain that runs North and South, to find soon again that the mountain, resembling the back of a gigantic crocodile, is broken by canyons and ridges that in turn run east and west. To see the sky, they had to climb mountains or, in the jungle, trees. All directional movement was slow and usually relatives followed in order to lean on each other's shoulders. Often, the young pioneer returned home to bring a bride and his old folks. Once they settled down, there was no reason to go back across the abrupt ridges they had passed but not tamed. They had all there was to be had in their mountain cañon, if they could continue jointly the *lucha* they had started jointly. Thus tradition and geography crowded in on the Latin

American kin group.   In Brazil and Argentina, the plantation and the *estancia* helped in the development of an extended family, which was, in the final analysis, a nucleus of nuclear families, except in the *casa grande* where the owner-master was a patriarch. Although the main traditions are still alive, the Latin American family of recent times is on the move: geographically, it is moving to the urban centers; socially, it is moving upward along the rungs of the stratification system. However, the *kind* of relationships have not changed very much. Segmental studies conducted in Mexico City, Bogotá, Lima, Rio, Santiago, and Buenos Aires tell of the ties that still remain strong in the kinship system;[35b] ties that even connect city and town.[28, 29]

Geographic and social mobility has brought about some independence and emancipation but has not damaged the warmth characteristic of the kin group. In the absence of mother and father, the Latin American falls back on the familial and friendship network. Only its members can surely be trusted. Success would spread throughout the network, failure would tie fast the pristine knot. The man who does not share with relatives his success *or* failure is *orgulloso*. And *orgullo* (pride) stains anyone's prestige. A successful man enhances the prestige of his kin; a failing man who seeks refuge in their midst enhances their prestige also. Even more, a relative must always be backed up. *Con los tuyos con razón o sin ella;* your relatives right or wrong. This is, in short, the Latin American kin group. Now I will discuss the *compadre* system.

Compadres Everywhere

Compadres are made in a variety of ways. Originally *compadrazgo* was the extension to the parents of the religious bond established at baptism between their child and his godparents.[2] *Compadres* means literally co-parents. In fact, the Church was concerned with assuring the Christian education of the child by extending the obligation from parents to godparents. Moreover, if his parents failed, the child was placed under the custody of his godparents. In certain areas, in an obvious extension of the incest taboo, an ecclesiastical taboo was erected regarding the marriage between a widow and her *compadre* or between a widower and his *comadre.*

Similarly, with the administration of some other Church sacraments, *compadres* could be made. Some other religious rituals have been turned into occasions to make new *compadres.* Even purely social occasions are used to make more *compadres.* It is not necessary to number these occasions. What seems most interesting is to see how the *compadre* system stretches out into the Latin American social structure and how it operates in this structure. As intended by the early Church, the godparent was a sponsor. He was a Christian of good standing who had passed on the "good news" (the gospel) to the new convert, and who could guarantee his perseverance. Eventually, when children's baptism became an institution, the Church sought a double assurance that the gift of faith was not being taken lightly; in a real sense, she was extending her protective arm to the parents through the godparents. In fact, uneducated Christians were not accepted as godparents. Thus this religious linkage brought together lords and serfs, aristocracy and peasantry, to the service of Mother Church (*la Santa Madre Iglesia*). In this way the uneducated and illiterate (often poor) found himself tied to the educated and literate (often rich) with a double bond, that of Christian faith and economic dependency. In Latin America the *encomienda* perpetuated the bondage, as have the *hacienda,* the *estancia,* the plantation, and in latter days the factory.

Godparenthood and *compadrazgo* are still very much alive in Latin America.[11] When parents are in search of godparents, they much keep two things in mind, the good standing of the candidates in the eyes of the Church, and their status in the eyes of the community. For the parents, the relationship is often loaded with mobility aspirations, for the prospective godparents may represent prestige and power. The more godchildren (and *compadres*) a person has accepted, the higher his social visibility and the stronger his arm in the community. This does not mean, however, that a man would accept the burden indiscriminately. His very rank demands that he be selective.

There is no Latin American institution immune to the force of *compadrazgo.* Few social activities lie beyond its reach. Obviously *compadres* can enter where kin cannot. It also draws the person closer to the family and the kin group. Perhaps in recognition of these facts, the Church has never allowed a priest to be a godparent. One would think that nobody could be better qualified for the role.

To be successful, to pull the right string at the right time, one must have *compadres* everywhere: in government bureaus, in political councils, in business directorates, in scholarship committees, in all sorts of *juntas*. If you are applying for a job, bidding for a contract, pleading in a court, running for an office, bargaining for property, planning for promotion, looking for a bride, going anywhere—especially upward—find out first who is *compadre* to whom and their prestige differences. Then enlist one with the most prestige.

From the point of view of personality, the *compadre* adds warmth and security to the kin group that shelters the individual. He is often aware that the relation is one of exchange and reciprocity. Thus the extended kin group (family, *compadres,* friends) becomes a therapeutic institution: problems are discussed, troubles aired, plans consulted, projects analyzed, emotions calmed, errors prevented, aspirations stimulated, frustrations understood, fears overcome, anxieties diffused, hopes balanced, strategies laid out, and solidarities cemented. Psychiatry could not find a better ally. This is all to the good.

The Latin American societies would be the best in the world (therapeutically) if the extended kin group had only one side. It does have more than one side, however. In its orientation toward the larger society, the Latin American kin group is a source of conflict. It is precisely the realization of this fact that explains the Latin American's inclination to stretch his kin group *ad infinitum.* It is illuminating to record that in Colombia, during the late forties, when the contending political factions (liberals and conservatives) were deliberately leading the country toward civil war or dictatorship, a social movement was started to stimulate young men and women to marry into families in opposite parties. It was thought that perhaps kinship could mend what ideologies had cut asunder. Children bring prestige but they also bring *compadres.* To bring the outer world under control, the Latin American infiltrates it with *compadres.*

The extended kin group, although brisk, is very volatile. This is true as you approach its boundaries. Thus, unless communication and physical contacts are renewed often in warm *abrazos,* the system changes in membership and lines of solidarity with astonishing fluidity. To last, loyalty must be reasserted ritually in frequent gatherings.

The Unanswered Question of Illegitimacy and Prostitution

If the family is so strong, if the kin group is still further strengthened by *compadrazgo,* why is it that illegitimacy and prostitution are so common in Latin America?

One explanation is the very character of the Latin American extended kin group. First of all, the social intimacy has been diffused from the nuclear family to the rest of the kin network. Husbands communicate more readily in matters of sex with their intimate friends and *compadres* of the same sex than with their wives.[23] This communication seems to treat sex as a "man's business." On the other hand, wives are either pregnant or ambivalent enough about sexual intercourse so as not often to attract their husbands, who may come home late at night anyway from "talking with the boys and visiting the girls," to quote a North American expression. Quite often, the friend or the *compadre* is a single man who cannot, like Tantalus, drink from his own fountain, because, after all, he will only marry a virgin. Their parents, older brothers, the brides themselves realize that if people in general cannot be trusted, men in particular may not keep their promises and may dishonor the family by dishonoring the girl. Honor, like hope, *es lo último que se pierde,* is the very last thing to lose. Moreover, if at any one time a family retains its solidarity, it is when a girl has entered adolescence and is approaching marriage. In summary, the kin group contributes to extra-marital and premarital sexual experiences outside the home sociologically by diffusing intimacy, making sex a matter of concern of the monosexual peer group, and by protecting girls strictly from dangerous affairs.

Culturally, as suggested above, a man's sex role definition carries with it the idea of sexual freedom; a woman's, in contrast, of sexual restraint. The psychological consequences of this cultural emphasis are clear: rejection of group values implies ostracism and loneliness; moreover, the codes are too deeply ingrained in the personality for the individual to be able to violate them without feelings of shame.

Viewed from this perspective, prostitution (and illegitimacy) make perfect sense. The picture is complicated by other aspects of the structure of most Latin American societies and cultures. It is, first, the breach between rich and poor; the unbalanced sex ratio; the geographical mobility of young males; the value placed on having children regardless of the consequences; the sociability of the Latin American; the believed therapeutic effect of the sexual transaction; the weakened bond of religious beliefs.

The strengthening of the nuclear family may bring about the weakening of the kin group. This may be the price Latin America has to pay, at this level, for the control of illegitimacy and prostitution. A change in values, as has been often proposed, mainly by outsiders, may be another alternative. This means, in a sense, a change by definition. Other alternatives will be offered later, since, in my view, familial relations cannot be treated in a vacuum.

From the Latin American point of view, the Puritan standards of sexual morality have contributed heavily to the bitterness characterizing race relations in North America. In the same view, illegitimacy and prostitution are the most effective means of miscegenation. In fact, they constitute almost the very bottom of the genetic melting pot. Break it and you will have a racial-caste system. Thus, from an ethical perspective, illegitimacy and prostitution have been the cost of miscegenetic societies.

The previous statement, although somewhat exaggerated, contains enough truth to explain some of the processes that have produced in Latin America all forms of *mestizaje*. This point has already been elaborated. What needs to be added is that perhaps illegitimacy and prostitution, at least historically, have torn down the racial barriers to legitimate sexual relations; they have, in other words, weakened the stigma placed on mixed marriages. Brazil and the Circumcaribbean countries are the most outstanding examples. In the following chapter, two aspects of the larger social context in which the family operates will be discussed. It is my hope in doing so that the idiosyncratic aspects of the Latin American kin group, of which Latin Americans are so proud, will become clearer still.

References and Selected Bibliography

1. Agramonte, Roberto. *Sociologia Latino-Americana*. (University of Puerto Rico, Rio Piedras). 1963.
2. Azevedo, Thales de. "Familia, casamento e divorcio no Brasil." *Journal of Inter-American Studies*. Vol. 3, 1961, pp. 213–237.
3. Beals, Ralph L., and Norman D. Humphy. *No frontier to learning: the Mexican student in the U.S.* (The University of Minnesota Press, Minneapolis). 1957.
4. Beals, R. L. *Cheran: A Sierra Tarascan Village* (Government Printing Office, Washington, D.C.). 1946.
5. Buarque de Holanda, Sergio. *Cuminhos e Fronteiras*. (Livraria Jose Olympio editora, Rio de Janeiro). 1957.
6. Bunzel, Ruth. *Chichicastenango*. (Publication of the American Ethnological Society XXII, New York). 1952.
7. Fals-Borda, Orlando. *Campesinos de los Andes: Estudio sociológico de Saucio*. ("Monografías sociológicas," No. 7) (Editorial Iqueima, Bogotá). 1960.
8. Fals-Borda, Orlando. *Peasant Society in the Colombian Andes; A Sociological Study of Saucio*. (University of Florida Press, Gainesville). 1955.
9. Faron, Louis C. *Mapuche Social Structure: Institutional Reintegration in a Patrilineal Society of Central Chile*. (*Illinois Studies in Anthropology* No. 1). (University of Illinois Press, Urbana). 1961.
10. Faron, Louis C. "Araucanian Patri-Organization and the Omaha System." *American Anthropologist*, Vol. 53, No. 3, June 1956 pp. 435–456.
11. Flores, Elias, Munizaga, Carlos, Rodriguez, Fausto, et al. *Compadrazgo, estructura social y grupos de referencias*. (FLACSO, Escuela Latinoamericana de Sociología, Santiago). 1959. One of a series of six studies by Fellows of Latin American School of Sociology during its first year of operation, 1958–59.
12. Foster, George M. "Report on an Ethnological Reconnaissance of Spain." *American Anthropologist*, No. 53, July-Sept., 1951, pp. 311–325.

13. Freyre, Gilberto. *New World in the Tropics*. (A. A. Knopf, New York). 1959.
14. Fuente, Julio de la. *Yalalag, una Villa Zapoteca Serrana*. (Museo Nacional de Antropología, Mexico). 1949.
15. Godoy Urzua, Hernan. "Bosquejo Sociológico de la familia en América Latina." *Cuadernos del Sur*, enero-febrero, 1967, pp. 55–64.
16. Gomez Robleda, Jose y D'Aloja, Ada. *La Familia y la Casa*. (Instituto of IS of UNAM, Mexico). 1961.
17. Hayner, Norman S. "The Family in Mexico." *Marriage and Family Living*, Vol. 16, No. 4, Nov. 1954, pp. 369–373.
18. Hayner, Norman S., and Una Middleton Hayner. *New Patterns in Old Mexico: A Study of Town and Metropolis*. (College and University Press, New Haven). 1966.
19. Hayner, Norman S. "Notes on the Changing Mexican Family." *American Sociological Review*, Vol. 7, pp. 489–497.
20. Hill, Reuben, et al. *The Family and Population Control: A Puerto Rican Experiment in Social Change*. (University of North Carolina Press, Chapel Hill). 1959.
21. Labarca Hubertson, Amanda. *Evolución Femenina en el Desarrollo de Chile en la Primera Mitad del Siglo XX*. (Editorial Universitaria, Santiago). 1951.
22. Labarca Hubertson, Amanda. *Feminismo Contemporáneo*. (Empresa Zig-Zag, Santiago). 1947.
23. Hoyos, Arturo de & Genevieve. "The Amigo System & Alienation of the Wife in the Conjugal Mexican Family" in Bernard Farber (ed.), *Kinship & Family Organization*. (John Wiley, New York). 1966, pp. 102–115.
24. Landy, David. *Tropical Childhood: Cultural Transmission and Learning in a Rural Puerto Rican Village*. (University of North Carolina Press, Chapel Hill). 1959.
25. Lathrop, Carlos Segundo. "Las Santiaguinas." (Imprenta America, Santiago). 1883.
26. Lewis, Oscar. "An Anthropological Approach to Family Studies." *American Journal of Sociology*, Vol. 55, No. 5, March, 1950.
27. Lewis, Oscar. *The Children of Sanchez; Autobiography of a Mexican Family*. (Random House, New York). 1961.
28. Lewis, Oscar. *Five Families: Mexican Case Studies in the Culture of Poverty*. (Basic Books, Inc., New York). 1959.
29. Lewis, Oscar. *Life in a Mexican Village: Tepoztlan Restudied*. (University of Illinois Press, Urbana). 1951.
30. Lewis, Oscar. "Urbanization without breakdown: a case study." *The Scientific Monthly*, No. 75, 1952, pp. 31–41.
31. Mendoza, Jose Rafael. "Existe una peculiar sociología latinoamericana: la familia." *Boletin del Instituto de Sociologia* (Buenos Aires, Argentina), Vol. XI, No. 7, 1953, pp. 119–127.
32. Minturn, Leigh. *Mothers of Six Cultures*. (John Wiley, New York). 1964.
33a. Pierson, Donald. "The Family in Brazil," *Marriage and Family Living*, Vol. 16, No. 4, Nov. 1954, pp. 308–314.

33b. Ramírez, Santiago. *El Mexicano, Psicología de sus motivaciones.* (Editorial Pax-Mexico, Mexico). 1959.

34. Redfield, Robert. *Tepoztlán, a Mexican Village: a study of folk life.* (The University of Chicago Press, Chicago). 1930.

35a. Rubel, Arthur J. *Across the Tracks: Mexican-Americans in a Texas City.* (University of Texas Press, Austin). 1966.

35b. Smith, T. Lynn. *Brazil: People and Institutions.* (Revised edition). (Louisiana State University Press, Baton Rouge). 1963.

36. Steward, Julian H. (ed.). *The People of Puerto Rico: A Study in Social Anthropology.* (University of Illinois Press, Urbana). 1956.

37. Steward, Julian H. and Louis C. Faron. *Native Peoples of South America.* (McGraw-Hill, New York). 1959.

38. Strickon, Arnold. "Class and Kinship in Argentina." *Ethnology,* No. 1 1962, pp. 500–515.

39. Stycos, J. Mayone. *Family and Fertility in Puerto Rico.* (Columbia University Press, New York). 1955.

40. Stycos, J. Mayone. "Birth Control Clinics in Crowded Puerto Rico," in Benjamin D. Paul (ed.), *Health, Culture and Community.* (Russell Sage Foundation, New York). 1955, pp. 189–210.

41. Taylor, Carl C. *Rural Life in Argentina.* (Louisiana State University Press, Baton Rouge). 1948.

42. U.S. Army. *Area Handbook for Venezuela.* (Government Printing Office, Washington, D.C.). February, 1964 (SORO study).

43. U.S. Army. *Area Handbook for Brazil.* (Government Printing Office, Washington, D.C.). July, 1964 (SORO study).

44. U.S. Army. *Area Handbook for Colombia.* (Government Printing Office, Washington, D.C.). Second edition, June 22, 1964.

45. Vergara, Marta. *Memorias de una mujer irreverente.* (Empresa Zig-Zag, Santiago). 1963.

46. Whetten, Nathan L. *Guatemala: The Land and the People.* (Yale University Press, New Haven). 1961.

47. Whetten, Nathan L. *Rural Mexico.* (The University of Chicago Press, Chicago). 1948.

48. Whiting, Beatrice B. (ed.) *Six Cultures: Studies of Child Rearing.* (John Wiley and Sons, New York). 1963.

49. Willems, Emilio. "A estrutura da familia brasileira." *Sociologia* (São Paulo, Brazil). Vol. XVI, No, 4, October, 1954, pp. 327–340.

4

The Educational Means
and the Occupational Ends

For Latin America it has been precisely the opposite: occupational means and educational ends. That is, education has traditionally been an end in itself. Not only the gentleman of leisure, but many other people scattered unevenly throughout the social structure, have engaged in economic activities that would allow them to widen their vision of the universe. It is not unusual, even in remote towns of Latin America, to find an obscure physician, an unknown judge, and a humble school teacher well versed in philosophy, literature (mostly poetry), and history. With the winds of change blowing from abroad and with the titanic efforts in recent times to meet the newly-acquired sociocultural needs, mostly of a material nature, shaking privileged and underprivileged groups in every corner of the continent, education is becoming what it is in the United States, a means to "betterment," not so much of the person as of his environment. The time has come for Latin America to change fundamentally the physical as well as the social environment of man. We shall see what happens to man in the process.

Education for Being and Education for Becoming: The Ignored Issue

In the Weltanschauung of the Latin American, the physical as well as the social universe has been relatively fixed; the emphasis has been more on being than on becoming. Therefore, education has been oriented toward *understanding,* not *changing,* man's place in his universe. Even today in many universities, the largest enrollments are found in courses of philosophy and history. From the North American perspective, this is most impractical; from the Latin American perspective, this is most meaningful.

In this view, the repetitive lack of originality of Latin American educational programs tried off and on, country after country, does not seem to make sense. Nevertheless, it does. The Latin American has a tremendous imagination for works of art, fiction, and poetry. He cannot bring together the small pieces of reality that make the puzzle of human affairs. If he could, he would not spend his time mimicking France and England, Germany and Spain, and the United States, but would instead unleash the energies harnessed in the inner currents of his culture. Only Mexico has done so with relative success, given the point of departure.[20, 84] The rest of Latin America has been sending her politicians and educators abroad—the roles are often interchangeable—to borrow new ideas, frequently announced in press conferences upon their return, and to bring new systems to be superimposed on crumbling structures. As a result, the products of the educational mill will be unfit to stay but fit to migrate. This point will be taken up later.

Educational reform is not a new theme in Latin America. With practically every change in government in every country, the theme reoccurs. What is new is the tendency to replicate United States patterns and to emphasize technical skills to meet the new demands of modernization.

Presently, policy-makers and top administrators are engaged in a supranational effort to cope with common problems with the help of the Pan American Union, UNESCO, the Pan American

Sanitary Bureau, and the Inter-American Development Bank. The attempt is to change the structure of the system once more, this time at the level of a Latin American integration.

Latin America runs parallel educational structures in every country. In fact, there is no Latin American system of education. Within each country there are various structures. There is a public and a private, a denominational and a non-denominational, a professional and a technical, and sometimes a national and a state structure. In the same organization (*colegio*) there may be classes from kindergarten to high school, that is, pre-elementary, elementary, secondary, baccalaureate, and/or technical or vocational. This diversity, however, does not mean flexibility. Generally speaking, the ministry of education in each country lays out the programs that are to be followed by all schools if they expect accreditation. Within this framework, there is some room for choice by the individual school, but little choice for the individual student.

Thus the Latin American educational structure, like the familial one, is authoritarian. This holds true for the Latin American university, which is a poli-versity, few Latin American universities are communities sharing common physical and instructional services. They are usually made up of *facultades* or schools that run their ethnocentric business in separate plants scattered throughout the city, if not throughout the country; often each *facultad* is a small empire in which the social distance between the faculty and the student has the character of a sacred liturgy.

In this model of authoritarianism one would expect to find the end product imbued with awe, deference, and submission, but in fact the end product is a rebel with a cause. His own mind is his own cause. The Latin American student has a mind of his own. Parents know this, partly because they themselves followed the same paths of maturing. Thus they do not get excited about the liberties taken by their children. Strikes and riots among the students, like role-trying in adolescence, are considered part and parcel of the process of growing up.

Moreover, the Latin American student moves within the confines of knowledge, not just of learning. He is a generalizer, not an expert. He is an integrator of ideas. This is one of the consequences of an élitist educational system.

Elitist and Egalitarian Education:
A Hard Fact

To assume that education can be taken out of politics is as un-
realistic as to assume that military affairs, religion, and business
fall out of the realm of power struggles. The Latin American is a
political animal. In Latin America, every significant decision is a
political decision.

Students are not exceptions to these rules. On the contrary,
by virtue of his generation, the student is located right on the spot
where the future pounds on the present and dissolves into the past.
He is placed at the intersection of streams of knowledge and currents of opinion.

There is another factor affecting the student and lying beyond
the sphere of his control. In developing countries, a wide spectrum
of minor institutions are in the process of formation and the ordeal
of change is disturbing the traditional ones. By his very position
in these processes, the student is in a sense forced into action.

Moreover, he is well aware of being one of the few who has
survived the fine, subtle, and often dubious selectivity mechanism
of an educational sieve through which only the intellectual elite
may pass. He is aware of the fact that the number of students
rejected at every university is frequently larger than the number
of students who enroll. And he is aware of the fact that tens of
thousands of his fellow citizens have not reached high school and
that tens of thousands more never will. Thus he feels responsible
for the destiny of his country. As one of the chosen ones, he has
a sense of mission. How can he possibly remain at the margin of
politics?

In addition, he will realize upon reaching the top that brain
power does not rule alone, that family name and tradition are
requisites to complete success.* Shocked by these realizations, he
might decide to buck the system in revenge, which means that

* A striking exception to this rule may be Chile, where the upper classes
have been blamed for the almost century-old economic misfortunes of the
country.

after a short period of flirting with the right, he might go back to the left with which he had established an intellectual affinity during his harsh formative period. This affinity, however, may not last for life. Most Latin American intellectuals who have flirted with the left have moved toward the center with the passing years.

That the Latin American educational system is extremely selective has been proven beyond doubt. Nevertheless, a few statistics are provided in Tables 5 and 6 to illustrate the point. The

Table 5   Percent of Children Who Finished Primary
School in Latin American Countries

COUNTRY	PERIOD	PERCENT
Uruguay	1959–1964	53.0
Panama	1960–1965	47.0
Argentina	1959–1965	42.0
Chile	1960–1965	38.6
Costa Rica	1960–1965	36.6
Bolivia	1960–1965	34.7
Peru	1959–1964	29.5
Mexico	1960–1965	28.3
Venezuela	1960–1965	27.6
El Salvador	1960–1965	24.2
Brazil	1960–1963	22.0
Colombia	1961–1965	22.0
Ecuador	1960–1965	21.0
Paraguay	1960–1965	19.0
Cuba	1960–1965	17.6
Guatemala	1960–1965	16.2
Honduras	1960–1965	16.0
Haiti	1957–1962	13.9
Nicaragua	1960–1965	11.1
Dominican Republic	1962–1965	8.7

After UNESCO, *Evolución de la situación educativa en América Latina,* 1965, Table 18, pp. 42–44.

reader may notice there that no country (except Uruguay) carries to the end of the primary cycle 50 percent of the children who started it. The drop-out reaches the 90 percent rate in the Dominican Republic, followed by six other countries in the 80s and six

Table 6 Percent of Children Age 13–18 and 19–22
Enrolled in Intermediate and High Level
Schools, Latin America, 1965

COUNTRY	PERCENT AGE 13–18 ENROLLED IN INTERMEDIATE SCHOOLS	PERCENT AGE 19–22 ENROLLED IN HIGH LEVEL SCHOOLS
Argentina	40.0	13.0
Uruguay	39.0	9.0
Chile	33.0	6.0
Panama	33.0	8.0
Venezuela	28.0	7.0
Costa Rica	25.0	5.0
Cuba	25.0	4.0
Peru	23.0	8.0
Brazil	22.0	3.0
Colombia	22.0	4.0
Bolivia	18.0	4.0
Mexico	17.0	4.0
El Salvador	16.0	1.0
Ecuador	15.0	3.0
Paraguay	15.0	4.0
Nicaragua	12.0	2.0
Dominican Republic	11.0	2.0
Guatemala	9.0	2.0
Honduras	7.0	2.0
Haiti	5.0	.9

After UNESCO, *Educación y desarrollo en América Latina. Bases para una política educativa*, Santiago, April, 1966, Table 7, p. 24 (mimeo).

more in the 70s. From another, although no more encouraging, perspective—percent of children of school age enrolled at two other levels—the reader may strengthen his conviction that Latin American education is in serious disarray. A look at the illiteracy rates (Table 7) will further confirm this conviction. In addition, most Latin American countries spend a higher percentage of government expenditures in the military than in education (as occurs also in the United States). Elitism thrives in ignorance.

There is still another interesting fact contributing to the elitist character of the system. It is the character of the faculty. Few

Table 7   Illiteracy Rates Population 15 Years Old and Over
Latin America Circa 1960

COUNTRY	YEAR	ILLITERACY RATE
Haiti	1960	89.5
Ecuador	1962	69.4
Guatemala	1960	68.5
Bolivia	1960	61.2
El Salvador	1961	53.7
Honduras	1961	53.1
Nicaragua	1963	50.4
Dominican Republic	1956	40.1
Peru	1961	39.8
Brazil	1960	39.5
Mexico	1960	37.8
Colombia	1961	37.5
Venezuela	1961	33.5
Panama	1960	26.7
Paraguay	1962	25.8
Chile	1960	16.2
Costa Rica	1963	16.0
Uruguay	1963	10.0
Argentina	1960	8.6
Cuba	1966	3.3

After UNESCO, *Informe de la Comisión de evaluación del proyecto principal,* Santiago, Chile, February, 1966, Tables P-11 and P-12, pp. 15-16 (mimeo).

Latin American universities have a full-time faculty and most faculty members work on a part-time basis. Often successful professionals want to add prestige to their practice by lecturing at a university. The other faculty members are peddlers of knowledge; they deliver their commodity from *facultad* to *facultad* or from university to university. But normally they are all scholars. They have attained their status *luchando;* therefore, they expect their students to *luchar* also. If the professor has anything to say, his students will listen. Otherwise, they will go either to the library or to coffeehouses to debate on the essential parts of the course. They have an instinct for the essential. The crucial encounter between professor and student will be at the end with a panoply of knowledge.

There are other factors contributing to the selectivity mechanism. The most important are of course family name and tradition. This is particularly weighty in private schools of all sorts. It is not only that family name and tradition very often go hand in hand with status. A prestigious family name lends prestige to the institution. In return, the institution will render special educational services to the fortunate child who *nació de pie* (was born on his feet).

Efforts toward equality of educational opportunity have not been absent in Latin America. In fact, they began with the Conquest. Later, the French Revolution's slogan became the battle cry of the Wars of Independence. Voltaire, Rousseau, and Robespierre had inspired, like a sacred scripture, the founding fathers of the new republics. Throughout the 150-odd years of self-government, the Latin American countries have fought for *liberté,* but *égalité* and *fraternité* have been left for the future.[49, 55]

Effective efforts toward equality of educational opportunity can be traced back to the second third of this century, when the waves of revolutionary ideas coming from Mexico and Russia began to slash at the pyramidal rock of the educational structure. Still, at the beginning of the last third of the century, literacy rates remain low in most countries, (see Table 7—once more) and in the most literate ones, Argentina, Costa Rica, Uruguay, Chile, and Cuba, about 1.5 per 1000 of those who finish high school graduate from institutions of higher learning. The number of drop-outs from universities is not known and the universities do not care, because they cater only to the elite of the countries. (This statement may not be correct for Cuba.) Thus, the economic cost to society and the psychological cost to the individual have not been measured.

The Peasants: More Words than Deeds

The highest rates of illiteracy are found in the peasant societies, particularly in those countries in which Indian subcultures abound.[3, 63] Elementary education is compulsory in every country, in theory although not in practice; enforcing the laws is beyond any government's power. Very few countries have integrated their ethnic societies, certainly not in the rural areas.[33] Even the urban *barriadas*—named variously in various countries—are pockets of illiteracy and foci of peasant subcultures. Moreover, if thousands of families can hardly eat, it is simply unthinkable to expect that their children would go to school.

The preceding is just a sample of the problems affecting the Latin American peasant. It has been said that the evils are rooted in the very structure of Latin American societies and that only violent revolutions can change the structure.[87] Analogies have been drawn between the colonial wars of independence from the European metropolies and the decolonizing warfare with bloodshed and all between the peasant societies and the native metropolies that continuously subject the hinterland to merciless economic exploitation.[92]

There is no doubt that the Latin American peasant has been traditionally forsaken and that the peasant problem remains unsolved, even in Mexico despite a very costly revolution. Facts on the Cuban experience are lacking to allow a balanced judgment. In general, however, the evidence indicates that the conditions of the Latin American peasant have deteriorated in recent years.[35]

The most fundamental attacks on the problem have been the various forms of agrarian reform with which all Latin American countries have experimented from time to time. For the most part, the reforms have focused on land tenure rather than land utilization, with little or no attention to the education of the peasant for his new roles and to the function of agriculture in the context of national and international markets; not to mention the total disinterest in understanding the nature of the peasant community and the intricacies of the peasant psychology.[35, 87] Moreover, all the solutions have come from the top down; none has gone from the bottom upward. The reforms have been *for* the peasants, not *by* the peasants. Peasants are not thought to have common sense and if they are Indians, they may not even have a soul. Small wonder that peasant unrest is the burning issue from Northern Mexico to Southern Chile and that bitterness corrodes the peasants both body and soul. Confronted with soil erosion, unavailability of good land, hard credit, falling prices, distant markets, and erratic government support, they have developed a new consciousness, the consciousness of their power. They do not listen any longer, they want to see with their own eyes. In every country and city throughout the continent, they are taking over, forcibly, land for agriculture and lots for housing.

For the young peasant, the alternative to fight has been to migrate.[47] He circulates from region to region around his country or moves (even across international lines, as from Bolivia and Paraguay toward Argentina) to urban centers to crowd the already crowded *villas miseria*.[88b] If he is lucky, he may learn a skill and join the ranks of proletariat. If he is not, he may reach the depths of human degradation so well described in *Child of The Dark*.[62a] I have been in terribly blighted urban ghettos in North America without fear; I have shivered in my boots when I have visited Latin American pockets of urban misery. Here I have felt that physical violence hurts less than hatred.

The Proletariat's Revolutionizing Conservatism

The early formation of the Latin American proletariat was a strange mixture of numbers of European immigrants and native migrants, both peasant in origin.[6, 80] In recent years, the foreign migration has been predominantly urban, and smaller in number compared with that of the past. By contrast, the rural-urban migration in each country has doubled and tripled and the age of the migrant has been younger. Thus the cities have swelled with the most variant elements.

These have not been the sole basis of recruitment of the proletariat. In some countries (Chile and Argentina) at least two generations of proletarians have passed; that is, proletarians have generated proletarians, more so in Latin America than in the contemporary United States. As indicated in Chapter 2, Latin America has been industrializing quite rapidly since World War II. In fact, industrialization is the main goal of the movement at the top for Latin American economic integration, which is best expressed in the Latin American Common Market and in similar regional efforts among the Andean countries, Chile, Peru, Ecuador, Colombia, and Venezuela (Bolivia is not a member of Corporación Andina de Fomento). Thus, in a real sense, the heyday of the Latin American proletariat is just dawning.

However, the class consciousness of the proletariat is not just emerging. The original proletariat was extremely class-conscious and very politically-minded.[80] European socialism migrated with the immigrants. At the turn of the century, Buenos Aires and São Paulo were boiling with unionizing and labor politicking. It was not exactly the worker in the new factories that was doing the acting. It was mainly the craftsman, the shoemaker, the typesetter, the carpenter, the blacksmith, the stevedores, the bricklayers, and the ironworkers. In Chile it was the *salitre* mine workers.[62b] Sociologically speaking, the most striking common denominator among the variant groups coalescing into the proletariat was their subcultural incompatibility. The foreigner had come in a sense of adventure with skills and organizational resourcefulness. He settled his family and found time for the associations. The native migrant had arrived in the big city with some sense of adventure but with no skills and no organizational experience or exposure. The only organization to which he had been exposed besides his family, often not very well organized, was the local church, in which he had hardly participated. The local church had little structure, although it was a very authoritarian one, in which the *cura* (parish priest) was the *cacique*. Thus, the native migrant continued to be a peasant in the big city, with all the characteristics of a peasant. Some of these characteristics nevertheless turned out to be very useful for survival. He remained rebellious and he returned to the womb of his kin group when the going got rough. However, in terms of a competitive world, he was a failure, and his sense of frustration, already ancestral, was transmitted to his children and to his children's children. Therefore, the labor movement that emerged had to be a split one and a weak one. Mutual associations meant something; militant ones only had a meaning when it came to the extreme. The peasant migrant had acquired through the generations, in the church and otherwise, a sense of martyrdom but not a sense of victory.

The preceding analysis explains also, at least in part, why the Latin American labor movement has not been an independent one.[9] It did become dangerous to the stability of society from time to time. It was then politically wise to patronize it. The government has been the *patrón*. All labor laws, as well as the labor court system throughout the land, have had a paternalistic character. They have been acts of lordly charity, not really recognition of basic rights. In turn, the labor unions have been models of facade democracies. It is not only that elections are often run under intimidation and votes purchased, as in the political arena; it is that the literacy-illiteracy gap between leadership and following has always been abysmal. It is also, and this time on the plus side of the balance sheet, that the labor union, governmental patronage or not, has been the only effective means for the workers to attain a sense of human dignity and the feeling of power and prestige. Thus the union leader has built for himself the aristocracy of the working class, not better and not worse than the other aristocracy. For the worker himself, this labor aristocracy has at least the advantage of being closer; that is, within reach. Nevertheless, he is moving once again in the authoritarian atmosphere that surrounds a new pyramidal structure, with little or no room for him at the top. This means a new split. And so on, *ad infinitum*. In the meantime, management always presents a united front.

Within the present context, it may be easy to see that the Latin American labor leader would seek prestige in martyrdom, not in compromise. He is not a negotiator. He is a true believer. Thus, strike follows strike. Of course, management and governments are also true believers. Freedom is not negotiable. In such a frame of reference *Las Relaciones Patronales* (the very telling Latin American expression for labor-management relations) must often be at an impasse. Lopez Mateos in Mexico applied an "internal security of the State" law to a railroad strike; Frei did the same to the postal strike in Chile; and Ongania has practically dissolved the labor unions in Argentina, to mention only the most recent and well known cases.

The just-described attitude of the Latin American proletariat is what I call a revolutionizing conservatism. It is conservative because the distribution of power is authoritarian; it is conservative because in the face of an organized world of business, it has remained split with *caudillismo* and *caciquismo;* it is conservative because it has not been weaned as yet from the breast of the State; and it is conservative because every gain sought has been a gain for the proletariat; other groups must fend for themselves. Moreover, almost every labor leader is a capitalist at heart. He not only adopts a paternalistic attitude toward his followers and lives and travels in increasing luxury with increasing power, but he is primarily interested in profits (called benefits) for his union, with little thought of sharing the profits with the rest of his society.

However, this very conservatism has been revolutionary. It has been revolutionary because the appetite for power has spread to other sectors of society; it has been revolutionary because by becoming a privileged class among the working classes, the proletariat has stimulated social unrest even in the rural areas. This may not apply as clearly to the rural proletariat of the Brazilian plantation and the Argentinian *estancia* as it does to the proletariat of the *hacienda* of Mexico, Colombia, and Bolivia and of the Chilean *fundo.* This second type possesses two distinguishing characteristics: it is made up of farmers—some of them landowners—and it is distinctly rebellious. The proletariat, finally, has been revolutionary because by forming new social institutions, it has cracked the building of society beyond repair. This latter result is the most outstanding one from the sociological perspective. Some of these institutions have already been mentioned, such as labor laws and labor courts. In addition, the right to association has by now been written into every Latin American constitution. The right to strike has been recognized, and so has the right to bargain collectively. Even the right of property, the most sacred institution, has been revised to contain a social responsibility.

The proletariat has been a failure, however, in inspiring bloody revolutions—shades of vulgar Marxism. Only the peasants have rebelled with a resolution to die. Death is meaningless to the proletarian. He wants to have his cake and eat it. Thus, in the true Marxian sense, the proletariat has been revolutionary—unwittingly; in the vulgar Marxist sense, it has not.* *Perro que ladra no muerde* (a barking dog never bites).

* The political leanings of the proletariat will be taken up in Chapter 6.

The White Collar Cleavage

In consciousness of class, the Latin American white collar workers excel every other class. They are very much aware of being caught in the middle. To this feeling, the aristocracy and the proletariat have contributed generously. Relatively speaking, the middle class was more important during the colonial period and the first century of independence than it is today. To begin with, it was more homogeneous and it was second in power to the aristocracy. It was much smaller, of course; it was made up of the government bureaucracy, the few school teachers, and professionals, mainly lawyers. And it was at the mercy of the aristocracy that dominated the church, the government, and the military.

In modern times, say after World War I, the middle class has become gradually more heterogeneous and larger in the rapidly developing countries. The bulk of it is still constituted by government and private bureaucracies and school teachers. Some new semi-professions have been added very recently, such as nurses and social workers, and, of course, many loose clerical and sale workers. But it has lost the established professions, to wit, lawyers, physicians, engineers, and university professors, who have emerged as a powerful class very conscious of their distinctiveness and distinction.

The proletariat, made up mostly of blue collar workers, has no regard for the middle class mainly because, with the exception of school teachers and bureaucracies, it has resisted unionization. Moreover, the proletariat is imbued with socialist and communist ideologies of which the middle class is terribly afraid.

If the proletariat is split, the middle class is split in a thousand splinters. The white collar worker is as prestige-hungry as anybody else in Latin America. But instead of organized power the white collar worker prefers to use individual persuasion, charm, and self-salesmanship to climb even closer to the aristocracy without alienating their graces. The white collar worker's proneness to individual action could also be explained by the general Latin American immunity to collective action. This explanation is not sufficient, however. The white collar worker suffers from an anxiety to differentiate himself clearly from the blue collar (or rather no-collar) worker who sometimes dares to wear a white collar. There is still another, and perhaps more telling, reason. The white collar worker is an occupational transient. He has arrived where he is with little choice of his own. It was perhaps a tight economic situation in the family; it was maybe the elitist screening at the university, or even the published glamor, soon faded, of the position. In any case, he is going somewhere else, to a better job, to marriage. Now the white collar cleavage may appear delineated. The white collar class is a wedge between the other four classes; it is a thorn in their flesh. The white collar worker cannot be trusted. Politically, he moves back and forth, unpredictably, from the collectivizing and nationalizing efforts of the proletariat and the peasantry to the individualizing and internationalizing tendencies of the professionals and the aristocracy. Sociopsychologically, he is obsessed with a false conspicuous consumption and a nail-biting neatness. Sociologically, as stated, he is an occupational transient.

The Professional: An Open-Ended Question

Relative to the others, the professional class is simple in structure but very complex in ideas and ideologies. In contrast to the one in the United States, the Latin American professional is often also an intellectual. Not that all intellectuals belong in the professions; some belong in the aristocracy; some in the proletariat; and some just do not belong, but merely run through a series of identifications.

Power has accrued to the professions in recent times especially as a consequence of the Latin American awakening to modernization and to its participation in a widening world community.[68b] Latin American professionals are heads of states in most countries, representing their countries in international organizations and deeply engaged in the efforts for Latin American integration. At the national level, they fill the houses of congresses and legislatures and they have occupied the crucial positions in business directorates and in political councils. Sociologists and economists have lately joined the club, previously made up of lawyers, physicians, and engineers. The new socioeconomic developments have thrown wide open a tremendous number of opportunities to the at one time surplus of professionals. They have also found new markets for their skills abroad. As shown in Table 8, great quanti-

Table 8   Immigrants Admitted to United States from Latin American Countries by Major Occupational Groups (1958–1965)

OCCUPATIONAL GROUPS	ABSOLUTE	RELATIVE
Professionals	45,868	6.5
Farmers	2,470	.4
Managers	13,552	1.9
Clericals	40,698	5.8
Sales Workers	8,224	1.2
Craftsmen	27,571	3.9
Operatives	32,695	4.6
Private Household	41,128	5.7
Service Workers	14,414	2.0
Farm Laborers	24,528	3.5
Laborers	54,624	7.7
Housewives, children and others with no reported occupation	403,020	56.8
Total	708,846	100.0

Adapted from Tables I through XII from United States Immigration and Naturalization Service, *Annual Report(s)* for 1958 through 1965.

ties of professionals have migrated to the United States. Physicians and engineers (according to various sources) head this list of expatriates.[75] The surface investigations so far conducted indicate as reasons the shortage of opportunities for betterment at home, the lack of facilities for scientific research, political and economic instability, and governmental threats to security and freedom. They obviously expect to find all they want in the adopted country. In my view, these explanations have to be strengthened by more fundamental factors. The most significant seems to be the very elitist character of the Latin American educational system that has already been discussed. In other words, the professionals are trained for migration. It is a wonder that more of them do not migrate. As insinuated above, the intelligent student who has reached the top soon discovers that intellect alone does not count, but that he also needs family name and a tradition. Moreover, during the screening process he has not only been conditioned to better and better things, but he may have been alienated from the very society from which he proceeds and from the very culture of which he is a product. He has succeeded outstandingly; thus, he scorns the failure. He has no regard for mediocrity. The gap then between the professionals and the rest of Latin American society is frightening.

Politics have certainly been the best home outlet for the frustrations of the professionals, with the results to which Latin America has borne witness for generations. The mind of the professional boils with ideas and he is terribly fond of ideologies. He can spend hour after hour over a cup of coffee or a glass of beer suggesting magnificent solutions to the problems of the world. He is amazingly well informed on what is going on in Asia, Africa, Geneva, the United Nations, California and Alabama, the slums of the large United States cities, and even in regard to agrarian reform and economic integration. But when it comes to the fundamental social forces that have created the necessity for the agrarian reform and the economic integration of his own country, he knows very little. And if pressed further for information about the rebellion of the Indians up in the mountains or down south, or the marches of the farmers to the presidential palace and of the neighborhoods or *comunas* to the House of Congress, or about the strikes of the students at the university, he would reply with no embarrassment that these occurrences are insignificant when compared with the threat of annihilation in an atomic holocaust. A most intellectual answer.

Alienated from his own land in his own land, the professional is rarely in touch with the realities that form the undercurrents of change in his own society. Not even the most obvious ones such as the police headquarters, the juvenile court, the emergency room in the hospitals, the rural wasteland, and the urban ghettos. He may have forgotten where he came from. The Latin American social climber never looks backward. However, if the professional were charged with the responsibility of finding a solution to these problems he would be genuinely concerned with them. He would immediately take off to visit Europe and the United States to find answers to *his* questions. Or, if in a top government position, he would hire experts from abroad to make a three to six month study of the economy of the country—since ultimately all problems are economic—and to write a report fat with figures that only other experts will read: certainly not he. In short, the Latin American professional knows Greece and Rome, but he does not know Latin America.

Efforts to correct this anomaly have not been lacking. In fact, during World War II and shortly afterwards, Latin American governments rushed into a crusade to widen the professional spectrum in forgotten fields of industry and agriculture. Truman's Point IV program was the North American response to the great Latin American endeavor. The results have been very contradictory. It is evident that the spectrum did widen. However, two major unintended consequences have appeared. One has been the brain-drain of the last decade, mainly in the direction of the United States. The other has been the monstrous deformity produced in the educational structure: resources flowed to higher education with almost total neglect of the intermediate technical, vocational, and elementary levels, especially as they relate to the rural areas. The price paid has been dear. Rural unrest has worsened and agricultural production has not kept pace with the growth of population.*

Reactions to the tendency of the professional to ignore the empirical approach to national and local problems have come from time to time from the professions themselves and more significantly in the sixties.[23] The strongest reaction has come from centers of higher learning. The University of Mexico has been producing good works on Mexico; the University of Buenos Aires good works on Argentina, the University of Chile good works on Chile, the University of Colombia good works on Colombia, the University of Brazil good works on Brazil, and all of them good works on Latin America. There are some excellent centers of

* I am aware of other factors, of course, affecting the consequences just mentioned.

socioeconomic investigations in Rio de Janeiro, Santiago, Buenos Aires, San José, Bogotá, and Mexico City, all concerned with local and regional problems. The economic commission for Latin America of the United Nations, located in Santiago, has a competent team of Latin American professionals who keep in touch with Latin American realities.

There is a brain trust guiding the reforms sought by Frei in Chile; there is evidence of some brains returning to Brazil after the panic of Castello Branco; in 1967 Argentina was luring the brains the military literally beat in 1966; the 1966–70 president of Colombia was himself a well-equipped economist, and in Mexico the dialogues between the government and the professionals have borne fruit for a generation. Thus, throughout the continent, governments and professionals, particularly the intellectuals, seem to be entering an era of collaboration on more firm ground and much closer to the Latin American soil. They have finally learned that every problem insinuates its own solution.

This does not mean that consensus has arrived and ideologies have departed. Not at all. Certainly not ever in Latin America. It only means that the Latin American intellectual and professional will soon not be borrowing recipes from abroad any more; he will no longer be a merchant of solutions; he is beginning to manufacture them, and he manufactures them with native raw materials —from which, after all, the solutions must be produced.

Finally, what is happening to the Latin American man participating or involved in these rapidly moving processes? Perhaps I should start with the professions.

By the very character of his preparation and on the basis of the traditional deference rendered to the man of letters in the culture, the professional is at the wheel of the ship, giving both direction and impulse. It is not only that he may be considered an expert. It is that he has moved with his inner world into either business or politics, since so frequently they interlock. He is at the point of the whirlpool where the strongest forces of the hurricane are spinning. This constitutes at the same time the virtue and the tragedy of his fate.

Loaded with responsibilities and resilient to frustrating foreign advice, he is turning to his own sociocultural heritage for answers, well aware of what others have done. Thus he is learning to be totally committed to the mastery of his own destiny. The turmoils around him do not frighten him any longer; rather, they are beginning to stimulate him. When he turns abroad for help he expects to obtain it his way, that is, in a man-to-man transaction. He has come to know very well what sort of fire is burning under his feet. If rejected, he may blow on the fire.

The tragedy of his fate derives from the nature of the extended kin-group that surrounds him and from the kin-group character of the associations that he has joined. The stranger, the outsider, may hear about the event after it has happened. Neither rivalry nor competition could explain this phenomenon. If you are *there,* if you belong—at least potentially—and if you care to pick the link in motion then the chain would take you anywhere you are capable of going. And you must pick the link when it is offered, for it may not be offered again. The old Latin American attitude of polite resistance that invites insistence has faded away from the culture of the professional. It is not difficult to see that. Within this framework, the newcomer must be willing to join the clique. As a consequence of the *compadre* attitude, the waste of talent in the continent is considerable, although in this way intellect and leadership have come closer together. It may go without saying that what is characteristic of Latin American professional groups is not the existence so much as the exaggeration of this attitude. It may also be that I have touched here on another factor explaining the migration of Latin American professionals.

There is another aspect of this tragedy that must at least be mentioned now. The Latin American university student, the young professional, and the young intellectual have accepted the invitation to participate in the democratic process so seriously that they have frightened the elders who extended the invitation. The young generation wants democracy to be practiced in every institution. If institutions interpenetrate, they reason, education and religion cannot escape the influence of democracy. If these expectations fail to be realized, student riots would erupt and churches would remain deserted. Latin America has always been young and has always been disturbed by youth but the present disturbance is a particularly articulate disturbance.

The preceding analysis does not apply in the same degree, or does not apply at all, to the other social classes, which are almost totally unfit to participate in the democratic processes. They covet the spoils of the victory without the upheavals of the struggle. Perhaps the young proletarian may be excepted, but he is caught, whether member or not, in the machinery of the unions.

In the meantime, the old generations are frightened. As a consequence, they are losing their sense of balance and perspective. They are not only puzzled by the fantastic proliferation of heretofore exotic associations, always noisy and often intermittent, but they also hold fast to the very structures that are crumbling. In their desperate efforts, they are accompanied by the middle class and the aristocracy.*

* Generally speaking, Latin American aristocracies have changed very little in the past two generations. (Mexico and Chile differ, for different reasons, from the rest of Latin America.) Everywhere the aristocracies have been able to retain, almost intact, in the long run, their castles of prestige and power. In most countries they control the largest proportions of land, the best urban real estate, banking, and some types of industry. They have left some branches of government, the church for the most part, the military, and education to the others, as long as no drastic measures are taken to alter the tradition. If faced with these measures, they would quickly and skillfully set in motion every group that falls within their sphere of influence, not excluding foreign aristocracies and governments. In fact, the most intriguing aspect in the workings of the aristocracies, the network of supranational relationship through which they operate to remain firm in their position, has been totally ignored by investigators. In terms of numbers, the aristocracies never amount to more than 5 percent of the total population in any given country. They are followed by the professions another 5 to 15 percent; by the middle class falling somewhere between 10 and 30 percent; by the urban proletariat also between 10 and 30 percent; and by the peasants from 20 to 60 percent. To these one has to add the farmers and the marginals, that is, the many who are in the shady areas of transition. Figure 3 is given strictly for purpose of illustration. The statistics on which it is based, although the best available, are not reliable. Not having shoes, one has to wear sandals. However, I am more interested here in the *kind* than in the *size* of the phenomena. For the *kind* of phenomena, Figure 3 is a terrible oversimplification. Both the United States and Latin America are much more complicated, class-wise, than shown in the figure. Latin America's social class structure is complicated, tremendously complicated, by ethnicity. Each ethnic group has its own class structure and these structures seldom overlap. Color shades add new complications. A dark aristocracy is a dubious aristocracy.

Figure 3 Contrasted Class Structures of United States
and Latin America (Rough Estimates)

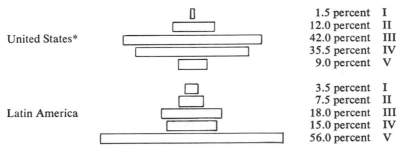

United States*

1.5 percent	I
12.0 percent	II
42.0 percent	III
35.5 percent	IV
9.0 percent	V

Latin America

3.5 percent	I
7.5 percent	II
18.0 percent	III
15.0 percent	IV
56.0 percent	V

Explanation (*Mutatis mutandis*)

   I. Made up of traditionally aristocratic families, landlords, or large
      estates, industrial oligarchies, successful political leaders, highest clergy,
      and military.
  II. Lawyers, physicians, engineers, university professors, lesser executives
      and managers of large corporations.
 III. White collar workers, government and private bureaucracies, public
      school teachers, and farmers.
  IV. Skilled workers, craftsmen, operatives, and industrial workers.
   V. Unskilled workers, farm laborers, and laborers.

   * Adapted from statistics given by Joseph A. Kahl, *The American Class Structure*.
New York: Rinehart & Co., 1957, p. 187.

In summary, revolutionary change is brewing in Latin
America in the midst of two characteristically contrasting groups,
the highly literate and the quasi-illiterate, the well educated and
the poorly educated, the professional and the peasant. They shake
trees. The others collect the harvest.

In general, the Latin American man is becoming more mate
rialistic, more competitive, and more shrewd than the North
American man and the United States has to take part of the blame.
In fact, the United States has unleashed some Latin American
sociocultural forces that cannot be stopped and that the United
States itself will regret.

True, the Latin American man has always gone after quick
gains. In the past he did so in order to take time off for philosophy,
history, and the arts. Now he is on the go for quick gains that

would lead to quicker gains still. And he would elbow out of his way anyone who interfered.

Likewise, the Latin American man has been very competitive. There has been a land rush and a gold rush and a black gold (rubber) rush and a liquid black gold (oil) rush in Latin America. There has been, within each country, a power rush and a prestige rush without relent. However, the power rush at the international level that the United States has unleashed in Latin America is a very recent phenomenon. If Latin America claimed a mission, it was a romantic and quixotic one, not one of power. It was with the highest cultural content: *Hispanidad, la raza,* idealism, literature, religion, trade, and educational exchange, not armed power. It was a generalized, impractical form of human brotherhood, not armed power to destroy. This is absolutely new.

Finally, the Latin American man has been shrewd. He has shown excellent ability to outsmart the Indian, the peasant, and the foreign firm. But there was always some heart in it. He was even artistically shrewd. He is becoming shrewd in a new form, in a cool rational way. In fact he has discovered that law and order often may pass as substitutes for justice. Thus laws are not infrequently passed and constitutions enacted to give a façade of legitimacy to unethical acts. It is a sort of due process in reverse. Castello Branco in Brazil and Barrientos in Bolivia have been the most recent and the most telling cases in order. And who has been their godfather? One may say that this is not new in Latin America, but it is. It is not a matter any longer of government by decree. It is government by "law," with Congress and Supreme Courts entering the act.

The dollar rush has entered the universities of late through AID and foundation funds (Ford, Rockefeller, and the like) and has turned into a double-edged blade: It is making the students hate the foundations and the country from which they came, and despise the Latin American professor who did not stay abroad long enough to master the language and his field.

The picture is not all gloomy though. There are plenty of aristocratic and middle class people who love the United States of America and all we expect is just a drop of love.

References and Selected Bibliography

1. Abernethy, David and Trevor Coombe. "Education and Politics in Developing Countries." *Howard Educational Review,* Summer 1965, *35:* 287–302.
2. Adams, R. N. "Change from Caste to Class in a Peruvian Sierra Town," *Social Forces,* March, 1953, *31:* 238–44.
3. Adams, Richard, J. P. Gillin, A. R. Homberg, O. Lewis, R. W. Patch & C. Wagley. *Social Change in Latin America.* (Harper, New York). 1961.
4. Ahumada, Jorge. *En vez de la miseria.* (Editorial del Pacífico, Santiago). 1958.
5. Alba, Victor. *Alliance without Allies.* (Frederick A. Praeger, New York). 1965.
6. Alba, Victor. *Historia del Movimiento Obrero en América Latina.* (Libreros Mexicanos Unidos, Mexico City). 1964.
7. Albornoz, Orlando. *El Maestro y La Educación en la Sociedad Venezolana.* (Kipuven, Venezuela). 1965.
8. Alexander, R. J. *Labor Relations in Argentina, Brazil and Chile.* (McGraw-Hill, New York). 1962.
9. Alexander, Robert J. *Today's Latin America.* (Doubleday and Company, Garden City, New York). 1962.
10. Arroyo, Dulio. "La Tragedia de la Clase Media en Panama." *Epocas* (Panama), Vol. II, No. 16, 1947.
11. Azevedo, Thales de. *Social Change in Brazil.* (University of Florida Press, Gainesville). 1963.
12. Bailey, Norman A. "The U.S. as *Caudillo." Journal of Inter American Studies.* (Wayside Press, Gainesville, Fla.). July, 1963, *5:* 313–324.
13. Banco Interamericano de Desarrollo. *La Educación Avanzada y el Desarrollo de América Latina.* (Imprenta Nuevo Mundo, Mexico). 1966.
14. Beals, Ralph. "A estratificacao social na america latina." *Sociologia* (Sao Paulo, Brazil). Vol. XVI, No. 3, August, 1954. Pp. 219–235.
15. Beals, Ralph, L. "Social Stratification in Latin America." *American Journal of Sociology,* 1953, *58:* 327–39
16. Beegle, J. Allan and Charles P. Loomis. *Rural Social Systems.* (Prentice-Hall, New York). 1950.
17. Bonati, Felix Martinez. *La Situación Universitaria.* (Universidad Austral de Chile, Valdivia). 1965.
18. Bonilla, Frank. "Sobre la Estructura de Clase en América Latina." *Ciencias Sociales.* (Pan American Union, Washington, D.C.). 1956.
19. Boorstein, Edward. *The Economic Transformation of Cuba.* (Monthly Review Press, New York). 1968.
20. Booth, George C. *Mexico's School-made Society.* (Stanford University Press, Stanford, California). 1941.

21. Buitron, Anibal. "La Educación Indígena." *Ciencias Sociales,* Vol. VI, No. 35. (Pan American Union, Washington, D.C.). 1955.
22. Burnett, Ben G., & Moises Poblete Troncoso. *The Rise of the Latin American Labor Movement.* (College and University Press, New Haven). Date not shown.
23. Bustamante, Norberto R., et al. *Los Intelectuales Argentinos y su Sociedad.* (Ediciones Libera, Buenos Aires). 1967.
24. Camilo, Joao. *Estratificacao Social no Brasil.* CLPCS, Brasil.
25. Carvajal, Juan F. "Observaciones sobre la Clase Media en Cuba." *Materiales,* 1950, pp. 31 ff.
26. Carter, Roy E. & Orlando Sepulveda. "Occupational Prestige in Santiago de Chile." *The American Behavioral Scientist,* September 1964, *8:* 20–24.
27. Castro, Fidel. *Fidel Castro Denounces Bureaucracy and Sectarianism.* (Pioneer Publishers, New York). 1962.
28. Chaplin, David. *The Peruvian Industrial Labor Force.* (Princeton University Press, Princeton, New Jersey). 1967.
29. Cochran, Thomas C. *El hombre de negocios puertorriqueño.* (Centro de investigaciones sociales, Rio Piédras, Puerto Rico). 1961.
30. Cochran, Thomas C., Ruben E. Reina & Sue Nuttal. *Entrepreneurship in Argentine Culture: Torcuato de tella and S.I.A.N.* (University of Pennsylvania Press, Philadelphia). 1962.
31. Comhaire, Jean L. "El campesino haitiano y su gobierno." *Ciencias Sociales,* Vol. VII, No. 38 (Pan American Union, Washington, D.C.), 1956.
32. Consejo de Bienestar Rural. *Problemas Económicos y Sociales de los Andes, parte II: Venezolanos.* (Consejo de Bienestar Rural, Caracas). No date.
33. Corredor, Berta and Sergio Torres. *Transformación en el Mundo rural Latino-Americano: Consecuencias económicas y sociales de las estructuras agrarias.* (Oficina Internacional de Investigaciones Sociales de Feres, Bogotá). 1961.
34. David, Pedro Rubens. *The Social Structure of Argentina.* (University of Illinois, Bloomington). 1963. (micro-film)
35. Delgado, Oscar (ed.). *Reformas Agrarias en la America Latina.* (Fondo de Cultura Economica, Mexico and Buenos Aires). 1965.
36. Denis, Lorimer and Francois Duvalier. *Le probleme des classes a travers l'histoire d'Haiti.* (Port-au-Prince, Collection "Les Groits"). 1948.
37. Dias, Everardo. *Historia da lutas sociais no Brasil.* (Editoria Edaglit, Sao Paulo). 1962.
38. Diaz, Demetrio. *La Educación en Brazil.* (Centro de Información en Sociología de la Obra de Cooperación Sacerdotal Hispano Americana, Madrid). 1961.
39. Diaz Soto y Gama, Antonio. *La Cuestión Agraria en Mexico.* (Institute of I.S. of U.N.A.M., Mexico). 1959.
40. Dominguez, Ranson. *Nuestro Sistema de Inquilinaje.* (Imprenta del Correo, Santiago). 1867.
41. Descoff, L. F. *Human Resources of Central America, Panama and*

Mexico 1950–1980 in Relation to Some Aspects of Economic Development. (U.N. Economic Commission for Latin America). 1960.

42. Erasmus, Charles J. *Man Takes Control: Cultural Development and American Aid.* (The Bobbs-Merrill Co., New York). 1961.

43. Fagen, Richard R. *Cuba: The Political Content of Adult Education.* Stanford: Hoover Institution Studies (4), The Hoover Institution on War, Revolution, and Peace, 1964. Contains the translation of several important revolutionary documents.

44. Fals-Borda, Orlando. *El Hombre y la Tierra en Boyaca: Bases Sociológicas e Históricas para una Reforma Agraria.* (Ediciones Documentos Colombianos, Bogotá). 1957.

45. Fonseca, Eugenio. *Clases sociales y desarrollo económico.* Santiago de Chile, (FLACSO, Escuela Latinoamericana de Sociología, Santiago). 1959.

46. Form, W. H., & A. A. Blum (eds.). *Industrial Relations & Social Change in Latin America.* (University of Florida Press, Gainesville). 1965.

47. Form, William H. and Julius Rivera. "The Place of Returning Migrants in a Stratification System," *Rural Sociology,* Vol. 23, No. 3, 1958.

48. Galenson, Walter (ed.). *Labor in Developing Economies.* (University of California Press, Berkeley). 1962.

49. Garcia, Antonio. *Reforma Agraria y Economía Empresarial en América Latina.* (Editorial Universitaria, Santiago). 1967.

50. Garcia, Luis Scherz. *Una Nueva Universidad para América Latina.* (Dept. de Copias Secretaria Central, Valparaiso). 1964.

51. Germani, Gino. *Estructura social de la Argentina.* (Editorial Raigal, Buenos Aires). 1955.

52. Germani, Gino. "La clase media en la ciudad de Buenos Aires." (Boletín del Instituto de Sociología, Buenos Aires). No. 1, 1942.

53. Germani, Gino. "La Clase Media en La Argentina con especial referencia a sus Sectores Urbanos," in *Materiales para el Estudio de la Clase Media en la América Latina.* (Union Panamericana, Washington, D.C.). 1950. p. 1 ff.

54. Godoy Urzua, Hernan. *Orientación y Organización de los estudios sociológicos en Chile.* (Edit. Universitaria, Santiago). 1960.

55. Gonzalez, Julio Ileise. *150 Años de Evolución Institucional.* (Edit. Andres Bello, Santiago). 1960.

56. Grompone, Antonio M. *Universidad Oficial y Universidad Viva.* (Universidad Nacional, Instituto de Investigaciones Sociales, Mexico, D.F.). No date.

57. Grupo Cubano de Investigaciones Economicas. *Labor Conditions in Communist Cuba.* English Translation by Raul M. Shelton. (Cuban Economic Research Project, University of Miami, Coral Gables). 1963.

58. Hamuy, Eduardo. *Educación Elemental, Analfabetismo y Desarrollo Económico.* (Editorial Universitaria, Santiago). 1960.

59. Havighurst, Robert J., and Moreira, J. Roberto. *Society and Education in Brazil.* (University of Pittsburgh Press, Pittsburgh). 1965.

60. Hutchinson, Bertram, et al. *Mobilidade trabalho: Um Estudo na Citade de São Paulo.* (Centro Brasileiro de Pesquisas Educacionais, Rio de Janeiro). 1960.
61. *International Joint Seminar on Geographical and Occupational Mobility of Manpower,* Castelfusano, 19th–22nd November, 1963, Paris: Manpower and Social Affairs Directorate, (O.E.C.D.), 1964.
62a. Jesus, Carolina Maria de. *Child of the Dark.* (Dutton, New York). 1962. (trans. by David St. Clair).
62b. Jobet, Julio Cesar. *Ensayo Crítico del Desarrollo Económico-Social de Chile.* (Editorial Universitaria, Santiago). 1955.
63. Johnson, J. J. *Political Change in Latin America: The Emergence of the Middle Sectors.* (Stanford University Press, Stanford). 1950.
64. Kahl, Joseph A. *Comparative Perspectives in Stratification: Mexico, Great Britain, Japan.* (Little, Brown & Co., Boston).
65. Kahl, Joseph A. *La Industrialización en America Latina.* (Fondo de Cultura Económica, Mexico and Buenos Aires). 1965.
66. Kneller, G. F. *The Education of the Mexican Nation.* (Columbia University Press, New York). 1951.
67. Labbens, Jean. "Las universidades latinoamericanas y la movilidad social." *Aportes,* Paris, Oct. 1966, pp. 67–79.
68a. Leonard, Olen E. and Loomis, C. P. (eds.). *Readings in Latin American Social Organization and Institutions.* (Michigan State University Press, East Lansing). Chapter on States and Stratification by Loomis, et al. especially p. 200.
68b. Lipset, Seymour M. et al. *Elites in Latin America.* (Oxford University Press, New York). 1967.
69. Loomis, Charles P., et al. *Turrialba.* (Free Press: Illinois). 1953.
70. McClean-Estenos, Roberto. *Clases sociales en el Perú.* (Universidad Nacional Mayor de San Marcos, Lima). 1941.
71. Mendieta, Lucio y Nuñez. *Las Clases Sociales.* (Universidad Nacional, Mexico, D.F.). 1957.
72. Monteforte Toledo, Mario. *Guatemala, Mongrafía Sociológica,* (Institute of I.S. of U.N.A.M., Mexico). 1959.
73. Muñoz de la Fuenta, Rene. "Altibajos de la reforma educacional." *NORTE* (revista de la U. del Norte), Nov. 1966, No. 1, pp. 19–27.
74. Othon de Mendizabal, Miguel, et al. *Las Clases Sociales en Mexico.* Mexico: Tlapali (Sociedad Mexicana de Difusión Cultural), undated.
75. Pan American Health Organization. *Migration of Health Personnel, Scientists, and Engineers from Latin America.* Scientific Pub. No. 142, Sept. 1966, (Pan American Sanitary Bureau, Washington, D.C.)
76. Pan American Union. *La Articulacion de la Enseñanza Media con La Primaria y Superior.* (Pan American Union, Washington, D.C.), 1965.
77. Pan American Union. *La Educacion Superior en America Latina y La Cooperacion Interamericana.* (Pan American Union, Washington, D.C.), 1961.
78. Pino, Raul Alarcón. *La Clase Media en Chile: orígenes, características e influencia.* (Editorial Tegualda, Santiago). 1947.
79. Poblete Troncoso, Moisés. *El movimiento asociacional profesional obrero en Chile.* (Colegio de Mexico, Mexico). 1945.

80. Poblete Troncoso, Moisés. *El movimiento obrero latinoamericano,* (Fondo de Cultura Económica, Mexico). 1946.
81. Prates, Susana. "Los intelectuales y la transformación político-social de América Latina." *Revista Latinoamericana de Sociología.* Vol. II., No. 3, 1966, p. 305.
82. Rama, Carlos M. *Las clases sociales en el Uruguay: estructura morfología.* (Ediciones Nuestro Tiempo, Montevideo). 1960.
83. Salcedo, Margarita. *Estructura y Contenido de la Educación en América Latina.* (Santiago). 1965.
84. Sanchez, George Isidore. *Mexico: A Revolution by Education.* (The Viking Press, New York). 1936.
85. Sariola, Sakari. *Social Class and Social Mobility in a Costa Rican Town.* (Inter-American Institute of Agricultural Sciences, Turrialba, Costa Rica). May, 1954.
86. Shils, Edward, "The Intellectuals in the Political Development of the New States." *World Politics,* April, 1960, *12,* 329–368.
87. Smith, T. Lynn. *Agrarian Reform in Latin America.* (A. A. Knopf, New York). 1965.
88a. Smith, T. Lynn. "Fragmentation of Agricultural Holdings in Spain." *Rural Sociology,* Vol. 24, No. 2, 1959.
88b. Smith, T. Lynn. *Migration from One Latin American Country to Another.* (International Population Conference, Vienna). 1959.
89. Soares, Glaucio, A. D. "The Active Few: Student Ideology and Participation in Developing Countries." *Comparative Education Review,* Vol. 10., No. 2., 1966.
90. Soares, Glaucio Ary Dillon. *Sociología de la Universidad: Algunas Areas de Investigación.* (Escuela Latinoamericana de Sociología, Santiago). 1967.
91. Stavenhagen, Rodolfo. "Changing Functions of the Community in Underdeveloped Countries." *Sociologia Ruralis,* Vol. IV, No. 3/4 (Royal Van Gorcum, Ltd.: Netherlands), 1964.
92. Stavenhagen, Rodolfo. "Classes, Colonialism and Acculturation." *Studies in Comparative International Development,* Vol. I., No. 6, 1965, pp. 53–77.
93. Torres Restrepo, Camilo. *La Proletarización de Bogotá.* (Universidad Nacional de Colombia, Bogotá). 1961.
94. Tumin, Melvin, and Feldman, Arnold S. *Social Class and Social Change in Puerto Rico.* (Princeton University Press, Princeton, N. J.) 1961.
95. UNESCO. *Proyecto Principal de Educación, America Latina.* Bulletin No. 14. (Editorial Universitaria, Santiago). April–May, 1962.
96. UNESCO. *La situación educativa en América Latina, la enseñanza primaria: estado problemas, perspectivas.* (Paris). 1960.
97. UNECLA/FAO. "Problemas y perspectivas de la agricultura Latino-Americana." Document to ECLA Conference at Mar del Plata, May, 1963.
98. U.S. Department of HEW. *Education in Peru.* OE-14104 Bulletin 1964, No. 33. (Government Printing Office, Washington, D.C.). 1964.
99. U.S. Department of HEW. *The Development of Education in Vene-*

zuela by George I. Sanchez. OE-14086 Bulletin 1963 No. 7. (Government Printing Office, Washington, D.C.). 1963.
100. U.S. Department of HEW. *The Current Situation in Latin American Education.* OE-14080 Bulletin 1963, No. 21 Feb. 1962. (Government Printing Office, Washington, D.C.). 1963.
101. U.S. Department of HEW. *Education and Social Change in Chile* by Clark C. Gill. OE-14111 Bulletin 1966 No. 7. (Government Printing Office, Washington, D.C.). 1966.
102. U.S. Department of HEW. *Education in Chile.* OE-14096 Bulletin 1964 No. 10. (Government Printing Office, Washington, D.C.). 1964.
103. U.S. Department of Labor, Bureau of Labor Statistics. *Labor Developments Abroad.* (Government Printing Office, Washington, D.C.). Sept. 1966, *Latin America,* pp. 8–10, "High-level Personnel."
104. U.S. Department of Labor, Bureau of Labor Statistics. *Labor Law & Practice in Bolivia.* BLS Report No. 218. (Government Printing Office, Washington, D.C.). 1962.
105. U.S. Department of Labor, Bureau of Labor Statistics. *Labor Law & Practice in Columbia.* BLS Report No. 217. (Government Printing Office, Washington, D.C.). Oct. 1962.
106. U.S. Department of Labor, Bureau of Labor Statistics. *Labor Law & Practice in Ecuador.* BLS Report No. 242. (Government Printing Office, Washington, D.C.). Feb. 1963.
107. U.S. Department of Labor, Bureau of Labor Statistics. *Labor in Peru.* BLS Report No. 262. (Government Printing Office, Washington, D.C.). Feb. 1964.
108. Uzcategui Garcia, Emilio. *Compulsory Education in Ecuador.* (UNESCO, Paris). 1951.
109. Vega, Julio. "La Clase Media en Chile," in Theo. R. Crevenna (ed.), *Materiales para el Estudio de la Clase Media en la America Latina,* III. (Pan American Union, Washington, D.C.). 1950 pp. 61–92.
110. Wagley, Charles (ed.). *Race and Class in Rural Brazil.* (UNESCO, International Documents Service, Columbia University Press, New York). 1963.
111. Whiteford, Andrew H. *Two Cities of Latin America: A Comparative Description of Social Classes.* (Logan Museum of Anthropology, Beloit College, Beloit, Wisconsin). 1960.
112. Williamson, Robert C. *El Estudiante Colombiano y sus Actividades.* (Universidad Nacional de Colombia, Bogotá). 1962.
113. Williamson, Robert C. "Some Variables of Middle and Lower Class in Two Central American Cities." *Social Forces,* Vol. 41, No. 2, 1962.
114. Wolf, Eric. "El Campesino Latinoamericano." *Ciencias Sociales,* Vol. V., No. 30., 1954.
115. Young, de Maurice. *Man and Land in the Haitian Economy* (University of Florida Press, Gainesville). 1957. Series sponsored by School of Inter-American Studies, University of Florida.
116. Yudelman, Montagne. *Agricultural Development in Latin America: Current Status and Prospects.* (Center for Research on Economic Development, University of Michigan, Ann Arbor). 1966.
117. Zeitlin, Maurice. *Revolutionary Politics and the Cuban Working Class.* (Princeton University Press, Princeton, New Jersey). 1967.

5

The Supernatural
and Its Symbols

After-Effects of the Conquest

It is not an exaggeration to state that the conquest of America was
done for the Church and to a great extent by the Church.[43] By the
spring of 1492, the Catholic monarchs Ferdinand and Isabella
had forced the Ottomans out of the Peninsula with the downfall
of Granada, thus consolidating the religious unity of the kingdom.
To strengthen this unity, a decree forcing into exile all Jews refusing to become Christians was promulgated the same year. And
soon the Inquisition would spread its powers as a burning flame—
burning often literally—throughout the land, including the New
World territories added to the Spanish Crown by Pope Alexander
VI acting in the name of God. In His name, Bishop Zumárraga
would burn Aztec codices in the central square of Tenochtitlán and
the Inquisition would continue hunting heretics in the rest of the
new continent for at least two hundred years more.[44]

Religious unity was to be achieved at any cost. The *encomienda* was set up primarily as a religious weapon. To this end, the
missionaries spared no sacrifice and the Crown no resources.
Schools were built to teach the Indians Castilian catechism, Span-

97

ish, and Church history with a sprinkling of writing, reading, and arithmetic. Often after a battle the surviving Indians would be herded to the front of an improvised altar for a *Te Deum* of Thanksgiving and a mass conversion. The battle blood still warm and the wounds unhealed, both the victor and the vanquished had their own reasons to be thankful. At the altar, the missionary would deliver a great sermon, holding a cross high in his hand while the *Adelantado* would hold in his the sword against the background of the king's banner. The cross and the sword have remained interchangeable symbols in Latin America ever since. A soldier would plant his sword in the ground to dedicate to God and the king his discovery, or would kiss his sword as a cross before dying; a missionary would hold his cross from the top to make a sword in the fight with the Indians. Both symbols would be raised against the background of the same banner. After each mass conversion, reports would flow toward the Peninsula for the queen. The missionaries were also good statisticians.

The conquest of symbols over symbols had just begun. Soon Indian temples were flattened and Christian temples built on their ruins; Indian gods were displaced and new prayers heard. In this way the Indian could continue his pilgrimages to the same places, and, in his mind, to the same shrine and to the same deity. The Lady of Guadalupe, for example, would take the place of Tonatzín —the Aztec mother of the gods—at Tepeyac. Mary would even look Indian.[16]

The bitter struggle between the two religious subcultures has never stopped, although some compromise has been reached after so much suffering has darkened the souls on both sides. Today most Indians still do not understand the dogmas of the Church and the Church tolerates native rituals coated with a religious orthodoxy that nobody cares to peel off. Whoever has visited Catholic shrines throughout the continent must have noticed the mixture, and, upon closer examination, one soon discovers that the mixture is one of oil and water. Naturally, this applies to the *mestizo,* the *blanco,* and Negro subcultures with the sole reservation that the latter has African origins as well.[20]

Some Popular Beliefs

The Roman Catholic Church has been able to maintain a lasting monopoly in the dispensation of the grace of God in Latin America for two basic reasons. One is that crucial elements in the belief system, in themselves extremely appealing to the masses, have been presented wrapped in a pomp as appealing to the masses as it is reminiscent of ancient Indian pomp. The other reason, to be discussed fully in the next section, is the authoritarian family, an authoritarian state, authoritarian education, and the military, not to mention the most recent economic institution introduced in Latin America, the authoritarian corporation.

Without doubt the cult closest to the Latin American heart, from generation to generation, has been the one of the Virgin Mary. Tradition has been given as the most powerful explanation for this phenomenon. If properly understood, tradition may be a good explanation. What began as a religious symbol (*quien sabe?*) has successively been given additional meanings. More than those erected to any other, shrines to Mary have been health centers and psychiatric clinics for the underprivileged. All this is evident. Less evident, and often totally ignored, is that the cult of Mary cements the linkage between the church and the military in a way that enhances the image of both in the eyes of the faithful, always the majority in the Latin American community. In many countries, the Lady of Mount Carmel (*La Virgen del Carmen*) is the patroness of the Armed Forces. Therefore, every 16th of July they celebrate their dedication to Mary with a *misa campal* and a procession. This type of devotional ceremony is normally followed by social gatherings in the Officer's Club, where the military plays host to members of the clergy, while the faithful return home deeply impressed and not totally unaware of the cemented linkage. Even in Mexico, the 1910 Revolution not withstanding, the cult of the Virgin of Guadalupe remains as a wedge in the popular conscience; the *basílica* remains a national shrine, and the church regains the lost powers. It is true that in the case of Mexico the wars of independence were inspired and led by the lower clergy under the banner of the Lady of Guadalupe (Hidalgo and Morelos were excommunicated for this reason) and that the religious history of Mexico is not typical of Latin America.[47] Nevertheless, every Latin American nation has been officially dedicated to Mary at one time or another; every identifiable segment of each country has a famous shrine, center of pilgrimages and of colorful annual celebrations; and almost every temple has altars erected to different advocations of Mary. Hills and *cañons,* valleys, mountains and meadows, highways and paths, and often *plazas* have statues of, or are decorated with, grottos to Mary. Not infrequently, these grottos have running water thought to be miraculous.

Not only the military and the nation are tied to the church by the cult of Mary but also the family, the neighborhood, and the community. It is at this level that the sociocultural significance of the cult is most apparent. There is no parish throughout the continent without an association (*hermandad, congregación*) named after some advocation of Mary. These associations are extremely important for two reasons. First, they touch on some fundamental human drives. To illustrate this point, the Congregation of the Daughters of Mary may be mentioned. It is composed of young maidens in their teens and early twenties who must excel in virtue. Through this congregation the church (the irreverent say the clergy) controls sex when it is most appealing. It builds a fortress of modesty, prayers, insignia, uniforms, interaction, and ritual that, paradoxically, make the young maiden a more visible target of masculine aggression. Thus the church unwittingly sharpens the war between the sexes. The young woman gets closer to God when the young man is getting closer to the devil. Then she becomes a missionary and he a heathen. On both sides, the main strategy utilized is that of sex dressed differently. At the end, she would save his soul from falling to the devil and he her virginity from falling to another devil. Rushed marriages are frequent in Latin America precisely among the most protected; the others do not rush; some may even not marry. It must be added that while the warfare lasts, the young man becomes jealous of the priest in general and particularly of the one who hears the young girl's confessions. Perhaps the occurrence throws some light on the Latin American male's religious indifference and anti-clericalism.

A second reason for the significance of the *congregaciones marianas* is that they constitute an intricate weaving in the neighborhood and the community which is very difficult to cut. Protestant missionaries have found this to be the case. Often they have not realized that to attack Mary is also to attack three basic Latin American sex values, femininity, virginity, and motherhood, around which Latin American societies have built a complex protective network of social relations. Mary is just the symbol of these values.

There is something more still. The Latin American male worships motherhood as symbolized by Mary but seldom joins a *congregación mariana*. In this regard, all the efforts of the Church have failed. In general, the Latin American man is not a joiner; he only joins when he can also climb. Local church organizations do not make any room for a man; they are always structureless, and the leadership is the exclusive privilege and final responsibility of the priest and the faithful followers. Focused this way, the success in Latin America of those denominations that share the leadership with, and allocate priestly roles to, any man who "hears the calling," may be seen clearly. It is not only through feeding and medicating the poor (shades of vulgar Marxism again!) that these groups make converts. In fact, in sharing leadership lies also the secret of success of the Communist party at the community level.

A second major belief-cult complex popular in Latin America is the belief in, and the cult to, Satan. For the Church, Satan is not just a symbol of evil; he is the personification, the hypostasis of evil; he is a real being; he is the commander-in chief of the fallen angels;* his head (he appeared in the form of a serpent to Eve in the Garden of Eden) was crushed by the foot of Mary, the Immaculate Conception. Her victory was not final, however; he continues to undermine the kingdom of God by tempting man. His most subtle tool is pride, instilled with hatred; his most universal one is sex, under the guise of love. In either case, you

---

* According to St. Thomas Aquinas each angel is a species. The sole non-theological reason for his statement that occurs to me, is that, being specifically different, two angels could not mate for procreation.

must check the source of your feelings with the specialist in the confessional.

Although Satan is a spirit that cannot be seen, he may nevertheless appear in various forms to either saint or evil man. The life of *Le Curé d'Ars,* a French priest who lived in the last century, is full of Satan's tempting and tormenting.* Since Latin America has not produced any native mystic of fame, it is difficult to find accounts of the Devil's schemes against saintly persons. Popular folklore has it, however, that Satan uses all sorts of strategies (such as rubbing his fairy tail over your eyes to make you lazy) to lead one into temptation. This folklore has been a very effective means of socialization. It has been used not only by parents, priests, and missionaries, but also in catechism classes and Sunday sermons.

There are other spirits beside Satan. The most spoken about is *el duende.* When Michael and his angels forced Satan and his angels out of heaven, many of these did not reach hell; some stayed in the air and some in the caves under rocks along the rivers. These latter may be seen by young maidens and small children. A *duende* is a friendly but mocking devil that appears in some regions dressed as a small man wearing a big hat, and long whiskers and hair, smiling, teasing, and inviting. He is a funny kidnapper who may take away a small child to raise her to youth. She may then return to tell fantastic stories of delightful places. A *duende* is not a harmful spirit. He just bothers his victims beyond endurance. Naturally, all this takes place only in the rural areas. In fact, Satan himself is dead in the sophisticated urban areas. Also, one may stratify churches by the number of times Satan is mentioned and by the way he is mentioned in the sermons, if he is at all mentioned. A temple without Satan is automatically an upper class temple. The same principle may apply to families and to individuals. It may likewise apply to the practice of certain rituals performed in order to chase Satan away, such as burning blessed candles and blessed palms, crossing oneself, and sprinkling holy water.

The cult of Jesus has not captured the Latin American imagi-

---

* See Aldous Huxley's interpretation of these incidents.[27]

nation as have the cults of Mary and of Satan. The church has made gigantic efforts to popularize the devotion to the Sacred Heart of Jesus and to the *Santísimo Sacramento* (Eucharist), but without much success. The latter occupies the central place in the official liturgy and the theology, but this has never been properly understood by the layman. Not only the Indian may be burning candles and incense to his preferred saint (*al santo de su devoción*), but the educated and aristocratic lady may be kneeling and reading her *novena* to the *Milagrosa* or to Saint Anthony while the bishop or the priests are saying mass, the most important church ritual that commemorates the redeeming death of Jesus.

The fate of the Bible has not been any better in Latin America, nor has that of the New Testament that has been made available in pocket-size editions. Latin American hotels and motels would never keep copies of the Bible for their guests in drawers of bedside tables; "to each thing its place."

Lastly there is a cult that must not be forgotten if one is to understand the Latin mind and the Latin American community; it is the cult to the dead, dedicated to the souls in Purgatory. As with the calendar of the saints, this cult also has its *fiesta* day, called *el día de difuntos*. Its significance is great especially in the Indian and *mestizo* countries. On this day (November 2) tombs are cleaned and decorated, wreaths are either deposited around the tombs or hung from the crosses of the tombs in and out of the cemeteries, and prayers are said—often in groups led by a priest from grave to grave—for the souls of the departed. Indians may even bring foodstuffs to temples and cemeteries. These foodstuffs are sold in auctions so that the priests may say masses for the repose of the blessed souls (*ánimas benditas*) with the proceeds. In Mexico in particular, a man would travel miles and miles, loaded with flowers, to shed some tears over the ashes of his mother on the *día de difuntos*. As the patron-saint fiesta, about which so much has been written, the *día de difuntos* is the occasion for the migrant to return home to the closer kinship bonds, to renew acquaintances, and to relive old memories. The very particular and very Latin American characteristic of this day is the celebration and exaltation of the image of *el buen hijo* (the good son): he has come, rich or poor, year after year to fulfill his filial obligations. It is unnecessary to say how meaningful this is for the kin group and the community.

Holy Mother The Church:
A Changing Religious Oligocracy*

The formal structure of the Roman Catholic Church has remained identical since about the turn of the second century. The few changes that have occurred in the bureaucracy have been more apparent than real. The absolute powers of the Pope have not been curtailed by the creation of the College of Cardinals in the Middle Ages; on the contrary, the College has added to his powers. The dogma of his infallibility aroused some dissent at the end of last century, but it did not produce a schism. Thus, his powers remain absolute. Similarly any other bishop is an absolute monarch within the boundaries of his diocese, especially in Latin America. In Europe, his powers are somewhat limited in the sense that he cannot transfer *a cura* totally at will, for the *cura* may object by appealing to an ecclesiastical court; not so in Latin America. It is true that formally the canon law has a universal character. In practice, however, the bishop remains the absolute ruler. The small college of canons, non-existent in most Latin American cathedrals, is at most a cell of diocesan politics; its members are selected by the bishop and appointed by Rome. The diocesan councils, very seldom held, are very temporary debate assemblies and their rulings have no legal standing without the approval of the bishop. Within each country, the bishop has no superior and no organization can control him. Even the sacraments administered by the priests are just expressions of the episcopal priesthood. Not even in the Communist party does ideology (theology) permeate bureaucracy to a greater extent. This is, in my view, the most fundamental sociological reason for the relentless antagonism between Catholicism and Communism.

* Oligocracy (*oligos* = few, *kratos* = authority) has been coined here to describe the power and influence of the clergy and to avoid both the pejorative connotation of oligarchy and the "excellence" of aristocracy.

As I have suggested, dioceses are relatively small territories where Catholics are subject to the jurisdiction of a bishop. These territories are broken down into smaller ones governed by the *cura*. His authority is not as absolute as that of the bishop; in theory it is delegated; in practice, however, he is normally a local chief. Not only does he rule over his assistants, but, naturally, over his flock; he is the shepherd, and the faithful are his sheep.

Again, at the local level, there is no organization or council to curb the powers of the *cura*. Moreover, the position locates him where power flows in the community. The very location of the temple and the parish house, adjacent in most cases to the homes of the privileged class, suggests the power and status of the local pastor. If he chose to live otherwise, he would find it very hard. The best proof of this is that no Latin American *cura* has ever been added to the catalogue of church saints, the highest honor that the Church can bestow upon her loyal servants. Unfortunately, to be canonized one must be dead, a fact which tends to diminish the appeal of the honor.

It is obvious, then, that the Latin American *cura* is in a strategic position to perform either good or evil, normally both. He must tend not only to the essential tasks of his ministry, the administration of the word and of the sacraments, but also to the temporal needs of his flock; he must build hospitals, schools, roads, aqueducts, and homes for the wayward. He must protect his sheep against the intruder (the "wolf"), that is, the Protestant missionary, the Communist, the strange politician, and in some areas the geneticist and the agricultural expert. His success in any one of these endeavors increases his power.

Officially, the political arena has seldom been opened to the parish priest. Unofficially, this has not been the case. The pulpit and even the confessional have been used to influence the political choices of the faithful. From time to time, and in some countries, the parish houses or rectories have been foci of conspiratorial plots against legitimate governments. The best known cases occurred in Mexico as early as the time of Juarez, before the appearance of Maximilian, and as recently as during the period of Obregon and Calles.[46] The least known case occurred in Colombia during the second administration of Alfonso Lopez (1942–1946), when many clergymen openly condemned the efforts of his government to bring about the separation of state and church and secretly participated in the conspiratorial activities that ultimately produced the abortive Pasto coup and eventually led the President to resign (1945).

In very recent times, members of the clergy have either inspired extremely advanced government programs, as in Chile, or taken vigorous leadership in introducing drastic socioeconomic change, as in Colombia, Brazil, and Venezuela. There have been unthinkable instances of clerical participation in strictly revolutionary warfare, as in Peru and Colombia. The case of Father Camilo Torres is outstanding, not only because he was an intellectual and an aristocrat but because he died leading guerrilla groups against the Colombian army. No doubt these are exceptions. Nevertheless they are indicative of pregnant times. What they exemplify is a blatant interpenetration of the institutions. Soon unionized clergymen will be marching with the workers.

The preceding should not be taken as a statement favoring the assumption that the Latin American religious oligocracies are still monolithic. This would be a more serious error than to assume the oligarchies to be monolithic. Not only has the clergy been divided into lower and higher clergy, modernizing and traditional, etc., they have almost always split on every major issue that has split the countries. It is interesting to realize that Latin Americans have never seriously split on religious issues, at least never to the point of schism. Perhaps this can be explained by the fact that Latin Americans have never taken religion seriously, except when religious issues have been transformed into political issues, which has seldom happened. It has happened nonetheless. Perhaps the best example is Colombia. During the thirties and forties the bishops (around twenty) could not agree on a uniform approach to the political issues presented to the electorate in the presidential and congressional elections of 1934, 1938, 1942, 1946, and 1950. It was not only the changes in the new treaty between Colombia and Rome proposed by the Liberal Party, touching on such matters as marriage and divorce, birth registration, cemeteries, and education. It was mainly that the traditional intimate alliance between the Colombian Church and the Conservative Party had been questioned, somewhat diplomatically by the Vatican itself and quite openly by distinguished members of the clergy. It was also that the rivalry between the two centers of regional power, Medellín and Bogotá, was approaching its end. In any event, the bitterness* poured upon the political arena by the Colombian clergy in those years can only be fully understood within the image of a non-monolithic religious oligocracy. This religious bitterness has been one of the fountainheads not only of *la violencia* that has bled Colombia for over thirty years (around 300,000 dead so far), but of the streams of change and reform that are shaking the clergy. Moreover, when the unity of doctrine and discipline that had been given in testimony of the divine mission of the Church was obviously not there, the clamor for a democratic organization began to be heard everywhere. It is precisely in the Catholic centers of higher learning where this clamor is being heard strongest. In other words, Church control of its most fundamental prerogative, education, has been challenged by the very generations she would like to keep closest. In this respect, the June–July–August 1967 revolts at the Catholic Universities of Valparaiso and Santiago, Chile are symptomatic. In short, the structure of the Latin American religious oligocracy is flattening. At the same time, its interlockings with other structures are shifting.

Social scientists know very well that institutions interpenetrate and that their expanding structures crisscross into each other at various levels in every society. What is quite typical of Latin America is that the "systemic linkage" bridging these structures very often overlaps with the kin group network.[32] That is, kinship relations frequently tie together various institutional structures in very tight knots at the crucial points where opportunities for

* This bitterness was fed by the pastoral letters of such bishops as Builes of Santa Rosa, Martínez of Garzon, and Rodríguez of Ibagué, who not only threatened the Liberals voting for the candidates of their party with the denial of the sacraments, but made it a mortal sin to read *El Tiempo*, a Liberal daily of Bogotá. Thus, one could read it without sin in Cundinamarca but upon crossing the border to Tolima the faithful was to have his soul deprived of supernatural grace if he read it in Tolima. To this bitterness, Laureamo Gómez (leader of the Conservative party) contributed abundantly not only in his speeches in the Senate but by circulating literature accusing Bishop Concha's seminarians of homosexuality. Concha was the leader of the bishops sympathetic to the Liberals.

prestige and power begin to crystalize. This occurs in rural and urban areas with equal strength probably because the Latin American cities, even the large ones, are really overgrown villages, metropolitan villages, one may say. Perhaps only stratification differences might break this pattern, although relatives tend to follow relatives in the social ascent.

The best example of the interlocking, blatant to Latin Americans who walk on the edge of the real and the ideal, has already been mentioned in this chapter. It is the well known and traditional understanding between the church and the military by which, in patriotic and religious holidays that crowd Latin American calendars, the cross becomes powerful and the sword sacred. This is obvious. What has been less obvious, and what empirical studies have not touched upon, is the extent to which, in contrast with other societies, the kinship structures infiltrate the religious ones in Latin America, using them as levers to place their members in the ranks of the officialdom of the military through the process of upward social mobility. Naturally, the mechanism works in the opposite direction also.

From the same point of departure and following the same strategies, the movement flows from the religious to either the economic, political, or educational structures—all on an upward thrust. Again, the movement can begin in any one of them, in one or more directions. In the semi-feudal societies of rural Latin America, the landlord has built schools and chapels in collaboration with the clergy and the civil authorities. In doing so, he has strengthened traditional bonds for sure. He has also heard the religious calling of his own children, has placed friends and friend's children as teachers in the schools, and has wittingly and unwittingly enlarged the electoral forces of his political party. Often the chapel serves as school, the school as chapel, and both as halls of political gatherings, if the respective ideologies converge; it is very doubtful that any chapel has ever been used for meetings of the Communist Party.

In the urbanized societies, priests may just bless new bridges and cannons, dedicate government buildings and private factories, or even join unions and strike with the workers. The latter so seldom happens, however, that the well established alliance among the traditional institutional structures, after some strains at various times here and there, is emerging strong in the sixties, although in new forms. To maintain that the conditions of this alliance have not changed would not be factual. They do faintly reflect the pressures of the masses. In recent years, the Church has not only blessed programs of agrarian reform, but has rendered landholdings to the government in contribution to these programs. Textile industries have not only organized housing cooperatives for workers, but added educational programs in collaboration with the Church that had stimulated the economic reforms in the first place.

Perhaps the best symbolic expression of the new levels of interlocking is the clergyman without a clerical garb and the leftist union with a patron saint.

Religion and Politics: Church and Religion*

Whereas in Europe there is a priest for every 800 faithful, in Latin America there is one priest for every 5,000 Catholics.[40] From the point of view of the Church, this fact has obvious implications; it also has interesting consequences from the point of view of sociological analysis. There is one especially related to the present concern.

Being in charge of large congregations often dispersed in vast territories, the Latin American Catholic priest is forced to face a very clear political dilemma. He either joins without much effort the groups that hold the power in the community and that give his work part of their leisure, or he decides to produce power by helping the poor to organize. In either case, he is looking for a short-cut performance of an over-burdening role. No other alternative seems to be open to the parish priest in Latin America.

Aware of the dangers of remaining the church of the privileged minorities, Roman Catholicism is pushing its way to the

* This topic will be treated more fully in the next chapter.

masses through political action, mainly in the form of Christian Democratic Parties. However, this choice is bringing about new problems.

By drawing a line between church and religion, the old politicians gradually forced the clergy out of politics. In recent times, the Church has drawn a line between social and political action, claiming that the former is closer to religion than the latter. This distinction is not working in Latin America except in the countries where dictators are ruling. Or, to put it correctly, this distinction is not working in the Latin American democracies. Here social action is part and parcel of political action. Therefore, by refusing to accept the latter, the clergy may find itself deprived of the former and pushed further away into the sanctuaries of either faith or learning. In fact, it may not be an error to suggest that what seems to be emerging on the Latin American social horizon is the gradual de-professionalization of the priesthood. In other words, the priesthood may at last become a way of life and not a way of living.* Many Latin American priests are aware of this possibility and some see in it the final salvation of religion. If this ever happens, the traditional distinction between church and religion, so often used against the clergy, may become totally invalid.

Social Origins and Education of the Clergy

Every known bureaucracy has made efforts to recruit into its ranks members of the powerful classes of society. The Church is no exception. This is not to say that all members of the clergy have been members of upper class families. It means only that very often distinguished clergymen are also members of distinguished families. This is particularly true of those selected for the bishopric.

The majority of the clergymen who reached the shores of America during the first half of the Colonial period were neither the best models of the official standards of morality nor much better educated than the rest of the *conquistadores* and *coloniza-*

---

* Recently I have become aware of the writings of controversial Father Juan Illic and of his research center in Cuernavaca, Mexico.

dores. Many a clergyman even earned the dubious honor of leading bands of highway robbers. With the passing of decades, the standards of morality and literacy rose, and by the end of the Colonial period, the clergy had earned respectability.

It may go without saying that some clergymen were more respectable than others. As suggested above, the higher degrees of respectability did not come most often from virtue and learning but from the socioeconomic background of the individual clergyman. This has been the base of the traditional breakdown of the hierarchy into upper and lower clergy. In terms of estimated proportions (studies of this matter have not been conducted), the bulk of the Catholic clergy has been definitely middle class, in the sense used in the previous chapter. Few have come from the other classes, with the exception of the early Colonial period, when men were chosen for the priesthood more to fill vacancies than to fulfill the expectations of a calling.

The structure of the Church suggests very different standards to guide the selection of a candidate to be a bishop. Not only must his appearance, learning, reputation, and political ability be considered, but his loyalty to Rome must be unwavering.

The direct relationship between aristocracy and the higher echelons of the religious oligocracy has become erratic with the passing of the years; even the color of the bishops has darkened a little, although none has been pure Indian or pure Negro. When it comes to badly needed reforms, the most liberal bishops have not been the ones whose socioeconomic background may be traced back to the lower brackets of the stratification spectrum of society. In fact, this segment of the Church hierarchy has more often than not betrayed its social origins. It is therefore no exception to the picture of prestige rush that has been presented previously in this work. As stated previously, when a Latin American moves upward, he expects his past to be forgotten and readily adopts the attitudes and values of the class of destination. In general, this applied with equal force to *curas* and bishops.

In quantity, the clergy has not kept pace with the increase in population, although the quality of the education of the clergy has considerably improved with the passing of the years. The number of secular clergymen has increased more slowly than the number of religious priests. For example, whereas in 1912 there were 11,776 diocesan priests and 4,578 religious priests, in 1955 the numbers were almost even (16,145 and 16,010), and in 1960 the number of religious clergymen had exceeded by almost one thousand the number of diocesan priests (18,451 and 19,185).[22] One third of the total number of priests (37,636) were foreign in 1960 and more than half of the foreign priests had come from Spain. It seems that classwise the religious orders (the Jesuits excepted) are less selective of their candidates than the diocesan seminaries. This may explain, at least to some extent, the differential increase in the two branches of the clergy.*

For the greatest part of this century, the education of the clergy has been excellent. Often the priests working in the diocesan chanceries are graduates of Roman, Parisian, or other famous centers of higher ecclesiastical learning, and the Jesuits send priests to do specialized study all over the world. In fact, not only have the Jesuits had a virtual monopoly on higher education in countries such as Chile and Colombia for centuries, but they have produced great scientists, literary figures, and educators. In the rural areas, the Catholic clergyman is nearly always the most highly-educated person in the community. Close to 300 seminaries are dedicated to this end. The point could easily be made that there is a direct relationship between the standards of education of the clergy and the rapid change taking place not only within the Church but in the spheres of her influence. A revolutionary clergyman has never been an ignorant clergyman.

The preceding does not mean that the education in the seminaries has been flawless. Well-informed clergymen would list the flaws.[40] Just to illustrate, the seminaries are frequently totally

---

* It could go without saying that neither the phenomena nor the nature of the phenomena discussed in this chapter and related to the Roman Catholic Church in Latin America can be thought to be alike or to occur to the same extent or in the same degree in every Latin American country. Not in the least. Nothing in Latin America is homogeneous: the Church is no exception. For example: it was stated earlier that there is one priest for every 5,000 Catholics in Latin America. However, the differences are fantastic; Colombia, Ecuador and Chile have one priest for every 3,000 to 4,000 Catholics whereas Guatemala and Honduras have one for every 10,000 to 13,000.[22]

isolated both physically and emotionally from the community and the people. Programs of education themselves are often not only too specialized, but one-sided and negative as well. The student-priest is only partially exposed to current scientific controversies, and then almost always in a defensive way. Education in this fashion is not a widening but a narrowing of intellectual horizons and a sure path to a search for answers outside, and frequently against, the Church. This has been the most challenging problem to the Catholic hierarchy in recent years and the resulting pre-occupation has lead to serious studies. Nobody knows, unfortunately, outside of individual bishops, how many clergymen move to other professions in Latin American dioceses. The stigma placed on this mobility is so great that the Church keeps it under cover and the socially mobile individual moves away also. Moreover, in its anxiety to produce a perfect clergyman, the Church has de-humanized him, not, as is commonly thought, by depriving him of a family of his own making, but by alienating him from his society during the formative years. He learns plenty of Latin, philosophy, theology, exegesis of the Scripture, and Church history in the seminaries, but he learns little or nothing of his own sociocultural environment. At least for the parish priest, the program needs strengthening with studies in anthropology, sociology, and social psychiatry. This diet is only available in privileged areas for privileged clergymen.

The Newcomers from the North

Although instances of individual Protestants living in Latin America have occurred for a long time, the tidal wave of Protestant penetration in the continent is not yet 30 years old.[13] Some experts maintain that the turning point was the closing of many missions in the Orient (especially in China) and the signpost the International Missionary Congress at Madras, India, in 1938. However, prior to this date some Protestant Churches had long been officially established, even at the invitation of Latin American governments and politicians seeking in this way to curb the powers of the Roman Catholic Church. The first group to enter Latin America was the Presbyterians (Argentina, 1836; Brazil, 1859; Mexico, 1872; Guatemala, 1882), followed by the Methodists (Mexico, 1871; Brazil, 1886) and the Baptists (Brazil, 1881; Argentina, 1886; Chile, 1888). Other groups swelled the missionary wave at the turn of the century. By 1916 there were close to 70 organizations and 206 missionaries with a total of over 170,000 faithful scattered throughout the whole continent and the Caribbean. These figures had grown large by 1961, when almost 8 million Protestants were ministered by 6,541 foreign and 34,547 native missionaries in 42,420 places of worship.[13] By the end of 1967 every Protestant denomination had settled in Latin America and the figures continued to swell to astonishing size. To no one's surprise, the largest number of Protestants (over 8 million) is found in Brazil. Mexico has close to a million and so does Chile; these are countries where religious freedom has existed for over one hundred years. No matter how fast it has grown, Protestantism remains small indeed when compared with the Catholic Church. The reader may see that for himself by studying Table 9.

Sociological reasons for the influx are not difficult to find. Some of them have been suggested here. For example, all liberal governments and parties found it necessary to use the Protestant missions as a wedge with which to crack the power of the Catholic Church, which had become a state within the State,[36] and which had organized a tax-exempted land economy within a disorganized national (colonial) economy. In an expanding world of free thinkers, the personal Protestant approach to the interpretation of the Bible could help in setting the Latin American mind free from the dogmatic protection of the Church. Moreover, the Protestants found a fertile field among the underprivileged by building hospitals, sanitariums, and leprosariums; by opening schools in which new techniques of education were offered that appealed to the Latin American imagination, they were able to cut clear the underbrush in jungles of prejudice and misunderstanding. They could have been more successful still if dogma had given more way to mercy. However, too frequently the Protestant missionaries not only tactlessly attacked cherished Latin American Catholic beliefs, but engaged in home-to-home religious controversies that ended too

Table 9 Selected Statistics for the Roman Catholic Church in Latin America Years 1953, 1955, 1957, and 1960

	1953	1955	1957	1960
Catholic Population	149,774,000	159,323,000	170,572,000	180,548,000
Ecclesiastical Circumscriptions				
Archdioceses	65	67	71	78
Dioceses	202	215	248	270
Prelacies M	36	41	46	50
Vicariates Apostolicous	42	45	43	43
Prefecturae Apost.	15	15	14	15
Administrations Apost.	2	1	2	1
Missions	1	1	1	–
	363	385	425	457
Personnel				
Cardinals	10	9	9	8
Archbishops (including Cardinal Archbishops)	64	64	75	88
Bishops (including ordinaries and others)	325	336	382	393
Priests (total number)	30,779	32,700	35,613	37,920
Secular	15,241	16,226	17,184	18,258
Religious	15,538	16,474	17,954	19,662
Newly Ordained Priests	670	668	664	714
Seminaries (Major)	6,225	6,287	6,163	6,871
Religious Women	72,793	75,604	90,397	100,253
Parishes and Quasi-Parishes	11,983	12,383	13,103	14,038
Churches and Chapels (public and semi-public)	59,872	62,463	65,892	72,514

Source: Gibbons, W. J. and Research Associates, *Basic Ecclesiastical Statistics for Latin America 1958 and 1960*, World Horizon Reports, Maryknoll Publications. Courtesy of Maryknoll Publications.

frequently in fist fights and violent persecution. The most disturbing incidents took place in Colombia in the early fifties; they even reached the point of affecting the otherwise friendly diplomatic relations between that country and the United States. At present, the asperities of these battles have been softened and Protestants and Catholics have come not only to an understanding, but to actual cooperation in attacking major common problems.

To no one's surprise, the most successful groups have been those burning with the "Pentecostal fire" such as the Seventh Day Adventists, the Baptists, the Assemblies of God, and kindred sects. Reasons for their success have been not only that they have ministered to the poor (70 million in Latin America), but that they have given a feeling of belonging to men and women marginal in their own societies and have brought in fluid religious structures in which the opportunities for leadership are wide open. It is precisely here, in the latter point, where the Roman Catholic Church has failed.*

Emerging Sects, Emerging Values

The choice open to the Latin American believer is not only between Roman Catholicism and Protestantism, or between the varieties of each, but between them and the several currents of religious beliefs, rituals, and cults imported from Africa and the Orient. The African influence, almost as old as the Conquest, has received considerable attention from Latin American and other investigators. The Oriental religious strains have not been studied as well, probably because they are intricately interwoven with the close family and kinship system of a very small racial minority that has kept its beliefs strictly to itself.

A third, better known, but not very widespread form of heterodoxy has been Spiritism.[8] Not a religion in the traditional

* Some other reasons for the success of the Protestant groups in Latin America have been given at various times. For example, the impact of the missionary dollar, the appeal of the North American way of life, and the success of the North American economy so often attributed, even by contemporary social scientists, to the so-called Puritan Ethics.

sense, it has, nonetheless, greatly affected the quality of Christianity practiced by large sectors of the population, especially in the areas where the African influence has been felt most strongly, the Caribbean countries and Brazil. Although not alien to African and Oriental traditions, the most successful or persistent types of Spiritism came to Latin America by way of the English-speaking world. Unlike Protestantism, coming also mainly through that world, Spiritism has been a fad but not a church. It has not offered, accordingly, the opportunities for social mobility that a church can provide and that the Latin American world so desperately needs and so anxiously welcomes. The same analysis may apply to the African cults. In spite of the differences between these cults and churches, there is a common denominator to them all. They have been fountainheads of new values; openings to new freedom; points of contact with progressive societies; anticipations of approaching new forms of being; awareness of ignored or forgotten basic human rights; realizations of the feasibility of widening solidarities; in short, the acceptance of a more temporal and less personal form of salvation. Previously, Latin America was the land of absolute values; currently, the era of value relativity is on the upswing.

References and Selected Bibliography

1. Alonzo, Isidoro, et al. *La Iglesia en Venezuela y Ecuador*. Bogotá: Oficina Internacional de Investigaciones Sociales de Feres, 1962.
2. Araneda Bravo, Fidel. *Don Crescente Errazuriz Valdivieso* (separacion de la iglesia del estado). Santiago: Editorial Universitaria, 1952.
3. On the official Catholic position regarding social justice, social change and the emphasis on the community as well as labor relations see: Pope Leo XIII, Rerum Novarum; Pope Pius XI, Quadragessimo Anno; Pope John XXIII, Mater et Magistra; Pope Paul VI, Populorum Progressio.
3a. Azevedo, Thales de. "Vida religiosa en Brasil." Ciencias Sociales, December 1955, Vol. VI, No. 36, pp. 340–342.
4. Baez Comorgo, Gonzalo, & Grubb, Kenneth G. *Religion in the Republic of Mexico*. London and New York: World Cominion Press, 1935.
5. Braden, C. S. *Religious Aspects of the Conquest of Mexico*. Durham: Duke University Press, 1930.
6. Brinsmade, Robert B. "The Religious Crisis in Mexico: The view of a

118   *Latin America: A Sociocultural Interpretation*

liberal." *Southwestern Political and Social Science Quarterly,* Vol. 9, No. 1, June 1928. pp. 57–66.
7.   Bataillon, Marcel. *Erasme et l'Espagne.* Paris: Librairie E. Drez, 1937.
8.   Camargo, C. *Procopio de & Jean Labbens. Aspectos Sociologicos del espiritismo en Sao Paulo.* Friburgo: FERES, 1961.
9.   Castro, Américo. *España en su Historia, Cristianos, Moros y Judiós.* Buenos Aires: Editorial Losada, 1948.
10. Castro, Américo. *La Realidad Histórica de España.* Mexico: Editorial Porrua, 1954.
11. Chinchilla Aguilar, Ernesto. *El Ayuntamiento Colonial de la Ciudad de Guatemala.* Guatemala: Editorial Universitaria, 1961.
12. Correa, Gustavo. *El Espíritu del Mal en Guatemala.* New Orleans: Tulane University, 1955.
13. Damborina, Prudencio. "El protentantismo en la America Latina." Tomo I. *Etapas y Métodos del Protentantismo Latinoamericano,* Friburgo Suiza, Bogota, Columbia, Oficina Internacional de Investigaciones Sociales de FERES, 1962, Tomo II. *La Situación del Protentantismo en los paises Latinoamericanos,* ibidem, 1963.
14. D'Antonio, William V. & Frederich B. Pike (eds.). *Religion, Revolution & Reform; new forces for change in Latin America,* New York: Praeger, 1964.
15. De Camargo, Candido Procopio. *Aspectos sociológicos del espiritismo en São Paulo.* Oficina Internacional de Investigaciones Sociales de Feres, 1961.
16. De la Maza, Francisco. *El Guadalupismo Mexicano.* Mexico: Porrua y Obregon, 1953.
17. Dewart, Leslie. *Christianity and Revolution; The Lesson of Cuba.* New York: Herder and Herder, 1963.
18. Diaz, May N. *Tonala: Conservatism, Responsibility, and Authority in a Mexican Town.* University of California Press, 1966.
19. Fichter, Joseph Henry. *Religion as an Occupation.* University of Notre Dame Press, 1961.
20. Religion en Brasil, Estudio Sociológico. *Ciencias Sociales,* Vol. 36, pp. 340–42.
21. Galvao, Eduardo. *Santos e visagens: um estudo da vida religiosa de Ita Amazonas.* São Paulo: Editora Nacional, 1955.
22. Gibbons, W. J. & Research Associates. *Basic Ecclesiastical Statistics for Latin America, 1958.* World Horizon Reports, Maryknoll, N.Y. 1958.
23. Gill, Mario, *Sinarquismo.* Mexico, D.F.: Club del Libro "Mexico," 1944, pp. 114, 141, 148, 168.
24. Houtart, F. R. *La iglesia Latinoamericana en la hora del concilio.* Madrid: Rivadeneira 1963 (Publicación de la Oficina Internacional de Investigaciones de FERES Friburgo, Suiza y Bogotá, Colombia).
25. Houtart, Francois & Emile Pin. *The Church and the Latin American Revolution.* Translated from the French by Gilbert Barth. New York: Sheed and Ward, 1964.
26. Houtart, Abbe Francois. *La Mentalidad Religiosa y su Evolución en las Ciudades.* Bogota: Universidad Nacional de Sociología, 1959.
27. Huxley, Aldous. *Heaven & Hell.* New York: Harper, 1965.

28. Jiménez Rueda, Julio. *Herejías y Supersticiones en la Neueva España.* Mexico, 1946.
29. Kadt, Emanuel de. "Religion, the Church and Social Change in Brazil" in Claudio Veliz (ed.), *The Politics of Conformity in Latin America.* London: Oxford University Press, 1967, pp. 192–220.
30. Kelly, Isabel. *Folk Practices in North Mexico: Birth Customs, Folk Medicine and Spiritualism in the Laguna Zone.* Published for the Institute of Latin American Studies. Austin: University of Texas Press, 1965.
31. Kitscher, Gerdt. "Ritual Races among the Early Chimu" in *The Civilizations of Ancient America.* Selected papers for the 29th International Congress of Americanists, ed. Sol Tax. Chicago: University of Chicago Press, 1951, pp. 244–251.
32. Loomis, Charles P. "Systemic Linkage of El Cerrito." *Rural Sociology.* Vol. 24. No. 1., 1959.
33. Madsen, William. *The Virgin's Children: Life in an Azetc Village Today.* Austin: University of Texas Press, 1960.
34. Mangin, W. P. *The Cultural Significance of the Fiesta Complex in an Indian Hacienda in Peru.* Doctoral dissertation. Yale University, 1954.
35. Mariejol, Jean Hippolyta (trans. by Benjamin Keen). *The Spain of Ferdinand & Isabella.* New Brunswick, N.J.: Rutgers University Press, 1961.
36. Mecham, John Lloyd. *Church and State in Latin America: A History of Politico-ecclesiastical Relations.* Chapel Hill: University of North Carolina Press, 1934.
37. Menezes, Djacir. *Democracia y Misticismo.* Mexico: Instituto de Investigaciones Sociales.
38. Murphy, Robert F. *Munduruco Religion.* ("University of California Publications in American Archaeology and Ethnology" Vol. XLIX, No. 1) Berkeley: University of California Press, 1958.
39. Pike, Frederick B. (ed.). *The Conflict Between Church and State in Latin America.* 1st ed. New York: Knopf, 1964.
40. Poblete Barth, Renato. *Crisis Sacerdotal.* Santiago: Editorial del Pacifico, 1965.
41. Poblete, Renato. "Implicaciones religiosas de la sociedad latinoamericana en cambio." Unpublished manuscript. Centro Belarmino, Santiago, 1967.
42. Portes Gil, Emilio (President Mexico 1891). *La Lucha entre el poder civil y el clero; estudio histórico y jurídico del señor licenciado don Emilio Portes Gil, procurador general de la república.* Mexico: 1934.
43. Prescott, William H. *History of the Conquest of Mexico and History of the Conquest of Peru.* New York: Random House.
44. Roth, Cecil. *The Spanish Inquisition.* New York: W. W. Norton & Co., 1964.
45. Schaedel, Richard P. "Major Ceremonial & Population Centers of Northern Peru" in *The Civilizations of Ancient America.* Selected papers of the 29th International Congress of Americanists, ed. Sol Tax. Chicago: University of Chicago Press, 1951, pp. 232–243.
46. Tannenbaum, Frank. *Peace by Revolution.* New York: Columbia University Press, 1933.

47. Tannenbaum, Frank. *Mexico: Struggle for Peace and Bread.* New York: A. A. Knopf, 1956.
48. Toro, Alfonso. *La iglesia y el estado en Mexico (estudio sobre los conflictos entre el clero católico y los gobiernos Mexicanos desde la independencia hasta nuestros días).* Mexico: Talleres Gráficos de la Nación, 1927.
49. Valbuena Prat, Angel. *La vida española en la edad de oro según sus fuentes literarias.* Barcelona: Editorial Alberto Martin, 1943.
50. Vallier, Ivan, et. al. *Catholicism, Laity and Industrial Society.* Berkeley: University of California, 1967.
51. Vallier, Ivan. *Church "Development" in Latin America: A Five-Country Comparison.* Berkeley: University of California, 1967.
52. Viviani Contreras, Guillermo. *Pio XII y la Cuestión Social.* Roma: Instituto Gráfico, 1946.

6

The Development of Politics
and the Politics
of Development

There is nothing that better reflects the state of Latin American societies and that better portrays the complexities of the Latin American personality than the fluidity of the party systems. To begin with, all Latin American political parties have been carbon copies of European parties just as constitutions have been quilts of foreign constitutions far removed from national realities.[6] Even the issues have been European, varnished with Latin American romanticism, regionalism, and *caudillismo* (as defined earlier). The so-called autochthonous parties (APRA in Peru, Partido de Revolución Cubano, Partido del Pueblo Cubano [both now extinct], Partido Acción Democrática in Venezuela, Partido Liberación Nacional in Costa Rica, Partido Febrerista in Paraguay, Peronista in Argentina, and Trabalhista in Brazil) are no exceptions; not even the Movimiento Nacional Revolucionario in Bolivia, so stubbornly supported by the Indians.

The imported ideologies have been typical of each European period, except for the present. Now it is fashionable to be Asiatic, mainly so as to be clearly anti-imperialistic. During the 19th century, debates and wars on clericalism and federalism dominated the political scene throughout the whole continent, from Mexico to Chile. Ideas about mild socioeconomic reform have affected even the most conservative parties during the first half of the present century. The success of the Cuban Revolution, awareness of the Chinese strength, and concern with the Vietnamese struggle together with the impact of the tragic physical defeats of Camilo Torres and Che Guevara, have led the young generations to exert pressure upon the political parties everywhere, challenging them to venture into more drastic reforms and to reconsider violence as a legitimate means to gain power. Thus, up to the end of the fifties, revolutionaries had given support to "developmentalists"; now developmentalists have been seriously challenged to give support to revolutionaries. The goal is distributive justice.

Political maturity had previously been measured by national stability, but now it is measured by the ability of the party to change the social structure so as to allow for the rapid integration of the marginal groups of the society into a new form of national unity founded on the just sharing of the creation and distribution of the wealth of the country. Patriotism was the love of the fatherland no matter how few the beneficiaries. For the young political leader, only that fatherland is loveable which shelters, educates, and feeds *all,* because *all* are beneficiaries. The best political party is not the one that achieves this better but the one that does it faster. In this view, political parties only differ by the proposed speed to meet these expectations. The sorting of priorities for change has never been so crucial. Everybody in Latin America is a developmentalist and becoming a revolutionary, wittingly and unwittingly.

Clericalism is not the issue, federalism is not the issue; statism, collectivism, and individualism are not the issues; not even liberty is the issue. The issue is *how many* are well housed, well fed, and well educated, *if* the how well is defined by the people and not by the government. To talk about right and left does not make any sense. This perspective is horizontal; the new perspective is vertical.

The Party: An Elastic Measuring Rod

Latin American parties are shortlived. In other words, the mortality rate of Latin American parties is very high. Morever, they are extremely flexible. Lovers of consistency are mystified by the chameleon-like conduct of Latin American parties that "go to bed with God and get up with the Devil."

Cases in Chile, Uruguay and Panama have been chosen as illustrations. From 1925 to 1965, thirty Chilean political parties participated in different elections; in 1965, only thirteen appeared for the parliamentary elections. Then the Christian Democrats obtained very close to a million votes and the *Comandos Populares* just over three thousand. Uruguay, with less than half the population of Chile, has had, in approximately the same period (1925–1962), fifty-two political parties of which only twelve cast votes in the 1962 parliamentary elections. Two of them (*Nacional* and *Colorado*) obtained, in an almost even distribution, 91 percent of the total vote. Of the nineteen political parties in Panama, only nine survived the presidential elections of 1964 by obtaining the minimum of 5,000 votes that the law requires.

To survive, political parties often take shelter under *Uniones* and *Alianzas*. Obviously these are even more short-lived than the parties that compose them. These *Alianzas* may be found in practically every country and with the occasion of almost every election. The best known may be those of Brazil and Chile; Chile's has been the most durable, having endured for more than a decade.

The chameleon effect is the most fascinating feature of the Latin American political scenery. Without it the kaleidoscope would be colorless. A political party evolves, as all organizations evolve, but in Latin America it evolves beyond recognition in a short time. Examples abound. Outstanding in this regard seems to be the Socialist Party of Chile, which has just proclaimed (in a country so proud of its democratic traditions) violence as the only realistic means of gaining power and controlling the government. To be sure it has remained Marxist, but it has accepted nationalism in its program and has moved from a strategy of a democratic takeover of power in order to completely overhaul the social structure, to its current position of destroying it first and erecting a new one on its ruins later. The party is moving back to a mild form of supranationalism in the form of a Castroite type of Latin Americanism (*Organización Latino Americana de Solidaridad*,

OLAS). The Socialists, who tend to remain ideologically inconsistent, have split about once every eight years in recent times. Splitting, of course, is not the exclusive privilege of the Chilean Socialists in Latin America.

The *Partido Liberal* of Colombia may be another Latin American party that has been affected by the chameleon effect in just the last twenty years. For the Colombian Liberals, the chameleon effect has meant, in some doctrinal matters, total conversion. After being bitterly anti-clerical in the late thirties and early forties, its members now attend Sunday Mass and Holy Communion. In foreign policy and in administration and economic matters, they have become indistinguishable from the Conservatives. The sole remaining difference between the two parties is the family names that, according to contractual agreement, alternate power every four years. (This arrangement began in 1958 with Lleros Camargo; it will end in 1970 with a Conservative.) They alternate like Romulus and Remus under mother wolf.

As a final example, the Mexican government party comes to mind, although its ideological changes have been somewhat reflected in changes of label. As a *Partido Nacional Revolucionario,* it sought to organize (in 1928) the shambles of the revolution (1910–1917); as a *Partido de la Revolución Mexicana,* it sought to consolidate the achievements of the revolution; and as a *Partido Revolucionario Institucional* (PRI), it has sought to commemorate the Revolution. Calles made presidents and the party; Cárdenas continued, as president, making the party; now the party makes the presidents. In most policies, it wears the two faces of Janus. In economic matters, it nationalizes some basic activities (oil, telephones, electricity) and purchases bankrupt private industries, restores them to life, and sells them back to private investors. In foreign policy, it supports Cuba but remains silent about Viet Nam. In labor relations, it hands out packages to labor leaders, but if they demand larger handouts, the federal jail gets filled with labor leaders. In the sphere of religion, it lets churches act outside the constitution but occasionally condemns their street demonstrations. The economy grows strong but welfare programs slow down. Mexico (40 million population) contributes the largest number of migrants to the United States from any country in Latin America, except Castro's Cuba (population 7 million).

Other, even more colorful examples, could be cited, such as the Radical Party in Chile and the Communist Party everywhere. The main thing is that the elasticity of Latin American societies is faithfully reflected in the elasticity of the political parties.

Traditional Distribution of Power

The Latin American prestige rush finds its finest form of expression in the production and distribution of political power. The early organization of government was not a profitable enterprise, but a public service. Gradually it was realized that the interest groups that controlled the government could also influence the leanings of the economy. In this way the original political parties were merely expressions of specific pressure groups. In other words, parties and pressure groups were identical, because, among other reasons, the "masses" had no organizations of their own. In most countries, landlords and farmers grew into conservative parties, and the emerging bourgeoisie, not quite welcome by the landed aristocracy, joined the emerging proletariat, mostly of foreign origin, to form the liberal parties that Masons stimulated in their battles with the Church.*

As new pressure groups developed, speeded by the expansion of education, they eventually found it unprofitable to remain loyal

---

* This is admittedly a simplified version of the formation of the two parties, although not as simplified as the one most commonly given. In fact, anticlericalism was not a religious question; it was a land ownership problem; civil landlords against clerical landlords; newly-arriving land hunters against the incredible land monopoly of the Church that possessed at the same time the most effective power of taxation: tithes, collections throughout the countryside, fees for the administration of the sacraments and the performance of funerals, etc. Federalism, in turn, was an expression of regional interests—economic, administrative, religious, often ethnic—leery of the intentions of the few families that had inherited with wealth the ability to rule. It is interesting to notice that only large countries remain federations: Venezuela, Mexico, Brazil, and Argentina. Socioeconomically, Colombia has always been half its size. Incidentally, Liberal and Conservative parties have almost vanished from the continent.

for long to one party; henceforth, party and pressure groups became, if not divorced, at least separated.

Proliferation of pressure groups has been slow because Latin American economies have diversified slowly. The old powerful pressure groups—landlords, the Church, and the military—remain as inaccessible as ever. On the other hand, the professional groups, although accessible to many, have not become pressure groups, and the prestige they bestow upon their members has little glamor. Under these conditions, it seems evident that in prestige-hungry societies where opportunities are both accessible and glamorous, people should be concerned with politics.

The other glamorous alternative, higher education, has remained inaccessible to this day even in education-minded countries. And what is worse, Latin American universities have become gigantic castles of power, administrative giants vulnerable to and unshielded from party politics. Each university is a microcosmos of the larger society, a shrunken nation, and also a premonition of what will become of the country.

Latin American universities, lacking space, starving for faculty, rusting with seniority, and begging for equipment, with thousands of angry students knocking at their doors (23,000 students cannot find room for 1968 in Chilean universities), are called, on top of it all, dens of political iniquity. In the age of rights, our elders are still arguing about privileges.[31] What are these "leftouts" going to do? What they have been doing for a hundred years. They will swell the already bulging bureaucracy. Moreover, feeling trapped, they became easy pawns in the changeable political chess game. Few political parties in Latin America can claim stable constituencies.

In the meantime, the students have emerged as one of the most powerful pressure groups in the Latin American continent.[43] They have toppled *rectores,* ministers (government cabinet members), and presidents. This has been traditional. Students have also split the university power structure in an effort to construct programs of education sensitive to the problems of the country. Nowadays, when they take to the street they also carry with them workable solutions.

The development of strengthened pressure groups may not bring any closer the end of the pluralistic party system in the future of Latin America. Those ideologists who have sung their *requiem* in the end of ideology could have been singing their own *requiem*. Too often scientific rationality is an ideological garment. Many political parties are preaching rationality of the economy as the shortest path out of stagnation, defined, of course, in terms of profit maximization, rather than in terms of profit distribution. This latter definition is the one used by Socialists, Communists, and communitarianists, all appealing to the marginal groups, and, in this, being very rational. Rationality cannot exist outside a means-ends schema, and in the realm of the Latin American the relation between means and ends is extremely resilient. This explains why political parties, dealing as they do with different schemata and with this resiliency, are either so perishable or so flexible.

There is something else here. Latin Americans do not think that a two party system makes democracy more workable than political pluralism. On the contrary. Political pluralism allows for a wider representation and for more control in parliament of administrative decisions that affect increasing numbers of citizens. Moreover, they raise questions about a civil service that might choke the information process that begins with the people and ends at the desk of the decision makers. Has not this been the problem of the United States foreign policy in recent years? Remember the Bay of Pigs and the Dominican Republic!

Contrary to educated North American public opinion, the most articulate Latin American enemies of tradition are not the Communist or the Marxist parties. The Christian Democrats of the continent deserve this honor. Their intellectuals are seriously engaged in refining a theory and an ideology for the party based on existential realities. It is very ironic that the overzealous anticommunism of North American capitalism, when pouring in its vulgar Marxism, economic aid to the Latin American Church and her Christian Democracy, has helped develop a most effective and God-blessed form of anticapitalism. Perhaps this is exactly what our decision-makers in Washington had in mind.

Issues without Parties and
Parties without Issues

It was insinuated at the very end of the introduction to this chapter
that a horizontal perspective of the Latin American political scene
is most inaccurate. It would be more in accord with the nature of
things to talk about differences of degree rather than differences in
kind between the various political parties. Perhaps it would be
more accurate to talk about political factions rather than political
parties. The perspective should be vertical. A realistic model for
the Latin American political parties should look something like
Figure 4. On some fundamental issues, parties do not differ. To
issues, parties do not differ. To illustrate. There is no question
about the necessity for rapid socioeconomic change throughout,

Figure 4

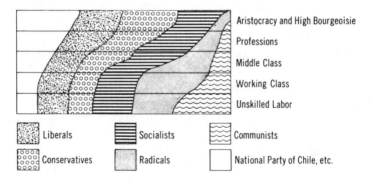

Liberals	Aristocracy and High Bourgeoisie
Conservatives	Professions
Socialists	Middle Class
Radicals	Working Class
Communists	Unskilled Labor
National Party of Chile, etc.	

They should be classified, then, as parties for the top, parties for the middle,
and parties for the bottom (depending on the layers of society from which
they are most likely to draw their constituencies). Thus, using Chile as an
example, National Party would be, in this perspective, a "top" party.

as demanded by population pressure, internal migrations, lingering
internal and external colonialism, widespread unemployment, fugi-

tive national capitals, low productivity, low rate of economic growth, falling exports prices, instability of foreign markets, rising imports prices, high revolutionary potential, etc, etc, etc. They all agree that the structure has to be revamped, thoroughly overhauled, and updated. It may not be a question of how deep the change either. It is a matter of priorities and strategies and timing. Some parties would begin with the legal system that seems to handcuff the rest of the society. These are the parties concerned primarily with order and authority. A few very small parties want violent total revolution, although without ever really doing anything about it. Similarly, the conservative parties are not really conservative. The real difference between Latin American political parties lies in the depth of their penetration into the layers of society.

There are causes that no political party has ever espoused. Concerned as they have to be with local and specific issues that need immediate solutions and forced to appeal to a terribly heterogeneous electorate, most parties rarely consider those causes. On the other hand, some parties appeal to very restricted constituencies. This is the case of Socialist, Communist, and revolutionary parties, as well as of those dominated by the so-called high bourgeoisie. One ignored issue in Latin America, no matter how much Puerto Rico has agitated it, is the frightening growth of population in the area, the fastest in the world. No real issue has been made of this phenomenon, although political parties do make innocuous statements about it from time to time.

The traditional position of Christians and Communists in this connection is well known. They both condemn birth control as a means of checking population growth, albeit for contrasting reasons. The Christians, because it would run contrary to the will of God, and the Communists because it is a capitalist device to shrink a labor supply that can conveniently be replaced by automation. They are all aware, however, that more fundamental cultural and socioeconomic reasons militate for large families in all Latin American social strata.

Regionalism buttressed by geographical isolation has been one of the most burdensome handicaps in the progress of Latin

America. Like most things in the area, transportation has been for the most part a privilege, not the satisfaction of a basic necessity. A look at a Latin American map will make the point instantly. Few roads run east and west, and those that run north and south either do not go far enough or degenerate in hair-thin lines. For thirty years the Latins have spoken sporadically of the Pan American highway and thirty more years will pass before it becomes the earthly bond of the continent. Even the most antimonopolistic parties dodge the issue.

Since Colonial times, bureaucracy has weighed heavily on the apportioning scale of government budgets and no political party has even touched it. Bureaucracy, assumed to emerge in the evolutionary path where rationality supersedes primary relations, has never been separated in Latin America from the kin group network, and probably never will. The recently imported corporation has often overcome the barriers of non-rationality by both the charisma of the president and manager and the splitting of functions along kin group lines. *Familismo, amiguismo, filhotismo* are not only well rooted in the culture, but no organization has yet been made free of primary relations. Add to this the Latin American *leguleyismo,* maintained not only by the high university enrollment in law, but by the legalism, against the common law approach, that places emphasis on jurisprudence more than on practice. Again, no party has made an issue of these problems.

Lest it be taken for granted that only government bureaucracies are burdened by the weight of these cultural imperatives, one must keep clearly in mind that in Latin America neither labor unions nor professional associations, neither the church nor the military, can be exempted; neither can the structure of the political parties. The most recent frontal attack against this problem, led by the army in Argentina, has been little more than a simple substitution. To place the blame in this case on the parties themselves, ignoring geography and ecology, the uneven growth of the economy, and the peculiarities of the social structure, is again a way to ignore the issue, in this instance by both military men and politicians.

Alianza Popular Revolucionaria Americana (APRA), the

party of the young, brilliant, and controversial Victor Raul Haya de la Torre in the second quarter of this century, made articulate attempts to interpret the plights of the Indians and *mestizos* of the continent. The issue has been snarled since in snares of *machetes* and bayonets, of diplomatic *leguleyismo* and electoral manipulations. In the end, the army has won in Peru. The Indians, in turn, never developed a class or political consciousness; they just escaped to tropical and urban jungles, and not even APRA has done much for them. The Movimiento Nacional Revolucionario reproduced, albeit more successfully, the Peruvian experience in Bolivia (1952–1964), but without grass-root consolidation, nevertheless. The Indian issue remains, thus, without a party.

Land reform has been an issue of every party at one time or another, the issue of very few parties sometimes, and the issue of all parties occasionally. Land reform laws have been passed in practically every country, in some with relative success. Land reform laws have focused exclusively on agricultural lands in an effort to solve both the endemic food shortage of the continent and the alarming agrarian problems. No attention has been paid to urban land reform. Land speculation, obviously, goes on unabated. Symbolically, Latin America has contributed to the international language with terms such as *favelas, barriadus, callampas, villas miseria*. The combine of realtors, banks, legislators, and family names is almighty and, like God, inscrutable. Scientific investigations on the subject have never been conducted. The party member who dares to scratch the surface of the monster ends up without fingernails. Some parties, like *Alianza Nacional Popular* (ANAPO) in Colombia, have timidly mentioned it. The answer of governments and parties has been mass-produced, uniformly boring, cheap housing, that, with un-Latin regularity, feeds the combine itself every political season.

Politicologists tell scientific yarns about how Latin American presidents cut themselves off from the little reality political parties unavoidably grasp. Few political parties spend time and/or money in researching social economic processes. They do not even study their own processes. Here again Latin America has contributed to the international language with a rich vocabulary: *personalismo,* *caudillismo, caciquismo, generalismo, golpismo, coronelismo, tenentismo, mandonismo, presidencialismo, matonismo, culatismo,** a most representative sample.

If political parties do not differ in regard to really fundamental issues, if their differences consist in ideological incidentals, and if many issues stay in oblivion, it seems that there should be parties without issues. Pragmatism, supposedly absent from the Latin American sociocultural experience, is at its very heart. In a traditional society, amazingly enough, it is a type of pragmatism without a past. In a world of ultimate causation the cause-and-effect nexus is not enough taken into account. Events just happen to happen. They are, in a sense, miracles. One sees the effect, one "knows" the cause; why bother about the nexus? In this context, experiencing does not at all carry the idea of experimenting. The present stands in itself and by itself. This seems to be the philosophy of people and party in Latin America.

Invariably, parties everywhere accuse each other of political opportunism. The disinterested observer, confronted with little or no ideological differences, often wonders, as almost any one who has studied the parties of Bolivia, Guatemala, Peru, and Panama may wonder. Most of them appear clearly to be parties without issues. Assuming this to be the case, what are the probable explanations?

The prestige rush that has been discussed is a good explanation, but it needs to be set in the socioeconomic context in which it works. For the Latin American of today, the universe is bounti-

---

* In 1950, Luís Ignacio Andrade, then Ministro de Gobierno under President Ospina Pérez, who had just come to his ranch in Baraya, Huila, Colombia to rest after achieving the "victory" for Laureano Gómez in the presidential elections of that year, told the author: "Lo que este país necesita es la disciplina de la culata" (What this country needs is the discipline of the gun-butt). In fact, it is in this way that he had achieved that "victory." What followed in Colombia is public history. A few years later, upon the death of his wife, Andrade left for Rome to become a Claretian priest making, of course, all the headlines. After his return, he came periodically out of his convent to pass ballots to farmers on election days and to show, dramatically if unwittingly, how religion and politics were jointly fighting the final battles. Father Andrade died in 1967; with him, hopefully, died a sinister era in Colombian politics.

ful and its potential limitless. Therefore, a "theory of limited goods" would not explain the scrambles. On the contrary, it obscures them. The very realization of this goodness, sometimes exaggerated, helps in understanding the political scene. Now, if the Latin American focuses on the present, on the quick and sizeable gain and on a rapid ascent, as he does, then the understanding increases. It must be added, in this connection, that there is no poor country in Latin America. Any student of economic geography knows this fact. There are poor (bad) governments and a marvelous mismanagement of each country's wealth.

On the other hand, most Latin American societies are just beginning to open. Through the few cracks that have opened, the vision of that bountiful world is telescoped; everybody has a view of what is to be had, and of the barriers that must fall. The parties are tearing down barrier after barrier. Again, the difference between them lies in how many people they are willing to invite to the banquet. The perspective *is* vertical.

This is what appears obvious to the young Christian Democrats of Chile. Christian Democrats have a whole cultural setting working in their favor in Latin America. The Communists do not. If the Christian Democrats fail, the sequel will be chaos, aimless violence, and urban guerrillas à la the North American Negro. The other alternative, civil disobedience, although not entirely unknown in contemporary Latin American history, seems alien to the traditions of bloodshed characteristic of every one of the countries. Perhaps it is true that there is a wolf within each man and a herd of wolves within each country.

The Oligarchies and the Masses

Unlike the political parties and the pressure groups that can be visualized in a vertical perspective, the oligarchies can be conceived only in a horizontal, albeit split, perspective. They are the groups that have controlled the dispensation of economic and political power from generation to generation, although without the stability of the landed aristocracies that preceded them or laid their foundations.[17]

There is no reason to believe that Latin American oligarchies present a united front under normal or abnormal conditions. In the first place, they neither share the same interests nor share them equally. One would think that the revolutionary movements that have made them targets of selective aggression would bring unity to their ranks. This has not been the case, because some members of the oligarchies either miscalculated the extent of the changes sought or thought it profitable to join the revolutionary forces. In Mexico, for example, members of the Mascareñas and Elías families, their large land holdings in Sonora notwithstanding, became representatives of the revolutionary government of Calles in the United States from the beginning of the famous upheaval. Similar instances can be found in less significant struggles, whether they are concerned with agrarian reform, highway construction, industrial development, policies on imports and exports, and what not.

Neither can it be maintained that oligarchies have presented a united front against employees, urban proletarians, or rural workers, as much political propaganda would lead one to believe. If they have not, it is only partially due to humane motives. The fundamental reason is structural. The National Associations of Manufacturers, The Associations of Cattle Raisers, of Cotton, Coffee, Rice Producers, of Realtors, etc., in which the oligarchies exert great influence, lack the agencies to interlock for the purpose mentioned. Moreover, in no Latin American country do the unions number more than 15 percent of the labor force.*

The Latin American masses are for the most part impermeable to ideas of organization because the evolution of society has not reached the point where unity means prosperity. It is well known that unions have not been organized in order to advance but in order not to regress, which may, of course, be said to be a form of advancement. To be a member of a union, one must know how to do something; there are no unions of those who do

* This does not imply that unionized labor can present a united front against the oligarchies either.

nothing. The great Latin American masses know nothing. The *peon* floats from farm to farm selling his physical energy, not his skills, for he does not possess any. The urban laborer tries at everything until he finds a niche that somebody has vacated. They all lack "consciousness of kind." There is still another angle to this picture. The lay-out of the Latin American city does not allow for much physical proximity of the underprivileged. Not all, not even most of them, live in *favelas, barriadas,* or *callampas.* Too often, wealthy sectors are dotted with dwellings of misery. Physically, at least, the underprivileged are frequently closer to the bourgeoisie than to the proletariat. In matters of ideology the masses—hardly lettered and skilled, very often letterless and unskilled—seem to prefer the ideology of the established masters over the ideology of the newly arrived ones called labor leaders.

In typical Latin American fashion, the geometry of the oligarchies coincides with the geometry of the kin group. As may be expected, the extent to which the groups overlap varies from country to country. In some countries, like Peru, Nicaragua, Honduras, Panama, Colombia, and Chile, the overlapping of these geometries is so striking that family names are symbols of easily identifiable nuclei of politicoeconomic power. In most cases these "clans" can not only control key industries, banks, and the insurance industry, but the most influential newspapers and best urban real estate as well.[17] Some of these groups have been studied a little, but most of them have not,[2b] because sociologists have only rarely been concerned with them. The oligarchies have been permanent targets of attack, but very seldom have they been targets of investigation. For the outsider, their boundaries remain unmarked and the extent of their influence hidden. It is well known that they are small in number although, when it comes to giving figures, there is a great deal of discrepancy. It seems that no more than ten kin groups make up the oligarchies of Chile and Peru, fourteen the ones of El Salvador, forty the ones of Colombia, and about five the oligarchies of Panama, Nicaragua, and Honduras. Some of these familial networks are international; soon, some will be continental. In contrast to this, needless to say, the masses have no international contacts, nor hopes of continental ones.

The Military: A Collective Messiah!

The military, the clergy, and the traditional professions (law, medicine, and engineering) have been the best, and about the only, channels of upward social mobility in Latin America until recent years. Literary success has been the other one, although its extent is obviously very limited.

It is also obvious that the military has towered above the others because of the prizes it can offer. The prizes are in the presidency and the cabinet. Only of late have the professions challenged the military in this arena. The Congresses, where they still exist, rank as poor second sets of prizes, inaccessible to the military.

In almost every country (except Mexico and Costa Rica) the ghost of the military haunts the presidency. There are three main reasons for this. One is that the legislative and the judiciary are extremely weak almost everywhere.[6] A second is that the legitimacy of presidential elections hinges too often on the largest minority, therefore making the support of the military a requisite for political survival. Finally, the little charisma built up by the victorious candidate soon fades away, filtered by the fourfold screen of the bureaucracy, the oligarchies, the aristocracy, and the religious oligocracy.

Of these three reasons, the most important, in my view, is the third one, because in all societies charisma is the shortest road to legitimacy.* This is particularly true in developing countries, where elections are by no means the most efficient sources of legitimacy and where political institutions are outdated. In this view, the "gap of legitimacy" is really a failure of charisma. For the Latin American mind, the latter makes sense while the former is meaningless. This is why the military emerges so often as a collective messiah.† Like the charisma of some presidents, the

---

* The reader must be aware of the fact that legitimacy is not identical with legality. An election may be legal without being at all legitimate.

† It seems evident within this context that an intelligent United States foreign policy would focus rather on stimulating the development of charismatic leadership, especially at the local level, than on reform of outdated institutions. More about this may be found in the last chapter.

messianic character of the military is always short-lived. In fact, only conservative historians in this country and in Latin America, supported by the four blocks mentioned above, think of the military for any length of time as a collective messiah. The peoples of Latin America have never thought this. The few contemporary military men idolized by a majority of Latin Americans ended by betraying the military: Parmenio Cardenas* in Mexico, Getulio Vargas in Brazil, and Domingo Peron in Argentina.

Without question, the Latin American military has been, especially after World War II, a solid foundation of political stability throughout the continent—a comforting circumstance for United States foreign policy makers who shiver from the memories of Guatemala and Cuba.[9, 14]

The monetary cost of this imposed stability has been paid by United States foreign military aid (See Table 10). The human cost has been paid by the great numbers of Latin Americans who die every week in desperate unrest and senseless starvation. On this there are no statistics. All we know is that malnutrition is the first killer in every Latin American country.

Awakened by the critics and aware of the power of the masses, the military has attempted to restore its image by joining the phalanx of developmentalists. In the attempt the military has done some good, at least indirectly. It has forced the young people in many a country, for example, to seek refuge in the churches, forcing them, in turn, to get closer to the masses. The very recent history of Brazil, Chile, and Argentina throws abundant light on the matter. In the attempt the military has done something more apparent: it has attracted larger sums of foreign aid from North America, which pleases to no end some sectors of the middle class and the newly-professionalized experts. To see this, one has only to turn to Bolivia, Brazil, and Argentina. In the attempt the military has succeeded in both delaying the revolutions and sharpening the minds of the revolutionaries. The tragic end of Che Guevara has resulted in new theoretical revisions of established revolutionary dogmas.

In war and peace the military has been a collective messiah

---

* Cardenas was not a career military man. With Obregon and Calles he was a product of the Mexican Revolution.

Table 10 United States Loans and Grants to Latin America

	Economic Aid*			Military Aid*			Grand Total
	Loans	Grants	Total	Loans	Grants	Total	
Argentina	380.0	8.8	388.9	1.0	49.5	50.5	439.4
Brazil	1,072.2	367.7	1,439.9	23.4	238.7	262.1	1,702.0
Bolivia	128.5	254.1	382.8	—	11.4	11.4	394.2
British Guiana	—	4.9	4.9	—	—	—	4.9
British Honduras	—	3.4	3.4	—	—	—	3.4
Chile	574.6	129.9	704.5	5.4	88.0	93.4	797.9
Colombia	383.7	105.4	489.1	—	66.8	66.8	555.9
Costa Rica	51.3	56.9	108.2	—	1.7	1.7	109.9
Cuba	29.2	4.0	33.2	—	10.6	10.6	43.8
Dominican Republic	50.9	51.5	102.4	—	11.8	11.8	114.2
Ecuador	101.5	53.4	155.0	—	37.5	37.5	192.5
El Salvador	46.0	26.2	72.2	—	3.9	3.9	76.1
Guatemala	45.7	132.3	178.0	—	8.7	8.7	186.7
Haiti	23.8	66.2	90.0	—	4.3	4.3	94.3
Honduras	25.8	34.1	59.9	—	3.5	3.5	63.4
Jamaica	12.8	17.3	30.1	—	0.5	0.5	30.6
Mexico	331.0	154.9	485.9	0.6	1.7	2.3	488.2
Nicaragua	28.8	44.4	73.1	—	6.6	6.6	79.7
Panama	55.4	68.5	123.9	—	1.6	1.6	125.5
Paraguay	32.0	36.1	68.1	0.3	3.7	4.0	72.1

	Economic Loans	Economic Grants	Total (a) and (b)	Military Loans	Military Grants	Total (c) and (d)	Grand Total
Peru	2?2.2	97.3	309.5	−2.1	97.4	95.3	404.8
Surinam	—	3.9	3.9	—	—	—	3.9
Trinidad and Tobago	12.7	27.4	40.1	—	—	—	40.1
Uruguay	71.5	9.2	80.7	—	32.8	32.8	113.5
Venezuela	243.8	24.0	267.8	43.9	11.7	55.6	323.4
Other West Indies	—	2.9	2.9	—	—	—	2.9
Total Economic Loans (a)	3,913.4						
Total Economic Grants (b)		1,784.7					
Total (a) and (b)			5,698.1				
Total Military Loans (c)				72.5			
Total Military Grants (d)					692.4		
Total (c) and (d)						764.9	
Grand Total (a), (b), (c) and (d)							6,463.9

* Total figures less repayments and interest. All figures in millions.

Adapted from *U.S. Overseas Loans and Grants and Assistance from International Organizations*, July 1, 1945–June 30, 1964. Loans imply assumed responsibility; grants outright donations. For some countries the economic aid in form of grants exceeds the one in form of loans. Military aid seems to take the form of grants with few exceptions, thus removing, one may think, local responsibility.

for the oligarchies and all other worshippers of order. In war it has been so for the underprivileged also, but only because war is a form of disorder. Civil war, that is, since the Latin American military has fought very few international battles.

The ties between the military and the oligarchies have been traditionally tight. They not only support each other in the name of law and order, but their children trade places from generation to generation in the higher rungs of the opportunity scale. The case of Argentina is typical of the rest of Latin America. The largest (28 from 114) single group of army generals and air force brigadiers have been children of traders and industrialists, and only two have been sons of working class fathers. (See Table 11) This is not surprising. No more surprising, but very significant nevertheless, and frequently forgotten, is the powerful unrooting effect that the military service has among rural Latin Americans.

Table 11 Parental Occupation of the Higher Officers

Assumed Level	Type of Occupation	Army Generals	Air Force Brigadiers	Total
Higher Middle Class	Landholders	5	5	10
	Trader-Industrialist	18	10	28
	University Professional	12	2	14
	Military	16	4	20
	Administrative Head	1	2	3
	Self-employed	4	—	4
	Home Builder	—	1	1
	Rentier	2	2	4
Dependent Middle Class	Journalist	1	—	11
	Employee (White Collar)	17	4	21
	Photographer	1	1	2
	Farmer	3	—	3
	Retired	1	—	1
Working Class	Mechanic	1	1	2
		82	32	114

From Horowitz, I. L. "The Military Elites" in Seymour Martin Lipset and Aldo Solari (eds.) *Elites in Latin America* (New York: Oxford University Press, 1967), p. 162. Reprinted with permission.

Few return to their villages. Most of them move to the cities in search for higher occupations. The consciousness of the prestige rush has been thusly awakened.

In recent years, the clergy has gradually disassociated itself from the military as a consequence of the rapproachment between the Church and the militant youth and between the lower clergy and the masses. The "mission" that the United States Army has set for itself in Latin America (as expressed in Project Camelot) has not been shared by the clergy and it has further alienated the clergy from the military. The ideology of insurgency has theological roots in Catholic Latin America. Thus, the Latin American military, previously identified with national sovereignty and patriotism, has become identified with the international crusade of the United States and its Defense Department to eradicate Communism and sexual immorality. As a result, the military is alienated from the newly emerging spirit of nationalism pervading Latin America. In fact, in the eyes of the people it has become a traitor to the national interests, an ironic side effect of United States military aid to Latin America.

It seems, in summary, that the image of the military as a collective messiah has been formed abroad with the support, naturally, of many Latin Americans.

Politics and Development: A Biased View

The development of Latin America is, in my view, primarily a structural problem, and only in this sense is it also political and economic. There are too many Latin Americans, or, to be more accurate, there are too many nations within each nation, or, more accurate still, too many countries within each country. This is not true only from the point of view of geography, which is simple in the case of Uruguay, or from the point of view of ethnicity, which is simple nowhere, but from the point of view of the structure of the political parties that reflects so faithfully the structure of the "national" societies.

Structuralists have been criticized for their emphasis on structural changes. Structuralist or not, one has to recognize some fundamental phenomena. For example, the distribution of the population is, without exception, uneven in every country. The cancerous growth of urban centers without urban mentality has pulled not only people, but resources too, out of the hinterland, creating an internal colonialism in both structure and attitude.[46a, 46b] The economic life of every group and every person is exploitive, not productive.

Few urban areas have grown as centers of industrial activity. Most of them have grown as places of refuge for drop-outs from the disintegrating agrarian life. Thus, the metropolis itself is a gigantic village. The urban-rural ratio is just a ratio, a quantitative difference that does not at all imply the qualitative differences most people tend to interpret.

The uneven growth has its antecedents and its consequences. It has been a product of governmental and economic administration geared toward extra-continental markets, the colonial heritage never lost. Latin America has not developed internal markets, and all governments have been just custom brokers, often unskilled ones, of the export-oriented economies. In the process, public and private bureaucracies have grown in direct proportion to their inefficiency. No bureaucracy has proven efficient and Latin American bureaucracies show this well by their very growth. In short, Latin American urban areas are administration centers more often than centers of production. Because services must be provided for the bureaucrats, a new growth emerges. Presidents, cabinet members, and bureau chiefs make sumptuous expenditures in monuments to their ancestors, in streets to their residences, and in public and private mansions, and thus a third growth emerges. In the meantime, the social distance has increased in proportion to the location of people along the ladder of political and economic power, and the urban masses remain as illiterate and poor and disorganized as the rural ones from which most of their members came.

Every large city in Latin America has been first a center of national or state administration and only second an industrial center. Only São Paulo in Brazil, Medellín in Colombia, and Monterrey in Mexico can trace most of their growth to industry. Obviously, the answer is government decentralization, easy to say but almost impossible to achieve.

A second example. In every country, a very small proportion of the population controls the largest proportion of agricultural land.[25b] This is true even for Mexico after fifty years of "revolution." The sole exception to this law is Cuba, which had to cut itself out of the inter-American system in order to achieve the miracle in a short time. And at what price! The rest of Latin America hardly wants agrarian reforms; not before violence, it seems.

The last example. At the end of the sixties, Latin America was still exporting about the same commodities that have left its shores for a hundred years: minerals, lumber, coffee, bananas, sugar, and oil. At the end of the sixties, Latin America was still importing huge quantities of manufactured products with an unfavorable balance of payments. At the end of the sixties, Latin America was still selling to and buying from the same countries. Little effort has been made to break these patterns. And who would dare to break the pattern of foreign investments that take out much more than they take in? Nobody. Latin America has produced only one Cárdenas and one Castro.

What is the answer? The answer, in my view, is an alternative: either charisma from the top or charisma from the bottom. Both must act (as they have in the past) outside the legal system. The charisma from the bottom has been called revolution. Modern revolutions—that is, guerrilla warfare—do not fit the Latin American modality. They require organizational discipline and Latin Americans know none. They require economic resources which the masses do not possess; international support has been a modern myth when compared with the support the military can attract. Witness the recent history of United States military foreign aid to Latin America. Moreover, Latin Americans have little respect for human life. Poorly planned and poorly financed revolutions are bound to end in mass murders of the poor.

The sole alternative, in my view, is therefore charisma from the top. Not the "national" leader that the military, with blessings from abroad, would promptly eliminate, or that would become the dictator Latin America experiences with un-Latin regularity.

But the local leader—a mixture of religious and political messiah —that Latin America has produced and will continue to produce. Hundreds of these leaders pack the Latin American scene today. Students and clergymen have in recent times been instrumental in helping these charismatic leaders to emerge. They respond to local needs with local strategies that governments and parties cannot at all ignore. And they are contributing, albeit unwittingly, to a meaningful Latin American integration that can only rest on solid ground when it is built on a local base. The other (ALALC, Latin American Free Trade Association) is the dream of Pan-American bureaucrats, and far removed from the soil soaked in blood and tears and sweat on which most Latin Americans die.

References and Selected Bibliography

1. Agudelo Villa, Hernando. *La revolución del desarrollo*. Mexico: Editorial Roble, 1966.
2a. Ahumada, Jorge. *La crisis integral de Chile*. Santiago: Editorial Universitaria, 1966.
2b. Alba, Victor. *Nationalists without Nations*. New York: Praeger, 1968.
3. Alexander, Robert J. *The Bolivian National Revolution*. New Brunswick, N.J.: Rutgers University Press, 1958.
4. Alexander, Robert J. *Communism and Latin America*. New Brunswick, N.J.: Rutgers University Press, 1957.
5. Alexander, Robert J. *Prophets of the Revolution*. New York: Macmillan, 1962.
6. Alexander, Robert J. *Today's Latin America*. New York: Doubleday, 1962.
7. Alvárez Andrew, Oscar. *Historia del desarrollo industrial de Chile*. Santiago: Editorial La Illustracion, 1936.
8. Andrzejewske, Stanley. *Military Organization and Society*. London: Routledge and Kegan Paul Ltd., 1954.
9. Arevolo, Juan José (President Guatemala 1904). *Anti-Communism in Latin America, an x-ray of the process leading to new colonialism*. Translated from the Spanish by Carleton Beals. New York: Lyle Stuart, 1963.
10. Arevalo, Juan José. *The Shark and the Sardines*. Translated from Spanish by June Cobb and Raul Osegueda. New York: Lyle Stuart, 1961. An Anti-U.S. polemic by the former Guatemalan president and leader of his nation's "social revolution."
11. Argulla, Juan Carlos. "Poder, comunidad y desarrollo." *Aportes*, October 1966, pp. 80–105.

12. Bailey, Norman A. (ed.). *Latin America, politics, economics and hemispheric security.* New York: Praeger, 1965.
13. Barber, Willard F., & C. Neale Ronning. *Internal Security and Military Power: Counter-insurgency & Civic Action in Latin America.* Columbus: Ohio State University Press, 1966.
14. Beals, Carleton. *Latin America: World in Revolution.* New York: Abelard-Schuman, 1963.
15. Benedetti, Adolfo A. *Arnulfo Arias, el caudillo.* Panama: Editorial Humanidad, 1963.
16. Blasco Ibáñez, Vicente. *El militarismo mejicano; estudios publicados en los principales diarios de los Estados Unidos.* Valencia: Prometeo, Sociedad Editorial, c. 1920.
17. Bourricaud, Francois. *Pouvoir et Societe dans le Perou Contemporain.* Paris: Librairie Armand Colin, 1967.
18. Bourricaud, Francois. "La formación de los elites en América Latina y los problemas del desarrollo." *Aportes,* Julio, 1966, pp. 122–151.
19. Castro, Fidel. *Cuba Confronts the Future: Five Years of the Revolution.* Toronto: Fair Play for Cuba Committee, 1964. Speech of January 2, 1964.
20. Castro, Fidel. *Fidel Castro Speaks on Marxism Leninism.* Toronto: Fair Play for Cuba Committee, 1962.
21. Castro, Fidel. *La Revolucion Triunfara en America* (II Declaracion de la Habana). 1963.
22. Chonchol, Jacques. "Razones económicas, sociales y políticas de la reforma agraria." in O. Delgado (ed.), *Reformas Agrarias en la América Latina.* Mexico and Buenos Aires: Fondo de Cultura Económica, 1965, pp. 100–126.
23. Correa, Oscar Domínguez. *Una Oportunidad en la Libertad.* Santiago: Editorial del Pacifico, 1961.
24. Costa Pinto, L. A. *La Sociedad del Cambio y el Cambio de la Sociedad.* Buenos Aires: Eudeba, 1963.
25a. Delgado, Oscar. "Revolution, Reform, Conservatism." *Dissent.* Vol. IX, No. 4, April 1962, pp. 351 and 359.
25b. Delgado, Oscar (ed.). *Reformas Agrarias en la América Latina.* Mexico and Buenos Aires: Fondo de Cultura Económica, 1965.
26. De Vries, Egbert, and Jose Medina Echavarría (eds.). *Social Aspects of Economic Development in Latin America.* UNESCO, Place de Fonteroy, Paris, 1963.
27. Di Tella, Torcuato S. et al. (eds.). *Argentina, Sociedad de Masas.* Buenos Aires: Editorial Universitaria, 1965.
28. Draper, Theodore. *Castro's Revolution: Myth and Reality.* New York: Fredrick A. Praeger, 1962.
29. Duverger, Maurice. *Political Parties,* translated by Barbara and Robert North. New York: Wiley, 1954.
30. Edwards Vives, Alberto. *La fronda aristocrática.* Santiago: Editorial del Pacifico, 1959.
31. *El Mercurio,* editorial, Santiago. Thursday, December 7, 1967.
32. Encina Armanet, Francisco Antonio. *Bolívar y la Independencia de la América Española.* Santiago: Editorial Nacimiento, 1951.

33. Encina Armanet, Francisco Antonio. *Las Relaciones entre Chile y Bolivia*. Santiago: Editorial Nacimiento, 1963.
34. Encina Armanet, Francisco Antonio. *Nuestra Inferioridad Económica, sus causas y consecuencias*. Santiago: Editorial Universitaria, 1912.
35. Febvre, Jean Louis. *Les tropiques des colonels*. Paris: Plon, 1961.
36. Fergusm, J. Halcro. *The Revolutions of Latin America*. London: Thames & Hudson, 1963.
37. Fluharty, Vernon Lee. *Dance of the Millions: Military Rule and the Social Revolution in Colombia, 1930–1956*. Pittsburgh: University of Pittsburgh Press, 1957.
38. Frei Montalva, Eduardo. *Sentido y forma de una politica*. Santiago: Editorial del Pacifico, 1951.
39. Galula, David. *Counterinsurgency Warfare: Theory and Practise*. New York and London: Frederick A. Praeger, 1964.
40. García Lupo, Rogelio. "El Ejército Argentino: mosaico dominado por la caballeria." *Política* (Caracas, Venezuela), May, 1967, No. 61, pp. 61–71.
41. Gerassi, John. *The Great Fear: The Reconquest of Latin America by Latin Americans*. New York: Macmillan, 1963.
42. Germani, Gino. *Política y Sociedad en una época de transición: de la sociedad tradicional a la sociedad de masas*. Buenos Aires: Editorial Paidos, 1962.
43. Gil, Federico G. *Instituciones y Desarrollo Político de América Latina*. Buenos Aires: INTAL (Instituto para la Integración de América Latina) BID, 1966.
44. Gil, Federico G. *The Political System of Chile*. Boston: Houghton Mifflin, 1966.
45. Gilmore, Robert L. *Caudillism and Militarism in Venezuela, 1810–1910*. Athens: Ohio University Press, 1964.
46a. Gonzalez Casanova, Pablo. *La democracia en Mexico*. Mexico: Ediciones Era, S.A., 1965.
46b. González Casanova, Pablo. "Internal Colonialism and National Development." *Studies in Comparative International Development*. Vol. I, No. 4, 1965, pp. 27–37.
47. Gozard, Gilles, *Demain, l'Amerique Latine*, Paris: Presses Universitaires de France, 1964.
48. Gutteridge, William. *Military Institutions and Power in the New States*. New York: Frederick A. Praeger, 1965.
49. Guzmán, German, et al. *La Violencia en Colombia*. Bogotá: Universidad, Nacional, 1962.
50. Halmos, Paul (ed.). *Latin American Sociological Studies* (The Sociological Review Memo, No. 11, Feb. 1967). Keele, Staffordshire: The University of Keele, 1967.
51. Heintz, Peter. *Sociología del Poder*. Santiago: Editorial Andres Bello, 1960.
52. Hirschman, Albert O. *The Strategy of Economic Development*. New Haven, Conn.: Yale University Press, 1960.
53. Hirschman, Albert O. *Journeys toward Progress: Studies of Economic Policy-Making in Latin America*. New York: Twentieth Century Fund, 1963.

54. Holt, Robert T. & John E. Turner. *The Political Basis of Economic Development.* Princeton, N.J.: Van Nostrand, 1965.
55. Horowitz, Irving L. *Revolution in Brazil, Politics and Society in a Developing Nation,* New York: E. P. Dutton, 1964.
56. Horowitz, Irving L. "The Military Elites" in S. M. Lipset & Aldo Solari (eds.) *Elites in Latin America.* New York: Oxford University Press, 1967, pp. 146–189.
57. Horowitz, Irving Louis. *Three Worlds of Development.* New York: Oxford University Press, 1966.
58. Hoselitz, Bert F. *Sociological Aspects of Economic Growth.* Glencoe, Ill.: Free Press, 1960.
59. Imaz, José Luis de. *Los que Mandan.* Buenos Aires: Editorial Universitaria de Buenos Aires, 1964.
60. Iscaro, Rubens. *América Latina en Marcha.* Buenos Aires: Grupo Editorial de Buenos Aires, 1967.
61. 'aguaribe, Helio. "La dinámica del nacionalismo brasileño." *Revista Latinoamericana de Sociología,* Vol. I, No. 3, 1965, p. 363.
62. Janowitz, Morris. *The Military in the Political Development of New Nations.* Chicago: University of Chicago Press, 1964.
63. Johnson, J. J. (ed.). *Continuity and Change in Latin America.* Stanford: Stanford University Press, 1964.
64. Johnson, J. J. *The Military and Society in Latin America.* Stanford: Stanford University Press, 1964.
65. Jobet, Julio César. *Ensayo Crítico del Desarrollo Económica-Social de Chile.* Santiago: Editorial Universitaria, 1955.
66. Lagos Escobar, Ricardo. *La Concentración del Poder Económico. Su teoría. Realidad Chilena.* Santiago: Editorial del Pacífico, 1961.
67. Lambert, Jacques. *América Latina: Estructuras sociales e instituciones políticas.* Barcelona: Ediciones Ariel, 1964.
68. Lhomme, Jean. *Pouvoir et Société Economique.* Paris: Editions Cujas, 1966.
69. Lieuwen, Edwin. *Arms and Politics in Latin America.* New York: Council on Foreign Relations and Frederick A. Praeger, 2nd Edition, 1962.
70. Lieuwen, Edwin. *Generals vs. Presidents: Neo-militarism in Latin America.* New York: Frederick A. Praeger, 1964.
71. Lipset, Seymour M., et al. *Elites in Latin America.* New York: Oxford University Press, 1967.
72. Maier, J., & R. W. Weatherhead (eds.). *Politics of Change in Latin America.* New York: Frederick A. Praeger, 1964.
73. Martz, John D. *Central America, The Crisis and the Challenge.* Chapel Hill: The University of North Carolina Press, 1959.
74. Martz, John D. *Colombia.* Chapel Hill: University of North Carolina Press, 1961.
75. Martz, John D. (ed.). *The Dynamics of Change in Latin American Politics.* Englewood Cliffs, N.J.: Prentice Hall, 1965.
76. McAlister, Lyle. *The Fuero Militar in New Spain.* Gainesville: University of Florida Press, 1957.
77. Mecham, J. Lloyd. "The Jefe Político in Mexico." *Southwestern Sociological Scientific Quarterly,* Vol. 13, March, 1933, p. 333–352.

78. Millikan, Max F., & D. L. M. Blackmer (eds.). *The Emerging Nations.* Boston: Little, Brown, 1961.
79. Moheno, Roberto Blanco. *Júarez ante Dios y ante los Hombres.* Mexico: Libro Mex, 1959.
80. Nun, José. "A Latin American Phenomenon: The Middle Class Military Coup." *Trends in Social Science Research in Latin American Studies: a Conference report.* Berkeley: University of California, 1965, p. 55.
81. Orsolini, Mario Horacio. *La Crisis del Ejército.* Buenos Aires: Ediciones Arayu, 1964.
82. Perlo, Victor. *Militarism and Industry Arms Profiteering in the Missile Age.* New York: International Publishers, 1963.
83. Petras, James. *Chilean Christian Democracy: Politics and Social Forces.* Berkeley: University of California, 1967.
84. Pinto Santa Cruz, Anibal. *Ni establidad ni desarrollo.* Santiago: Editorial Universitaria, 1959.
85. Pinto Santa Cruz, Anibal. *Chile. Un caso de Desarrollo Frustrado.* Santiago: Editorial Universitaria, 1959.
86. Poppino, Rollie E. *International Communism in Latin America; a history of the movement, 1917–1963.* Glencoe, Ill.: The Free Press, 1964.
87. Pye, Lucien. *Armies in the Process of Political Modernization.* Cambridge: M.I.T. Press, 1959.
88. Rostow, W. W. *The Process of Economic Growth.* New York: Norton, 1952.
89. Schmitt, Karl Michael. *Communism in Mexico: a study in political frustration.* Austin: University of Texas Press, 1965.
90. Schmitt, Karl Michael, & David Burks. *Evolution or Chaos, Dynamics of Latin American Government and Politics.* New York: Frederick A. Praeger, 1963.
91. Schneider, Ronald M. *Communism in Guatemala, 1944–1954.* New York: Frederick A. Praeger, 1958.
92. Silvert, Kalman H. *The Conflict Society: Reaction and Revolution in Latin America.* New Orleans: Hauser Press, 1961.
93. Silvert, Kalman H. *Expectant Peoples: Nationalism & Development.* New York: Random House, 1963.
94. Silvert, Kalman H. *Reaction and Revolution in Latin America; the conflict society.* New Orleans: Hauser Press, 1961.
95. Toledano, Vicente Lombardo. *La Perspectiva de Mexico Una Democracia del Pueblo.* Mexico: Ediciones del Partido Popular, 1956.
96. Tomasek, Robert D. *Latin American Politics.* Garden City, New York: Doubleday & Co., 1966.
97. U.S. 86th Congress, 2nd Session, Senate Document No. 125, *United States–Latin America Relations.* Washington, D.C.: Government Printing Office, 1960.
98. Vega, Luis Mercier. Trans. by Roberto Bixio. *Mecanismos del Poder en América Latina.* Buenos Aires: SUR, 1967.
99. Veliz, Claudio (ed.). *The Politics of Conformity in Latin America.* London: Oxford University Press, 1967.

100. Whitaker, Arthur P. & David C. Jordan. *Nationalism in Contemporary Latin America.* Glencoe, Ill.: Free Press, 1966.
101. Wolf, Charles. *United States Policy and the Third World.* Boston: Little, Brown & Co., 1967.
102. Wolf, Eric R. "La formación de la nación: un ensayo de formulación." *Ciencias Sociales.* 1953, *4*:50–62, 98–111, 146–71.

7

How Not To Tie
The Bundle: Anti-Utopia

The kaleidoscopic complexities of Latin American societies must by now appear dazzling to the reader. Everything in Latin America is moving, and moving at incredible velocities, although not in the same direction. For Latin Americans care more for freedom than for order. Having lived for far too long in an unstable universe, they have grown tired, at last, of an immobile social structure and have finally lost their innocence. They have sinned. They have come to realize, after four hundred years of Catholicism, that poverty is not a shortcut to heaven unless one voluntarily renounces richness. And who does that? Jesus Christ had nothing to renounce, and he only lived thirty-three years. This is the mood of most of Latin America today. The 15 percent at or close to the top continue to think that stability means order and that order is the hat from which a messianic magician, yet to appear, will pull out rabbits of liberty, together with the "carrots" of material prosperity.

Against all expectations, the United States has contributed greatly to this mood. Firstly, because only foreign aid pennies filter down to the bottom of society; larger coins are trapped at higher levels. Secondly, because, in various ways, the United States has been able to project an image of prosperity and well-being that fascinates the imagination of the hungry. Myth-loving Latin Americans share the utopia but do not agree about how best to get there. In fact, they do not even want to make the journey. Raised in a culture of miracles, they want miracles. Moreover, to weigh they do not use scales, but balances that can be tilted a little. Even the balance of Fortune can be tilted.

A Latin American Political Pluralism

Against this background Latin American political pluralism can be understood more easily. Political parties are there to tilt the balance of distributive justice. A gradual, scaled change is obviously inconceivable. It can only be "balanced." Retaining an ideal justice is recognized as practically impossible, and a minimum of injustice retained is recognized as a more nearly attainable goal. Here lies the functional significance of multiple parties. To impose upon Latin Americans a simple, dual political system or a government form of checks and balances, is simply contrary to the complexity of its societies. In all its complexity, the North American sociological scene is anchored on three or four gigantic bureaucracies: the governmental, the military, the industrial, and the labor bureaucracies. The United States is an employee (84 percent of the labor force) society. The Latin American nations are characteristically societies in which the self-employed and the unemployed predominate, and in which the most powerful bureaucracies are the governments and the armed forces, whose relations are often in collision rather than collusion.

If one were to rank Latin American governments in a "most-least" democratic scale, the countries located at the "most" end of the scale would be characterized by political pluralism. Chile and Uruguay are typical examples. At the opposite end of the scale, obviously, one finds dictatorships. In every instance, if political parties are still in operation, the tendency has been for them to be coterminous with pressure groups. In this regard the profile of the party, and therefore the perspective one must take to understand it, has to be vertical once more. Only in recent times, the reader must remember, have the two, party and pressure group, moved toward increasing differentiation. The reader must also remember that private industry is weak throughout Latin America and that governments frequently control, and can intervene in, certain types of large extracting industries such as oil, copper, and tin, and that they own, almost always outrightly, such services as telephones and telegraphs, railroads, and television networks, thus making the largest industrial bureaucracies the outstretched arms of governments. Under these conditions, as countries move from dictatorship to democracy, the pressure groups project themselves on the pluralistic party system. In a real sense, it must be remembered, the political struggle is a socioeconomic struggle for upward social mobility. Soon the artificial stability imposed by the dictator will dissolve in a joust of political and personality rivalries which eventually will bring about a new dictator. And the cycle will continue to spiral, to open, to infinity.

What is the answer? Mexico has offered one: a periodical referendum called presidential elections. The Mexican one-party system is a conglomeration of pressure groups struggling to be heard in the councils that make the politicoeconomic decisions for the nation. A man is chosen by these councils to execute their decisions. The country is then asked to respond in voting to the degree of charisma that the chosen one has displayed in the campaign. If, in his presidential role, he failed to measure up to the size of his mandate, strikes would erupt and marches on Mexico City would begin; a mobilization of unhappy pressure groups. Soon the pressure of the council would be felt, public opinion would be mobilized, and whatever wounds come open would be taped.

Workable as the Mexican experiment seems to be, it will not work in the rest of Latin America; in fact, it has not worked in Mexico. Here, in my view, are the reasons, in inverse order of their sociological significance.

The Mexican one-party system has been a product of the most generalized and bloody revolution that has ever occurred in this continent. Every institution was touched by it and the memories of the blood bath remain vividly alive. A product of the Revolution has been a striking identification of a people with their land and their rich, proud past. No other revolution in the hemisphere has reached this cultural depth. The Bolivian Revolution has failed and the Cuban Revolution has not yet matured. The latter might even prove to be more fundamental than the Mexican one. It seems to be so already. To succeed, a revolution of this type must have deep roots in the traditions of the culture and be placed in jeopardy by foreign powers. To this day, no other Latin American social movement has ever fulfilled these two conditions, and there are no indications that any will, in the foreseeable future. The so-called 1964 "revolution" of the Brazilian military was just a regular Latin American coup d'état, and the party subsequently organized to imitate Mexico and Cuba has not reached the masses at all, and never will. The pluralism of the Brazilian political scene, although repressed, has survived.

The Mexican Revolution has successfully weakened the military. This is the second reason. To succeed, the Brazilian "revolution" should have not only organized "the party of the revolution," but de-escalated the power of the military. Peron did just that. In turn, he failed to transfer his power to pressure group councils *a la Mexicana*. In the end, the military once more won out. Besides Mexico, every government in Latin America, including perhaps even Costa Rica, rules under the aegis of the military. Chile and Uruguay are no exceptions.

In Mexico, in the third place, the ecclesiastical bureaucracies have been kept under control, languishing in rituals almost totally empty of Catholic theology, and the labor bureaucracies have not only been creatures of the party, but have been given a strong voice in the decision-making councils. This may become more apparent when viewed in the light of the last reason to be offered presently.

In Mexico, two gigantic institutional structures have skillfully developed interlocking systems strong enough to prevent the development of any others but sufficiently sensitive to the internal struggles of the internal pressure groups. The balance has been maintained by a very idiosyncratic characteristic of the Mexican economy not found in any other Latin American economy, namely, the tourist trade. Tourism, in Mexico, is not a state enterprise. Every Mexican firm and organization has a free (and often dirty) hand in it. It would inflict a hard blow on the Mexican economy if shackles were clamped on the free (and often dirty) tourist trade. It is in the tourist trade that the checks and balances have been built for the Mexican sociopolitical case. Political pluralism, in short, has yielded way to pressure group pluralism under the blessings of the almighty and omnipresent dollar.

What about those other societies of Latin America? They fall somewhere in between. Between Mexico and Cuba on the one hand, Chile and Uruguay on the other.

A New Religious Synthesis in Diversity

The religious phenomenon is complex in itself and has added complexity to kaleidoscopic Latin America. It is simply not accurate to speak of a monolithic Church in Latin America. Every bishop is a monarch in his own diocese, one step removed from the top and one step removed from the bottom of the very simple Catholic hierarchy of priest, bishop, and pope. It is not accurate either to talk about a tightly-knit, horizontal ecclesiastical organization for Latin America. Neither is it accurate to talk about a uniform ideology cementing the fundamental dogmas of the Church with practical socio-politico-economic matters. The official pronouncements, no matter what the source, are always broad enough and flexible enough to generate diversity without endangering theological unity. The Reformation made the Church quite pragmatic, highly resilient to the incursions of the sciences of man and the men of science, and politically alert to a world where every thing, person, group, institution, and value is changing. The updating (*aggiornamento*) is penetrating the Church from Mexico and Panama to Central America, from Colombia and Chile to Ecuador, Peru, and Bolivia. The theme for Latin America is the awakening of the community in keeping with the social personality of the Latin American anchored in the kin group and the locality.

From decade to decade and century to century, the Church has placed a high value on parish life, symbolized by the patron saint and given local flavor by folkloric rituals and myths. Only the leadership has not been local. The parish priest has always been brought from the outside, although he has been trained to strengthen parish life. The outlook was, in any event, otherworldly. The Protestant missionary brought a more temporal, this-worldly type of salvation, but one which was still oriented toward the community. Finally, the Communist missionary arrived, not only preaching a here-and-now sort of salvation but stubbornly rejecting any other one that could not be seen and touched and smelled by everybody in the community. Protestants and Communists created local leadership. The meeting of these forces was explosive at first, accommodative later, and cooperative now. Ideologies remain clearly distinct but strategies are shared. During the struggle, governments became partners at times of one or the other of the contending forces and mediators of late. At least blood is no longer shed on this account.

The synthesis has been made in a new (for Latin America) meaning of man. Man does not mean humanity, as it used to. Man means, or begins to mean, you and me and the fellow next door and around the street corner; up the stream and down the stream; up the hill and down the valley. Man has become real at last.

This man, however, is not an individual *a la norteamericana*. He is and will continue to be what he has always been, an extension of the kin group and the community. Religion, therefore, is not a personal matter. To make it so, the Latin American has to migrate still. In other words, the conversion of a man often implies a shift of the whole kin group in the same direction. Otherwise, a lone convert would find himself uprooted.

If the new religious synthesis is being made around the existential man, member of a kin group and a community, the diversity that begins to emerge in Latin America staggers the imagination. Within the Catholic Church, power is gradually shifting from bishop to priest and from priest to faithful, under the impact of Protestantism and Communism and along with the concomitant upsurge of the community. The trend is toward decentralization. By the same token, the accent has been removed from faith and placed on action, action turned toward man and his surroundings. Thus, in the ideological arena, Catholicism, Protestantism, and Communism—three very different horses—are pulling the same cart in the very same direction, but in such varying circumstances that whatever outward unity they may show is continuingly threatened by an incurable Latin American localism.

From this perspective, an intelligent foreign aid program would not try to extend assistance to any one given denomination under any circumstances. It would attempt to help the individual local leader engaged in immediate local action. The standards of choice for aid would not be determined, therefore, by ideological considerations, but by the concern of the community already expressed, not in paper, only in action. This, of course, has been done occasionally here and there, as any reader of Congressional records may attest. But it has not been done either systematically or consistently.

The Professional Visionaries and the Realists

There is no tradition of scientific inquiry in Latin America. There is a tradition of prophets. They arise in the churches, in the labor unions, in the halls of congress, in the military barracks, in the *favelas* and *barriadas*. And they arise in the universities, where one would think they could not arise.

The Latin American is a dreamer. His is a world inhabited by spirits, ghosts, *duendes,* souls returned from Purgatory, tribal ancestors either asking for prayers or retracing ancient familiar routes. His is a world glowing with visions, with apparitions of the Blessed Virgin, and of Satan. His is a world penetrated with *mana,* a supernatural power that some have and some do not. The prophets walk through this world announcing the advent of a new era. A time when man will not have to labor. When he will leisurely stretch his hand toward the fruit hanging from the bending branch. The traditional prophets have *mana.* The new prophet, to be accepted, must show his extraordinary power too. He is the veterinarian, the agronomist, the nurse, the social worker, the social planner. The realists! They obtained their *mana* in the halls of knowledge that their predecessors never, or hardly ever, visited. In the eyes of the multitudes, the experts must also be magicians. Not being so, and having to proceed with limited knowledge and extremely limited resources, they are condemned to failure. Thus, government cabinets are frequently reshuffled; governors are removed; city mayors replaced; police sergeants transferred; experiment-station personnel shifted; and schoolteachers rotated. Only the bureaucracies remain firm, tied to their desks, entrenched in their traditions, harnessed to their unions. The people do not expect miracles from the bureaucrats. These are the real realists! The experts are not. They cannot possibly be.

The irony of it all is that the phalanx of professional visionaries has been swelled by the advent of the experts. It could not be otherwise. The experts are invited to improvise, with limited knowledge and extremely limited resources, quick solutions to pressing emergency situations, for Latin America seems to move in an uninterrupted state of emergency. The result of this approach is a multiplicity of projects halfway finished. The landscape of the continent is marked with buildings halfway built, streets and highways under permanent construction, bridges brought but never mounted, truncated monuments still waiting for the statue, railroad lines that do not quite reach the station. The irony of it all is that the continent is nevertheless progressing by leaps, in various fronts but in approximately the same direction, thanks to the visionaries and in spite of the realists.

The amazing thing is that there is much less waste in Latin America than in the United States, partly because Latin Americans use whatever they halfway construct. They may even use it for purposes not originally intended. It is not unusual to find in Latin America unfinished bridges used as shelters by the poor, incomplete chapels used as elementary schools, temporary railroad stations which have become distant barrios of a nearby city, unopened highways that are traversed by jeeps, at least during the dry season, bankrupt factories taken over for dwellings by compound family units, and even truncated monuments used by peddlers to expose their wares in fiesta, fair, and market days. North Americans, good realists that they are, find this quite illogical. And of course they are right. Latin Americans have never claimed to be logical. They claim to be creative. The famous names in Latin America belong to the writers of poetry and fiction: Rubén Darío, Amado Nervo, Rafael Pombo, Rivera, Montalvo,

Chocano, Rodó, Mistral, Borges, Neruda, Fuentes, Márquez, and to frustrated redeemers: Bolívar, Juárez, Balmaceda, and Getulio Vargas. All visionaries. The sun of the realists has not risen. To this day, the Latin American culture offers no room to the routinization of charisma.

Against this backdrop, and in the light of previous discussions, it appears that a realistic foreign policy would shy away from offering solutions to the uninterrupted state of emergency in which Latin America seems to move, and would allow Latin American visionaries and realists to work their way out of their problems, free from foreign advice. Few foreign experts have been successful in advising Latin Americans, and, without doubt, Latin Americans have been too hasty in seeking foreign advice. It would not be too difficult to make a long list of experts whose services have been sought by Latin American governments alone in the last 25 years.[10b] The results are visible, although no one can tell how things would have been otherwise.

The Fruits of Miscegenation

The great accomplishment of Latin America has been the mixture of races, unparalleled in history and unencumbered by religious taboos that make sex relations out of wedlock sinful. No law in Latin America forbids racially mixed marriages, and public opinion, although not entirely favorable to these marriages, has created appealing images of the striking products that often come out of heteroracial sex relations. Whatever bias may be found against such relations is based more on class differences than on race differences.

As may be surmised, the Latin American sex folklore has it that cross-fertilization, good across racial fences, is better across class barriers; thus, low-income women and upper-class men are believed to produce the best human types when the crossing is doubled by race. One might think of this as a most novel (and noble!) extension of the traditional incest taboo.

The fact is that Latin America has contributed to an already colorful human species with astonishing new shades in a broad spectrum tinted black-violet on the one side and red-white on the other. The Spaniards institutionalized around 17 types in between for most of Spanish America, as did the Portuguese for Brazil. Colonial scribes were very meticulous about them. Today most Latin American men (if not women) have become color-blind, especially for such practical purposes as the betterment of *la raza.*

No matter how permissive the mores concerning miscegenation might be in Latin America, it is still true that the upper classes remain white everywhere with the possible exception of Mexico, and even here the old aristocracy is much lighter than the new one that emerged, for the most part, with the Revolution. It is also true that only Mexico and Paraguay are proud of their Indian heritage and Brazil of its African races and subcultures. The other countries of the continent would bleach themselves snow-white if they could, no matter how much they speak out against United States racism. On the other hand, the feelings of racial purity characteristic of Uruguay, Argentina, and perhaps most of Chile, are well-known throughout the hemisphere. Within each country, color remains a clearly differentiating social category, and whatever pride may be expressed when referring to the human types produced in the historic process of racial mixture, families would not only avoid it when possible but would be hard put to recognize it in their genealogical trees under inquiry. Questions related to the subject remain embarrassing. Recognition of Negro or Indian heredity in one's ancestry might be useful under certain conditions to achieve political (but seldom social) success.* In the Latin American prestige race, the dark color of a man's skin is still a barrier.

Neither theological nor social attitudes have stopped the miscegenation process, and they certainly never will. There are some very strong cultural values and expectations, as well as group pressures, that stimulate the sex urges, which know no racial boundaries even when the races appear well defined. Some of these

---

* Jorge Eliécer Gaitán, for example, the great popular Colombian leader and presidential candidate whose assassination, on April 9, 1948, exploded an abortive but costly revolution known as *bogotazo,* was a very dark *mestizo.* He made excellent use of this color characteristic in his short but fantastic political career.

values, expectations, and pressures have been discussed in previous chapters, such as frequent sex experiences made the best expression of masculinity, the emphasis on fertility for both sexes, and the group ridicule against those members who do not communicate with friends their experiences and give no signs of heterosexual aggression. For this the opportunities abound. It is not only the large numbers of prostitutes available everywhere, but the accessibility of maids, servants, and employees. The statistics on illegitimacy are just weak indicators.

What is salient for the present purposes, however, and what must be reiterated, is that the racial color spectrum is extremely rich in Latin America and that many striking types of magnificent physiques can be found, without much search, everywhere. It is very unfortunate that no investigator has made them known skilfully and systematically.

Latin America and North America: Two Ways of Becoming

North Americans emphasize action for achievement; Latin Americans emphasize action for living. North Americans emphasize doing, producing, filling time and space, moving. Latin Americans emphasize being, creating, feeling time and space, expecting. North Americans emphasize going, Latin Americans emphasize returning. North Americans work for a purpose, Latin Americans simply work because they have to. North Americans emphasize learning as a means to an end; Latin Americans emphasize learning as means and end. North Americans understand love as an art; one must work at it. Latin Americans understand love as an experience; one must repeat it. North Americans take faith as an escape; Latin Americans take faith as a question mark. North Americans have brought the future into the present. Latin Americans have made the future await the present. North Americans want to make history; Latin Americans want to change history. North Americans think order should be kept; Latin Americans think order ought to be made. North Americans see law as a condition for order.

Latin Americans, on the contrary, place order as a condition for law. For North Americans, justice should be made when broken; for Latin Americans, justice has to be created; it has not been broken because it has never been. Authority in North America is a social expression; in Latin America it is an individual expression, which means, to be delegated in the first case, to be taken in the second case. That is, North Americans tend to differentiate power from authority; Latin Americans tend to confuse them. In fact, North Americans fear power and respect authority whereas Latin Americans seek power and resent authority. North Americans see things in black or white, good or evil, whereas Latin Americans see them in changing colors, mixed, both good and evil. The North American works on destiny; the Latin American has a partnership with destiny. The former thinks he is in debt to his country; the Latin American thinks his country is in debt to him. The North American believes freedom to be indivisible; the Latin American believes freedom to be a matter of more or less. The North American sees himself as an introjection of others; the Latin American sees others as extrojections of himself. The North American fears death and tries to flee from it; the Latin American sees death as the ultimate embrace. What a contrast! Obviously the ethos of the two cultures are poles apart. Polarity, however, does not mean opposition.

No one in his right mind would try to interchange them, to convert them into each other, since they complement one another so well. Yet many North Americans have been trying to produce such a transubstantiation for many years. It is precisely here where foreign policy has often failed, when the diplomat becomes a missionary.

When societies are changing rapidly, it is easy to see they have a future and a present but not a past, because having many alternatives to follow it is extremely difficult to see the continuity between past, present, and future. This fact, so confusing to contemporary North Americans, is even more confusing to Latin Americans, because, among other reasons, observing the world around them they would prefer to change the course of history. They do not see today's world as simply divided between East and West and Third World in which latter they have been pigeonholed. In other words, while many North Americans see the world as triple, Latin Americans think of it as a very complex multiplicity. Having many models, the Latin Americans are not interested in imitating anyone alone. They seem to be interested in locating what is good for them no matter where they find it, east or west, north or south, zenith or nadir. They are coming to realize that what is good for them cannot be found anywhere else but within themselves, in the wombs of their own societies and cultures. This is precisely what the United States has done when faced with failures in Viet Nam and in the ghettos: dig deep in the ethos of the culture, not as it was, but as it is. This is what Latin America has begun to realize and what concerned North Americans must help to accomplish.

Nominalism and realism aside, the fact is that the phrase "Latin America" does correspond to a sociocultural reality in spite of its intricate complexity. True by itself, this is also true by contrast. With every new day the Castilian language becomes more Latin American than say Mexican, Colombian, Peruvian, or Argentinian. Common economic problems are bringing about shared solutions; the Latin American Common Market is just one of the expressions. Although religious tolerance has increased among governments and peoples, Catholicism remains, and will most probably continue to remain, the major religious force in Latin America. It is too deeply entangled with other traditions of the culture. Moreover, there is a Latin American way to be Catholic (or Protestant). Political alliances are also contributing to the shaping of a Latin American identity in a way which is quite clearly Latin American.

In recent years, Latin America has found common enemies that serve to strengthen the previously dormant bonds of solidarity. For dissimilar reasons, Latin America has had to face the threat and challenge of Cuba and the relative indifference of the United States and Europe. In response to Cuba, the laboring classes have become objects of courtship for practically all political parties and all governments. The courtship has not brought together governments and labor but has cemented a horizontal solidarity of labor with labor and government with government across the continent, the first to exert pressure for reform, and the second to protect international borders from revolutionary infiltrators. At the same time, unable to obtain any meaningful aid from the United States, which is tied to a war that its people despise, the Latin American governments have been forced to turn to each other for closer cooperation and to Europe and the Communist Bloc for loans and trade. In freeing themselves at least a little from a United States that can only help with conditional loans, the Latin Americans have undertaken broader trade and have broken with ideology. In doing so they have produced a double effect: they have thrown cold water on the anticommunist crusade of the United States policy-makers, and they have simultaneously demoralized the subversive groups that claim linkage with the Communist Bloc.

Moreover, in tune with the ethos of her culture, Latin America is moving away from capitalism, Socialism, and Communism in the direction of a new social world. The inspiration has come from philosophies and ideologies which are marginal to Catholicism but which the Church will eventually place in the center of the doctrinal stage. Young forces are engaged in creating what they call a new society, the communitarian society, in which, they claim, man will arise, like the Phoenix, from its ashes, and "the system" will be buried in its place.

Boiling Societies: Multiple Identities

When reading or following the history of Latin America, one can easily come to the conclusion that its very essence is a relentless restlessness. It is not only the internal migrations, rural-urban, from area to area, from city to city, from *barrio* to *barrio,* the settlement and resettlement of agricultural land, the abandonment and penetration of forest, or the laboring in farm after farm for better pay. It is not only the crossing of international lines heading north by stages in the whole continent. Or, more specifically, north to the United States from Mexico, northwest to Mexico from Central America, and mainly northeast to Brazil in South America. It is also the everlasting stream of processions, marches, demonstrations, rallies, pilgrimages, fairs, carnivals, weddings, baptisms and funerals, political parties and union meetings, church revivals at all class levels, community and neighborhood dances, mass attendance to sports and races, etc. The Latin American never stays at rest. The Mexicanized image of a man sleeping under his hat, the cactus, and the sky, is a wishful fiction. The Latin American identifies freedom with motion and motion with power. The most powerful is the most free to move.

Sobre los llanos la palma	Over the plains the palm tree
Sobre la palma los cielos	Over the palm tree the skies
Sobre mi caballo yo	Over my horse myself
Y sobre yo mi sombrero.	And over me my hat.

Add to this the intermittent search for a better life, the seeking of class ascent, the social anxiety to hear and see. Moreover, every group of Latin Americans is a cast in which the same actor may play different roles, with all the actors often speaking at the same time. What a stage! With the peculiarity that when a man speaks, he is really making a speech. Making it he moves his head, forehead, and eyebrows, positions his eyelids and lips, balances his shoulders, stands up, walks up and down, leans back and forth, and designs with his arms, hands, and fingers. He is in motion. Latin America is in perpetual motion, in a relentless restlessness. Why?

How can anybody tell? Some have said it is a result of the inferiority complex of the *mestizo*. Others find the cause in the Latin imagination. Some in the uncertainties of the physical environment. Others in the closed quality of the social structure. I subscribe to an integral, eclectic explanation, with emphasis on the multiple identities of Latin American man and Latin American societies.

In infancy, the Latin American is passed from bosom to bosom and from hand to hand within his usually large kin group. He is learning, one may say, the various patterns of warmth and grip. During childhood he learns to identify with many significant others, the knots of his kin group network. He learns that they are extensions of his parents whom he has learned to love, please, respect, and obey. Most probably his locality is dotted with them and very likely some of them hold positions of power and prestige that he might wish but never have. As an adolescent he plays at his father's role of sharing responsibilities and noticing escapes, without daring to question either. As a young man he leaves, unrooted by either college or the army, attracted by tales of prestige, power, and wealth to be found beyond the familiar hills that have kept the horizon small and warm. Thus he has to develop new identities for which he had acquired strong powers nearing pathos. In the process he learns also that the effects of his attacks on the rigid society cannot be predicted, and to shift easily from love to hatred, from sufferance to anger, from submission to rebellion.

While at least in some other parts of the world history has been steadily purified from myth, in Latin America history continues to be mythologized. Every important actor, whether individual or group, writes his own history. It often happens that, with a new party in power, a new revision of the history textbooks is readily introduced. Bolivar, for example, a demigod for the Conservatives, has been a demon for the Liberals. Juárez, a hopeful symbol for the masses, has been made a target of attack by old aristocrats and clergymen. The Latin American has not yet encountered the true image of his country's past. In addition, too many Latin American governments have too frequently sought and obtained support from foreign powers to stay in power when the peoples wanted them out of power, blemishing therefore the source of their legitimacy, blurring the emerging national identity, and forcing the people to identify with the community and the region. In a meaningful sense, there are only two nations on the olive-skinned continent, Mexico and Cuba. They have developed national identities. The other countries are just states. Some—Venezuela, Brazil, Uruguay, Argentina, and Chile—labor under the burden of large numbers of immigrants who stubbornly retain European identities and despise the *mestizo* ruling groups. Others—Guatemala, Ecuador, Peru, and Bolivia—remain culturally split by ancestral tribal loyalties which are more comforting than the promises that are often made but never kept. Colombia has not yet outgrown regionalism and aristocratic bickering. Honduras, Nicaragua, El Salvador, and Costa Rica still fluctuate between local and Central American identities. The Dominican Republic and Panama, so strategic for the United States defense blueprints in the Caribbean, think of themselves as pushpins in the maps of the warlords of the hemisphere. And Haiti and Paraguay continue to be what they have always been, estates. Not counting the fact that some countries have yet to settle their territorial claims,* international boundaries are for the most part just points of demarcation, not anchorage points for national identities. This is particularly true for the thousands of Latin Americans who have crossed them in search of peace, bread, and shelter for many years.

Within each territory the societies are boiling, urged to seek what is tangible. Within each society man finds multiple identities because it has come to pass for Latin America that man's heart is where his treasure is. Patriotism has obtained a new meaning. A man's land is not where he was born; that idea has been left behind. A man's land is not where he will die; where that will be, he does not know. A man's land is that one which cares for him; for that land, he cares.

A Latin America Manifesto

At last, after four hundred years of delivery, Latin America is being born. The midwives have been Spain, France, England, Spain again, and the United States of America. The gestation has been a period of establishing a configuration, of developing an identity, of achieving recognition. And great pains have accompanied the formation of this recognized identity, which has obviously not yet been completely carved out of the block of civilization from which it is arising. What can Latin America do and how can the United States contribute to the finishing strokes in the emergence of this identity?

Listen Latin America! It is not at all realistic to imagine that history can be reversed; it can only be altered. In the process of consolidation and further differentiation of the class structure and

---

* Chile with Argentina, Ecuador with Peru, Honduras with England, Venezuela with England, Argentina with England, and Panama with the United States.

under the influence of a moralistic middle class traditionally engaged in copying mores from the aristocracy and from foreign middle classes, particularly North American, the impetuous early process of miscegenation has slowed down. Waves of racism, from Germany in the thirties and from the United States at all times, have blown out of all Latin American proportions the aversion to the contact—sexual and otherwise—between the races. Thus the dream of the race visualizing a *mestizo* continent, where polarities of color would fade away in a wide spectrum softened by feelings of racial equality, has been frustrated. Had the attempts been successful they would have added a new element of discord to a scene already tortured by dissension. In spite of this failure, they did open old wounds, those inflicted on the society at the time of its conception, firstly with the enslavement of the Indians and secondly with the Negro slave market. Neither the repentance of Las Casas nor the self-imposed slavery of Claver has washed away from the new soil the blood that ran for too long from Indian and Negro ankles, wrists, and shoulders. In fact, the bells of emancipation have never tolled for the Indians. They still carry cargoes on their shoulders for the masters through the steep and abrupt pedestrian trails of the Andes. When it comes to economic exploitation you, my spiritualistic Latin America, have competed successfully with the materialistic areas of the world. You have added the irony of chapels in the plantations and missionaries in the mines and have made the master pay for the funerals of his slaves.

More concerned with becoming whiter than with the betterment of *la raza,* your native aristocracies have traveled abroad generation after generation trading green- or blue-eyed wives to beget stubbornly brunette children. Soon thereafter, disgusted with the dull life of the plantation, the *estancia,* the *fundo,* and the *hacienda* and disillusioned with the artificially civilized life of the semicolonial metropolis, the unaccustomed wives of your aristocratic males would demand the establishment residences in Europe and North America. Your culture would have then a chance for its revenge. The landlords, feeling terribly lonesome, would suddenly find beauty in the virgins hiding in the small huts that purport to shelter the laboring hands that minister the estate. Then your landlords would claim again to be contributing to the betterment of *la raza,* no matter where the wives had come from. Neither biological nor cultural evolution can be reversed; they can only be altered. But why do not you, Latin America, allow to occur again what was happening at the time of your conception? Why do not you let the cultural meet the biological instead of trying to force the biological to fit the cultural?

Your split (professional and clerical), moralistic middle class, bureaucratically ubiquitous as ever and as ever engaged in imitating whatever happens or is done in Europe and North America, has fallen victim of its own trap. Eager to climb fast the prestige ladder, it has appealed to contraceptives in order to protect its crumbling patterns of consumption. Always begging higher incomes and never willing to fight against inflation, the middle class has no alternative no matter how biting the religious conscience and how strong the peer group pressures. Then once more the cultural imperatives riding on instinctual horses would drive the middleclass male to procreate among the poor in the *barriada.* His wife in the meantime would go to confession monthly, driven by the guilt of contraception. Again history and cultural evolution cannot be reversed; they can hardly be altered. Free your people, then, from the newly imported values and try to match instead the old mores with eugenics. Perhaps in this way more prodigies would be made in the guise of Sonora, Cuba, Cartagena, and Rio, where races from all over met to melt their clay in molds of beauty never known before.

Use your brains before they run away and do not cry when they are gone. It is too late. You seem to love the paradox, the contradiction. Not making room for the ones who reach high levels of competence in your own midst, ignoring their efforts, and often ridiculing their dreams, you let them go to the United States and Europe and then, upon the emergence of problems that had or could have been foreseen, you hire foreign experts to rush through frequently inadequate solutions. In this way you can, of course, blame the foreigner for your failures, but that is not accomplishment. Break the vicious circle. Get loans without the planning experts imposed upon you by the granting agency. Borrow, do not beg. Business relations are not primary relations, at least not in the capitalist system, to which you have been so far forced to bend your knees.

Of course the big trouble with your culture is still that the dispensation of prestige, for which all crave, has always been done in recognition of charisma and that legitimacy itself is related only to charisma. Knowledge is not enough. One has to have charisma. Authority is not enough. Whoever exercises it must have charisma. In a distributive society, charisma helps perhaps in the balancing of justice; the very opposite obtains in competitive societies. In your land charisma has practically always stimulated further inequalities precisely because the charismatic leader can seldom find knowledgeable men able to translate his dreams into practical decisions.

The solution is quite simple and has been offered by students throughout your land from time to time, even against the opposition of their teachers: bring the universities much closer to the people; split the power structure within them; rotate the power holders; make knowledge a response to the conditions of society. Knowledge for knowledge's sake is a dead issue in the contemporary scene.

What you need most, Latin America, is not money, but a more comprehensive concept of responsibility. Responsibility is not only to take care of oneself, one's family, and one's kin group. Unless the community, the region, and the country enter the circle of everyone's responsibility, famine, illness, illiteracy, and hatred will continue to impede the search for your identity.

You have betrayed your past, Latin America, and you may soon betray your future because you seem to be totally unable to become the master of your own affairs and of your own destiny. You are always begging, imploring, borrowing, consulting, mismanaging, and wasting. You can do nothing by yourself. You cannot even protect your own natural resources from raiders from abroad. Many of your leaders, in fact, have played host to these raiders.

Have you begotten any children of lasting international renown, other than dictators? Yes! Some poets and writers, one or two composers, two or three painters, one or two presidents. No scientists, no philosophers, no historians, no theologians, no linguists, not even one great humanitarian. Why? Because you have never searched into your soul. The zest of life of your children is exhausted in very intimate relations. Beyond the immediate circle, life and death are chips in a gamble. Within his own self man is too lonesome.

While seeking prestige in sumptuous living and in political maneuvers, your ruling groups have lost portions of your land, have rented others out, and have turned over to international cartels your richest natural resources and control of your economy. To this day the cartels control your coffee, sugar, banana, cotton, rice, wheat, and lumber markets. They control the exploration, exploitation, transformation, and marketing of oil (the second richest supply in the world), copper, tin, iron, uranium, and paladium. They control the sea and they control the air. In the meantime, your local companies languish and unemployment swells to 15 and 20 percent of the labor population. Then, when violence erupts, your ruling groups shout "Fire!" denying that they themselves set up the kindling and stroked the flint.

Press for roads leading north and south, lift the lid of international frontiers, let your people move freely, and then you shall see the direction they will take. Over 125,000 Latin Americans move to the United States every year, not counting those whom your governments exile; and 6,000 of them are classified as "brains." These are professionals. Why do they all leave? They have lost hope in you, Latin America. Dante, when approaching the gate of Hell, saw this inscription on its lintel: "Abandon all hope, those who enter." Is your land becoming Hell? Are you progressing or regressing? Have you abandoned the search for your identity?

Nationalism is in the upswing on your continent. Let it rise to surges; blow it to a cosmic fire. Perhaps you have to crystallize your identity by fire. Your people seem to be ashamed of you. Italian immigrants remain Italian, the Germans remain German, the Spanish remain Spaniards, the French French, the British British, the Orientals Oriental, etc. Thave have never called themselves Latin Americans. They have not changed to a new identification. They have come to exploit and then return to the "mother country" to live on their exploits. As for the *mestizos,* the Negroes, and the Indians, one can hardly say that they are proud of being Latin Americans. Indeed they offer apologies for it. They all feel transient. And perhaps they are. They seldom own the land on which they walk and their countries seldom own the main sources of wealth. They cannot even run the affairs of their states without foreign influence.

Your hopes are in your youth, Latin America. Do not quench their rebelliousness too soon. Listen to them first. Ask them to join in the political process and in the processes of change. Move with them. You are a young continent. Over 50 percent of your population is under twenty. Let them run your business. Let them make mistakes. Their mistakes cannot be any worse than the mistakes of their elders.

For one thing, they have developed, more so than their elders, a Latin American identity. They have a fairly clear conception of what it is and what it ought to be. They have models. The models that your ruling groups and their *patrones* from abroad so wholeheartedly detest: Cárdenas, Sandino, Castro, and Che Guevara. Not that your youth remain uncritical and follow their admired predecessors blindly. They only have faith in you, in your culture, in your people, and their own ability to change a society corroding with injustice, and burning to ashes with hatred.

Their battle cry is distributive justice. They are seeking the democratization and declassization of the university; the democratization of the electoral process; the deconcentration of land ownership without falling back on the extreme parcelling of stripes; profit and management sharing in industry; returning the ownership and management of natural resources to the country; the opening of markets to the country's products in all corners of the world; the liberalization of trade barriers; the public control of urban real estate, of public transportation, and of utilities and banking; the joint ownership of those industries crucial to the welfare of the nation, such as housing; and the socialization of health services and credit. Socialism? Communism? Not in the least. Distributive justice, shared responsibility, with deep foundations in the Judeo-Christian tradition that their elders have either shelved or placed in high niches "for worship only, do not touch." Your young have even thought that seminaries and military academies alienate their inmates from society. Therefore, they too should be opened for reform. More still. They hope that man the killer is to become a lamb. They have borrowed from Isaiah a 2,500-year-old dream. The paradox is that they plan to achieve what has been said and more that has not been said by any means, thus showing that they are just as human as humans have ever been.

Latin America, let your youthful generations dream and let them build on their dreams. Just try once to let them peacefully build on their dreams.

Perhaps the most perplexing stance of a human society has always been the balancing of power with ethics. This has been particularly difficult for the United States of America, because almost unwittingly it became one of the most powerful nations before reaching adolescence. Unable to set his mind on hairsplitting ethical distinctions and overconscious of his strength, the overgrown pre-adolescent makes the band of the norm coextensive with the range of his fist. The records of the United States' relations with Latin America are very dirty. Any historian knows that. In just the 145 years of the Monroe Doctrine, the United States has meddled in the internal affairs of the various Latin American republics about once every year on the average, most of the time shamelessly and always with arrogance, first with a carrot and a stick and later with the diplomacy of the dollar. Although the intervention in Guatemala in 1953, in Cuba in 1961, in the Dominican Republic in 1965, and the threats to Venezuela in 1958 and to Panama in 1964 were nothing but the swinging of the stick at mid-twentieth century. Why does this have to happen?

Listen North America! Yours is a culture of power. You tend to confuse bigness with goodness, knowledge with wisdom, modesty with weakness, and to associate wealth with virtue, white with grace, black with dirt, poverty with sin, ignorance with malice, right with might.

You seem to believe that the electoral process is the sole path to legitimacy and that the elected official, once invested with authority, is also invested with infallibility. Thus, your vote cast, you withdraw to the television set and the murder mystery while he, believing what you believe and not hearing from you, begins to claim infallibility.

Yours is a society of bureaucrats. Not over 20 percent of your labor force lie outside bureaucratic structures in which frictionless relations have become meaningless relations; where the efficiency of the machine has been attributed to the organization; in which the hierarchical allocation of responsibilities has resulted in refusal to share responsibilities; where the individual's personality hides behind his position and man is not a man but a customer. You should feel lucky that the ever-expanding opening of new positions has at least injected some flexibility above the middle of your rigidly stratified society, because otherwise a few bureaucratic giants would strangle your democracy. But what are you going to do when the machine-god eliminates human labor, if you still hold fast to the idea that man shall win his bread with the sweat of his forehead? Rehearse, at least, by liberating the poor from their misery.

Not quite proud of their past and already bored with the present, your children, as from a prison window, can only look at their future wantonly. They do not even look around their feet to see the earth cracking. Their efforts seem to center on bringing the future to the present, without their ever resting long enough to enjoy either.

Worshippers of power and seers of the future, your children, North America, have erected a million shrines to youthfulness. For youth speaks power and represents the future. But, as with their dead gods, aging North Americans do not wish the new idols to mix in their mundane affairs. In revenge, the idol has begun to desecrate its own temples. The new youth has little respect for bureaucratic power and wants to cash all promises today.

Let the young reap the harvest. They know only too well that your values have become the sole shackles in the true human success of your unparalleled technological development. You must realize, before it is too late, that the contemporary struggle is no longer between nations, or social classes, nor between the oppressors and the oppressed. The struggle is between the older and the younger. You must realize also that the struggle is ideological and ethical, not physical. Do not waste your funds. Turn to your inner self. Love again. You must realize, finally, that the young are not departing from your principles, but are only building upon them exactly what you would if you could be young once more.

Here springs the fountainhead of your misunderstandings, Latin and North America. You are both ruled by older generations that correctly attribute power and responsibilities to knowledge but mistakenly associate knowledge with experience. The younger generation know that knowledge is not entirely associated with experience and that experience is extremely fallible if deprived of systematic observation. Exposed as these young generations are to all sources of knowledge, they want to share the power and responsibilities concentrated in the hands of their elders. On this Latin and North American youth agree totally. Moreover, new values are emerging, spurred not only by the failure of the physical sciences to bring about social order, but because it is in the nature of values to alter as they are put into practice. For more than 2,000 years knowledge has been showing man that men are equal. Only gradually has man moved to new levels of equality. The equal access of man to his gods has been recognized, after much bloodshed, but it has not been assured. The equal access of man to the administration of justice has only vaguely been recognized, and hardly assured. The equal access of man to the bounty of nature and technology is very far from being recognized, as is his equal access to decision-making. The younger generations are just trying to take the premises to their logical conclusions. They no longer see how man can be equal in one sphere but not in others. In respect particularly to decision-making, they can no longer accept it if the people affected by decisions are deprived of the right to participate in making them. If democracy has worked anywhere, democracy may work everywhere. Latin America, a young continent, shares all these values with the youth of North America. Only the ruling groups of Latin America resist, together with aging North Americans.

The struggle between generations has taken the form of nationalism which by implication carries a harsh indictment against those "too old to shout." It has been shown in university reforms, in party splits, in new definitions of religion, in early marriages, in migrations of all sorts, in revolutionary planning and plots, and in thousands of other ways.

What have you, North America, done? You have always lined up with the wrong side of the struggle. Ignoring the exploitation of the poor you have sided with the bourgeoisie and the aristocracy. Blind to the tight grip of your international cartels, you have made them official representatives of your people by sending your marines in defense of their monopolies. Trapped in bureaucratic snares, you have yet to produce a generation of diplomats able to project a faithful image of yourself (shades of "the ugly American"!), with the exception of an exceptional few, who do project the true image. Imbued with messianic aspirations against purely imaginary Communist monoliths, you have, with one exception, discouraged your reform-minded friends. Doubtful of the value of free scientific inquiry, you have allowed your Defense Department and the Pentagon to buy in shameless trade scientists and universities while dealing mortal blows to the local acceptance of sciences. Preaching peace and brotherhood with a big mouth, you have let the merchants of death sell millions in arms under the table to Latin American totalitarians and have burdened your foreign aid with military hardware and technocrats while letting the masses go hungry with only the crumbs from your table. Sick with hallucinations of purity, you have denied passports to the "unfriendly" while pushing them further into the lap of your enemy. Dizzy with dreams of democracy, you have made some agencies inscrutable centers of terror, a paradox that your enemies cherish and your friends deplore, thus undermining democracy. Affected by religious and political schizophrenia, you have let cardinals and congressmen bless and embrace Latin American dictators while self-denying missionaries and plain generous people, not even wearing official badges, have created an image of bountiful America for which millions long in despair, including the young, the wave of the future.

Listen North America! Give the little man at the bottom a chance; the small man at the top has had it. Open literacy courses to cardinals and congressmen. Welcome all visitors no matter what color they wear at that time; they often change color. Stop trading guns for bread. Set free your centers of learning and those scientists who care. Be loyal to your manifest destiny of bounty. Cut cold your diplomatic snarls. Let the cartels fend for themselves; they have means. Ignore the anti-Communist clamor of native colonial exploiters; they mean to cry for your teats. Channel your aid through international banks, in a businesslike way. Listen to the entreaties of the young. Let Latin America come of age, at last!

References and Selected Bibliography

1. Albuja, José Ignacio, et al. *Integración Communitaria.* (FLASCO., Escuela Latinoamericana de Sociología, Santiago). 1959.
2. Lagos, Gustavo. *International Stratification and Underdeveloped Countries* (University of North Carolina Press, Chapel Hill). 1963.
3. Burr, Robert N. (ed.). *Latin America's Nationalistic Revolutions.* (The Annals of the American Academy of Political and Social Science, Philadelphia) 1961.
4. Delgado, José Hernández. *La Confianza Como Factor Decisivo en el Progreso Económico y Social de Mexico.* (Nacional Financiera, S. A. Mexico). 1963.
5. Dillon, Dorothy Rita. *International Communism and Latin America: Perspective and Prospects.* (University of Florida Press, Gainesville). 1962.
6. Erasmus, C. J. *Man Takes Control: Cultural Development and American Aid.* (University of Minnesota Press, Minneapolis). 1961.
7. Fals-Borda, Orlando. "The Ideological Biases of North Americans Studying Latin America." University Christian Movement speech, December 2, 1966.
8. Goldenberg, Boris. *The Cuban Revolution and Latin America.* (Allen and Unwin, London). 1965.
9. Gonzalez Casanova, Pablo. "Internal Colonialism and National Development." *Studies in Comparative International Development,* Vol. I. No. 4, 1965 pp. 27–37.
10a. Grompone, Antonio Miguel. *Filosofía de las Revoluciones Sociales.* (Imprenta Peña Hermanos: Montevideo). 1932.
10b. Hirschman, Albert O. *Journeys Toward Progress: Studies of Economic Policy-making in Latin America.* (Twentieth Century Fund, New York). 1963.
11. Hoffer, Eric. *The Ordeal of Change.* (Harper, New York). 1952.
12. Huberman, Leo, and Sweezy, Paul M. *Cuba: Anatomy of a Revolution.* 2nd ed. (Monthly Review Press, New York). 1961.
13. James, Daniel. *Cuba: The First Soviet Satellite in the Americas.* (Avon, New York). 1961.
14. James, Daniel. *Red Design for the Americas: Guatemalan Prelude.* (John Day, New York). 1954.

15. Juliao, Francisco. *Que sao as ligas camponesas?* (Editoria Civilizaca Brazileira, Rio de Janeiro). 1962.
16. Lannoy, Juan Luis de. *Los Niveles de vida en América Latina. Estudios sociológicos Latino-americanos No. 6.* (Bogotá: Centro de Investigaciones Sociales, 1964 and Friburgo, Suiza: Oficina Internacional de investigaciones sociale de feres). 1964.
17. Larrain Acuna, Herman. "Una opinion sobre la juventud." *Revista Mensaje,* Vol. 10, 105, Dec. 1961.
18. Lederer, William J. & Eugene Burdick. *The Ugly American.* (W. W. Norton & Co., New York). 1958.
19. Matthews, Herbert L. *The United States and Latin America.* (Prentice Hall, Englewood Cliffs, N.J.). 1959.
20. Mendieta y Núñez, Lucio. *Teoría de la Revolución.* (Instituto of IS of UNAM, Mexico). 1961.
21. Mills, C. Wright. *Listen Yankee: The Revolution in Cuba.* (McGraw-Hill Book Company, New York). 1960.
22. Nurkse, Raynar. *Problems of Capital Formation in Underdeveloped Areas.* (Oxford University Press, New York). 1962.
23. *Obra Revolucionaria.* (Imprenta Nacional de Cuba, Habana). 1961.
24. *Obra Revolucionaria.* (Imprenta Nacional de Cuba, Habana). 1962.
25. Pablo, Vicente E. de, & Ezcurra, Marta. *Investigación social en agrupaciones de "villas miserias" de la ciudad Buenos Aires.* (Comisión Nacional de la Vivienda, Buenos Aires). 1958.
26. Paddock, William and Paddock, Paul. *Hungry Nations.* (Little, Brown & Co., Boston). 1964.
27. Prebisch, Raul. "La Estrategia del Desarrollo." *El Mercado de Valores.* (Nacional Financiera, Mexico). Vol. XXVI. No. 39, 1966, pp. 963 968.
28. Quadros, Janio. *Message to the Congress of Brazil Covering Foreign Relations.*
29. Ramos, Alberto Guerreiro. *Sociología de la Mortalidad Infantil.* (Instituto de Investigaciones Sociales Universidad Nacional, Mexico). 1955.
30. Ruiz, Ramon Eduardo. *Mexico: The Challenge of Poverty and Illiteracy.* (Huntington Library, San Marino, California). 1963.
31. Senior, Clarence. *Land Reform and Democracy.* (University of Florida Press, Gainesville). 1958.
32. Serrano Palma, Horacio. *Por que somos pobres.* (Editorial Universitaria, Santiago).
33. Shapiro, Samuel. "Castro and his Critics." *The New Republic,* Vol. 143, No. 24, Dec. 5, 1960, pp. 11–13.
34. Silva-Solar, Julio & Jacques Chonchol. *El Desarrollo de la nueva Sociedad en América Latina.* (Editorial Universitaria, Santiago). 1965.
35. Silvert, Kalman H. "American Academic Ethics and Social Research Abroad." *American Universities Field Staff.* Vol. XII, No. 3 (American Universities Field Staff, Inc., New York). 1965.
36. Smith, T. Lynn. *Current Social Trends and Problems in Latin America.* (University of Florida Press, Gainesville). 1957.
37. Socarras, José F. "Alimentación de la clase media en Bogotá." *Anales de Economía y Estadística* (Bogotá), March 5, 1943.
38. Stavenhagen, Rodolfo. "Seven Erroneous Theses about Latin America." *New University Thought,* 1966.

39. Tepaske, John J., & Sydney Nettleton Fisher. (eds.). *Explosive Forces in Latin America*. (Ohio State University Press, Columbus). 1964.
40. Utria, Rubin D. "Los Factores Estructurales del Desarrollo y el Problema de la Vivienda en América Latina." *Boletín Económico de América Latina*, Vol. XI, No. 2, 1967.
41. Wallis, Victor. "La experiencia del Brasil con una política exterior independiente." *Estudios Internacionales*, Ano I, No. 2, July 1967, pp. 189–211.
42. Zeitlin, Maurice and Scheer, Robert. *Cuba: Tragedy in Our Hemisphere*. (Grove Press, New York). 1963.

8

Some Suggestions
for Policy

Every book written on Latin America has, explicitly and implicity, made suggestions for policy. Because I am a Latin American-born United States citizen, I shall be doubly generous. For the United States, I will suggest a policy of deliberate isolation; for Latin America, a policy of alerted responsibility. I propose to develop this chapter by following the order of the headings of the preceding chapter.

Latin America's Political Pluralism

Like most societies those of Latin American have followed idiosyncratic paths of development. It would be an error to assume that the same labels symbolize identical phenomena in every country in which they appear. This rule applies to every political party as well as to other political institutions. Neither the Communist Party nor the Christian Democratic Party nor any other party is identical throughout the continent, even assuming that each constitutes a solidary organization in each country, which it does not.

179

I have explained why. They are trying to respond, often inaccurately, to situational realities of incredible complexity, not excluding the split in generations. The young Christian Democrats, the young Communists, and the young what-nots are not only refusing to mimic their ideological ancestors, but they are rebelling against them.

Under these conditions, a dualistic party system will not work in any Latin American country. Why then place all our political eggs in one basket in an effort to polarize the contending forces into a dual alignment? It does not make any sense. We spent millions in the 1964 national and municipal Chilean elections helping Frei carry his Christian Democrats into power against the alliance of Socialists and Communists headed by Allende. We have continued to pour massive economic aid into Frei's government in order to make it a democratic reply to Castro's revolution. So far, the results have been not further polarization but a further split of the party in power. New elections will bring with them new alignments and new coalitions.

We put all our political eggs in one basket in Bolivia, the MNR party, with resulting corruption and subsequent downfall under a military rule we now bless, and we exalted *Acción Democrática* in Venezuela in a similar manner. Perhaps it is time we put our political eggs into as many open baskets as we can find. What Latin America needs is political education. Every party needs a good dose of it, even the Communists.

Judging from the American experience, it seems that political sophistication goes hand in hand with nationalism. Genuine nationalism, however, is not necessarily reflected in Latin American constitutions. Thus, constitutional governments do not necessarily guarantee legitimate government. When the military acts to protect the constitution, it does not necessarily act to protect the interests of the people. The boundaries between legality and legitimacy are so blurred in Latin America that the United States would be wisest to leave contending parties to settle their quarrels among themselves. Since the genuinely nationalistic parties are often closer to the people, they deserve our aid, not to win elections but to educate the masses in local and national responsibility.

Our foreign aid is from government to government, as required by the Punta del Este charter. In light of what has just been said, the reader may see why the more we spend in Latin America the more Latin America moves away from us.

I suggest that we defederalize our foreign aid. It could be channeled through international agencies, as Senator Fulbright has proposed, or it could be reoriented, through our tax structure, to stimulate the small farmer, the small businessman, the small university, and the student to join in Latin America's development efforts. The Peace Corps has done wonders. A diversified movement of citizens, unencumbered by the dead weight of a bureaucracy, would do more wonders. The movement must go from community to community, from school to school, from organization to organization. What the United States government has to do is stimulate, guide, inspire.

From her colonial status, Latin America has inherited burdensome bureaucracies that are expanded and perpetuated by every input of foreign aid. Bureaucrats consume, but they do not produce. As consumers, Latin American bureaucrats are oriented toward foreign products, hurting, therefore, not only the national balance of payments but the demand for national goods. By rejecting the local, they identify themselves with the foreign, again hindering the emergence of nationalism.

Moreover, these two bureaucracies, one at the shipping, the other at the receiving end of the foreign aid path, come closer and closer together in the process, increasing in size and decreasing in effectiveness. Here international understanding works well. Left aside, the students and the masses have become more and more conscious of the effectiveness of political action as a means of influencing the distribution of the socioeconomic rewards in each society. Sometimes this action borders on disorder. Then the guardians of order march in and the chances for political growth fade away. Under a defederalized foreign aid program, it would not matter who ran each country; and, since the aid would reach the people immediately and directly, at least some of the causes of unrest would disappear. In this way, governments would cease being substitutes for Divine Providence.

The Religious Diversity

With the inroads into some governments made by Liberalism since early in the last century, many Protestant denominations have grown steadily, especially during the last forty years when they have grown by leaps and bounds. This religious pluralism has received the encouragement of United States agencies, private and public alike. Under this impact, Roman Catholicism has opened to ecumenism at last. Today, Latin American youth is refreshingly unconcerned about the religious issues that produced bloodshed in years past.

More than Roman Catholicism has, Protestantism has emphasized the community basis of organized religion. The Protestant sect that has become a church started from the grassroots upwards and has remained fairly faithful to the wishes of the people. The Roman Church has preferred to be "the Congregation of faithful Christians" rather than a confederation of congregations. Thus, the role of the community is unwittingly deemphasized and with it the role of the laiety from which spontaneous leadership emerges. If both Roman Catholicism and Protestantism are to be meaningful to the Latin American of today, they have to stimulate local leadership with maximum support and minimum interference. It is here where our private foreign aid should focus. The doors have been opened and a great deal has been done, but too much effort is being spent in the areas of dogma and theological issues at a time when practice is needed; action is more convincing than a thousand sermons. This seems to be true not only for churches but for the State Department, whose ideological penetration has decreased with increasing propaganda efforts.

Recent events have indicated that to inject foreign aid into the Catholic Church under the assumption that it is the strongest barrier against Communism may not be the wisest decision. Unexpected alliances, with a strong anti-American flavor, have emerged, and in some instances they have emerged as a direct response to the foreign aid received. Fortunately, the Communists have experienced the same reactions for depending on Soviet assistance and for emphasizing dogma over action. In any event, there are myriads of community projects sponsored by religious bodies. All of them deserve support although the granting agency should set its priorities. It would be a thankless task to try to make specific suggestions here.

There is one area, however, in which the churches can play a crucial role and about which I would like to be specific. It is the area of population growth. All the figures given in an earlier chapter, and many others that have been assembled by investigators, clearly prove that in population Latin America is the fastest growing continent. It is also true that the official pronouncements of the Roman Church condemn the use of contraceptives and oppose the disemination of birth control information. However, those members of the clergy best informed in demographic problems tend to interpret the pronouncements more broadly than those who have not been exposed to the advancement of knowledge in the matter. In the same vein, those clergymen exposed to the thinking and behavior of the young generations offer also their own views of the official regulations. For this reason I suggest a policy of exposure and confrontation. The granting agencies should create the appropriate situations. This can be done at the universities both in the U.S. and in Latin America.

The universities have isolated themselves from the clergy with the exception of an occasional clergyman who happens to teach in a lay university, and with the obvious exception of those universities which are run by the clergy. In all instances, the contact with the young is sporadic and the exposure to demographic problems limited, in theory and practice.

A fundamental approach could be the acceptance, as part of the university curriculum, of theology, philosophy, church history, and other courses now offered in the seminaries. In other words, the seminary, so far the most alienating institution, should become an integral part of the university system, physically, and from the point of view of programming. This requires basic changes in outlook in both the church and the university. The Latin American church has feared the lay universities. If an experimental university could be founded in which the clergy were accepted as a legitimate occupation and the challenges to dogma faced squarely, both the church and the university would become more relevant to the Latin American struggle for growth and development. Ideological differences do not need to disappear, but only to be recognized and respected. This is the real meaning of civilization.

None of these ideas is new. All of them have been presented and discussed here and there, in small groups and in obscure publications. Very seldom have they reached the general public, and then only because the church has questioned their orthodoxy.

The Visionaries and the Realists

In the land of magic and miracles, of poetry and adventure, of oratory and history, one might well expect philospher-kings, although mostly without kingdoms. These Quixotes have crossed the continent from corner to corner, accompanied, on occasions, by the realists. I have distinguished two kinds of realists, the ones entrenched in ossified bureaucracies, and the technocrats of latter day arrival. A new breed, a hybrid of visionary and realists, is in the offing. It constitutes a small minority in the universities and in the young branches of most political parties. The new breed seem to be a sort of domestic peace corps, dedicated to the solution of pressing local socioeconomic problems and to the task of building nations in which working men, peasants, and intellectuals, can sit at the same round table. In fact, many of them have joined forces with our Peace Corps volunteers, who dare to work weaned from close bureaucratic guidance and with outstanding consequences.

These are the people that North Americans should support most enthusiastically. First of all, they are trying to bridge the gap between the man of letters and the unlettered man. They are trying to build theories on situational realities. They are trying to articulate the needs of the masses, who comprise the largest portion of the Latin American population, into political philosophies for political action. And their enthusiastic dedication is affecting younger generations at lower levels of education. These visionary realists deserve our attention.

Why not encourage university and high school students throughout the nation to spend summers in the urban and rural ghettos of Latin America, learning Spanish or Portuguese; collecting fauna, flora, and cultural specimens for our homes and laboratories; teaching English; and just simply socializing, free, on their own; without bureaucratic and parental supervision? What better summer camps can be found than in the villages of Mexico, Central America, and the Andes?

The North American realists have left the human enterprise of aid to developing countries to "the appropriate agencies," that is, to the federal government. Which means in the final analysis, that the North American realists, frequently opposed to centralized government, are truly supporting the very centralization they oppose.

Democracy is a mixture of realism and vision. Our North American realists, however, seem to have turned realism upside down. They fear the power of the president, of the bureau chief, of the executive; all are social fictions, or perhaps just social realities we have created. They fail to ask for the name of the man who happens to be president, bureau chief, or executive. These men are not social fictions. We have to learn to break the barriers these men have created to match our proneness to myth making. This is what the young rebels are teaching us now, both here and in Latin America.

The young generations want action. It is perhaps their turn.

Has Miscegenation Stopped?

With the rise of the middle classes, with the bureaucratization of labor, with the migrations from Uruguay, Argentina, and Chile to other Latin American countries, with the penetration of the culture of the United States into the continent, a new wave of racial puritanism has swept even the bottom of society. In the past, the *hacienda* and the urban slum were relatively free of inhibitions concerning racial mixing. Today, even the urban slums are spotted by ecological ethnicity. Brazil may be the only country where economic success and personal charm still tend to erase racial boundaries.

Signs of a reverse trend are not lacking, however. The continent has closely followed the struggles for the liberation of the blacks in the United States ghettos and has reacted with praise and admiration for the United States government's positive drive toward equality. Cuba, by emphasizing the exploitation of the Negroes in the U.S., has made salient their conquests. In turn, the Indian is awakening anew in southern Mexico and Guatemala, and in southern Colombia, Ecuador, Peru, and Bolivia, and not all of those who reach higher levels of education are betraying their ethnic ancestry. They are contributing to the gradual liberation of their peoples.

The process of identification with the nation is being mediated by a process of identification with one's racial and ethnic group. There is no more emphasis on *mestizaje,* mostly because this was the dream of the intellectuals not of the *mestizos.* Those who today proclaim nationalism are the heirs of those who advocated *mestizaje* in earlier decades. In the meantime, the masses are turning to themselves; they are facing local common problems united in terms of those characteristics that may bring them closer together, whether in terms of kinship or ethnicity or race or foreign nationality. Group competition is the order of the day. The mixing may come later.

All this means that there is a higher awareness in Latin America of socioeconomic standards than ever before, and that miscegenation is now more an accident than an expression of life without concern. In terms of control of population growth, the preceding considerations are very significant, as they also are in terms of the development of multiple identities, a subject to be treated again later. If groups consolidate on ethnic and racial foundations to break the artificial barriers to their advancement, it seems obvious that cross-cultural relations must weaken. In other words, the price of growth and development may be heightened ethnic tensions.

There are some forces counterbalancing these tendencies. The high degree of political and economic instability makes for some downward social mobility. Under these conditions, successful brown or black men may rescue those families which remain caught in the scramble. In this form, the prestige of money saves the prestige of skin color and puts brakes on the antimiscegenation forces. In contrast with that of past generations, however, the results of this miscegenation are meager.

For policy purposes it may be advisable to stimulate the sharpening of ethnic differences so that group competition may result in further development. There is no problem in this matter with regard to the various European or Far Eastern nationalities. The problem is with the native groups that century after century have been forced to erase their identities. Some countries, such as Mexico and Bolivia, have been relatively successful in awakening the latent pride in the oldest Indo-American ancestry.

Mexico has been particularly skillful in stimulating pride in cultural diversity, not only by protecting tribal rights and traditions but by creating a national and international market for the products of the various regions. Less successful attempts in this direction have been made in Guatemala and in the Andean countries that remain inaccessible to most North American tourists. Moreover, there is little consciousness of tourism in these latter countries where, in spite of the regional and cultural diversity so appealing to foreign visitors, appropriate facilities are lacking, transportation is terribly deficient, information is frequently misleading, sanitary conditions are highly questionable, and even the local traders are grabby. A continental campaign in education for tourism is still badly needed. Will tourism help in crystalizing ethnic identities and will it further slow down the process of miscegenation? I think so, although the final answer should await additional empirical evidence.

Two Ways of Becoming

Most of North Americans are justly proud of their country and its traditions. Some proud North Americans have maintained that the "American way of life" should be made the way of life of other societies. This has been apparent in the conduct of U.S. foreign policy since the Monroe Doctrine, and, in recent year, since John Foster Dulles. It is interesting to observe, by contrast, that Latin Americans, while rejecting, especially since Cárdenas, the intervention of the U.S. in the internal affairs of their nations, have always welcomed the penetration of the North American culture. It is even more interesting to observe that those North Americans who have spurred this penetration are frightened now by its revolutionary impact. Latin Americans are not happy with crumbs any more; they want a piece of the pie. In fact, they want the whole pie. This is quite consonant with both the culture of equality of opportunity and the culture of miracles.

North Americans have done a marvelous job of advertising their wares. Latin Americans have done a marvelous job at stretching out their hands in the traditional gesture of entreatment. North Americans take risks and invest in Latin America. Latin Americans take refuge and invest in U.S. companies. On the one hand you have the culture of entrepreneurship, on the other the culture of security. I am talking of course of those who can invest. The majority of Latin Americans cannot; they struggle. These are the ones who are anticolonialist and antiimperialist; they attack internal colonialism and external imperialism. They create small industries of all sorts in collaboration with their relatives in city and town. These are the ones that deserve our aid. They are developing a form of communal capitalism; one finds family enterprise everywhere, even in the *barriadas* and *favelas*.

Up to a point, Latin American governments have been concerned with these people. There is an array of banks purposely, but not effectively, organized for them such as Banco Agrario, Agrícola y Ganadero, Banco Comercial, Banco Industrial y Minero, Banco de Crédito Ejidal, Banco Agrícola e Hipotecario, Caja de Crédito Territorial, Caja Agraria,* etc. and all the thousands of credit unions and cooperatives that often enjoy legal privileges. The Inter-American Development Bank has helped the small business people also. However, the distribution of this help has been defi-

---

* These names are not identical throughout the continent, but the examples are quite representative of the titles and nature of the banks serving small industries, farmers, etc.

nitely lopsided in contravention of the stated purpose of the Alliance for Progress.

North Americans think that Latin American states are Socialist because they own the railroads, most of the power plants, telephones and telegraph communications, air-lines, merchant marines, the mines, and the oil. What these North Americans do not realize is that Latin America is not one nation but 22 nations; that there have never been wealthy enough capitalists to own and exploit these services; that there is not one Latin American market but hundreds of little markets; that Latin America is not an industrialized continent; that some countries are not states but estates. The governments own these industries and services out of necessity. The alternative would be not to have them at all. These North Americans have forgotten that the U.S. federal government subsidizes the oil companies; subsidizes the banks; subsidizes the railroads (after giving them large portions of federal lands), etc. But this is not of my immediate concern.

In previous chapters I have especially emphasized a contrast between the U.S. and Latin America at the value and norm levels. I would like to address myself to those North Americans of good will who are interested in fostering a kind of international relation based on the recognition of existing differences. Some of these differences, I have maintained, are complementary, and now I suggest that they be respected and even stimulated.

Some illustrations follow. North Americans love freedom and so do Latin Americans. The two concepts of freedom are not identical, however. Latin Americans think of freedom as an environment in which each man can express himself, not only without fear and coercion but without total commitment. Laws are not sacred, contracts are not inviolable, the word may be retracted. What counts is man, a man who moves in a transactional situation; who negotiates with the others at every step of his career; whose immediate future does not depend on what is written but on what is settled and done. Freedom is, therefore, negotiable.

As such, freedom is for man, not man for freedom. It is inconceivable for the Latin American to fight a war that is not an immediate response to an immediate injury. In this sense, freedom is not "there"; it is "here," between you and me, in this situation, now. Perhaps if the U.S. were 51 nations instead of one, U.S. citizens would find freedom, in this sense, conceivable. But being a big nation and a big power has made freedom remote and abstract, a matter of commitment, indivisible, nonnegotiable. Perhaps the one view balances the other and will save mankind from ultimate conflagration.

The Latin American has not practiced political democracy, because in his mind democracy cannot coexist with inequality. In the meantime, Latin American societies continue to be both undemocratic and elitist. If our foreign aid could be detached from our (official) diplomacy, perhaps our influence on Latin America's move from elitism to egalitarianism could more readily be felt. As things now stand, it seems that our foreign aid has been hardening rather than mellowing the traditional social class structure, except, of course, for the expansion of bureaucracies.

Democracy has been defined and used differently by everybody in Latin America for at least 150 years, even by the Communists and the military. Development has been the catchword in recent years; now it is revolution. But development and revolution have been defined and used differently by different people. Thus the skepticism of the Latin American often borders on cynicism.

It is here, in my view, where the practical genius of the North American comes into play. For generations the holders of power in Latin America have talked about doing things, and then along come the North Americans, who do things first and then talk about them later. This is truly revolutionary. Development makes sense. Democracy may work after all. However, this is the thought of the masses. The holders of power have felt, on the one hand, the revolutionary content of the North American influence and have seen, on the other, that investing in Latin American enterprises does pay after all. Now they want to do something for the masses and they want to gain full control of the economies. Nationalism, thus, has found support both in the masses that are asking for more and in the oligarchies that want sure profits. Obviously the role of our foreign aid is to do more, small as it may be, but everywhere. At present our foreign aid is concentrated in such "show countries" as Chile, Colombia, and Brazil.

It seems that no matter what the U.S. does for Latin America,

Latin America is going to move in her own way. In the sixties we saw new dictatorships established in Argentina, Brazil, Bolivia, Peru, and Panama, not counting a short-lived one in Ecuador and another one in the Dominican Republic. Social unrest has not subsided anywhere. Why not make our foreign aid truly "American," as the term is used in the U.S.? Why not make our foreign aid the aid of the people, to the people, by the people, for the people? In this way, at least the people would take part of the blame and Latin Amrica would find her identity.

Multiple Identities

Latin America has not one, but many identities. The little Latin America there is has emerged in a very long and painful process. In other words, Latin America has not been homogenized. Regionalism and localism still prevail. People identify themselves first with the locality and only secondly with the region and only weakly with the nation. When they move, most probably to the city, they remain loyal to the community from which they came no matter how harsh living there may have been. This is why, among other reasons, agrarian reform makes so much sense.

That practically no land reform has been successful in Latin America speaks for the inability of the governments to overpower the landed oligarchies. And that the U.S. has not been able to reach the masses with its foreign aid also speaks for the power of the Latin American oligarchies.

The U.S. as a nation was born from a series of identifications. In fact, the last states did not enter the Union until this century. There is a tremendous identification with the community in the country, obviated by such institutions as the jury system, the school board, and hundreds of educational and philanthropic organizations. Often these organizations elect their boards so that the people's participation becomes paramount. Not so in Latin America, where too frequently elections are replaced by appointments from the top, so that one can visualize power flowing not from the people to their representatives but from the almighty

(Almighty) to the masses. In Latin America, when something needs to be done in the community, people do not turn to themselves, but to the government; not the local government, which is powerless, but to the central government, from which "all good proceeds." The Mexicans have labeled this illness in their system "señor-presidentismo." It is an illness of all Latin America.

Efforts to correct this providentialistic attitude have been made, with varying degrees of success, in Mexico, Colombia, Venezuela, Chile, Argentina, and Uruguay, not by changing the political system but by developing community awareness of power focusing on issues. The literature on community development is abundant. Many U.S. universities have contributed well in this endeavor. Cornell, Michigan State, Wisconsin, and Florida come to mind. Citizens' organizations have done precious little in this regard, because when it comes to foreign aid North Americans have preferred centralization.

It is the pride and organizational genius of the North American neighborhood and city dweller that has not been sent abroad with our foreign aid to stimulate a healthy community identification able to transcend the boundaries of kin group alignments.

The North American melting pot has ceased to melt in recent years. Waves of ethnic self-awareness have swept the nation. Black and Mexican-American militants are fearlessly unearthing the buried gold of their cultures, not to destroy America but to beautify America. *E pluribus unum.* The unity of the nation is not to be disarrayed by their ambitions, no matter what a few radicals may say. And unity is meaningless without diversity.

There is no reason why similar healthy competition should not be further fostered in Latin America by both North Americans and Latin Americans. The North American society is responding with justice to the poor. There is no reason to doubt that Latin American societies will respond likewise under combined pressures from within and from without. President Kennedy moved Latin America. His mistake, as Victor Alba has demonstrated, was in setting an alliance of governments rather than of people. Also, in my view, his Peace Corps was not sufficiently ambitious, and was soon burdened with bureaucracy. Moreover, his Peace Corps did not create a counterpart in each nation, except, again, at the bureaucratic level. New knowledge often derives from old errors. The true spirit of the Alliance has not died.

President Kennedy became a symbol of the young. The young everywhere are restless. They feel capable of sharing responsibilities. If President Kennedy were alive today, he might have changed his historic inaugural address for the late sixties, to read like this: "My fellow Americans, ask not what you can do for your country. Ask instead what you and your country can do for the peoples of all nations."

Postscript: Latin America in the Seventies

Postscript: Latin America in the Seventies

When this book was completed at the end of the 1960's, Latin America was experiencing a cathartic process of self-evaluation, emerging as a continent composed of multiple identities. Clearly manifested in this effort were two opposite phenomena. First was the stream of Latin American realities breaking, like sea waves, at the walls of industrial and commercial plants and at the sanctuaries of faith and knowledge. Population was increasing at world record rates, natural resources were rapidly becoming depleted, and the rural areas were being abandoned for the crowded urban slums. Transportation, imitating the industrialized countries, was becoming a private car affair; the traditional linkage of local oligarchies to foreign capitals was becoming tighter and shifting to new industrial enterprises. Education was more universal at the lower levels but less accessible at the higher levels. The family was more exposed to the employment of women and their liberation; the Church more involved in basic socioeconomic and even revolutionary change; the proletariat more consumption-oriented in imitation of the middle classes; and the peasants more aware of their exploitation and impotence. Even the military, a traditional barrier to social reform, was moving leftward.

The 60's was a decade of hope for the masses and of concern everywhere for the entrenched oligarchies. The model of democracy was of course Chile. For at least two generations the country had been able to change its leadership by constitutional methods and through the electoral process. Eduardo Frei, whose term of office closed the 60's, had responded to the needs of the people by moving his party clearly to the left. Rodomiro Tomic would try to move it still farther in the elections of 1970 in which Allende, a declared Marxist, was elected with only a 36% plurality of votes. Democracy was to be of a leftist, perhaps Marxist, type.

Then there was a second stream—the ideological one. Latin American intellectuals and politicians were trying to develop conceptual schemes to deal with the complex realities they had to confront. Since no scheme was to be found locally they had to look elsewhere. There were two "overarching paradigms" [Bernard— (1973)] for which they could reach: capitalism and Marxism. The first was exemplified by the unbending orthodoxy of rostow (1962) as practiced by the Democratic White House of the 60's and as early as the 50's by Raul Prebisch (1950) as first General Secretary of the new UN Economic Commission for Latin America (ECLA) with headquarters in Chile. Prebisch's modified, anti-imperialist capitalism would guide the political economy of the period that ended in 1970 with his famous report to the Inter-American Development Bank (IDB). Best known, although not loyal, followers of this line of thought in Latin America have been Celso Furtado (1963, 1970a, 1970b, 1971) and Osvaldo Sunkel (1969, 1970, 1971).

Within a relatively orthodox Marxism that sees Latin America as an appendix to imperialistic capitalism, Andre Gunder Frank (1967, 1969, 1972), Theotonio Dos Santos (1970, 1973), James Petras (1973) and Allende himself seem to be the most articulate representatives. Other outstanding thinkers of development fall somewhere in between the capitalist and Marxist positions. The following names come to mind first: Cardoso (1964, 1970), Quijano (1966, 1968, 1973), Jaguaribe (1969, 1973), Pinto (1969, 1965). Those major Latin American realities that seem to be most relevant in shaping the future of the area have been chosen, without making any claims to orthodoxy in either camp. From the analysis the reader should be able to derive the explanatory perspective taken.

In the discussion of the Latin America of the 70's the most salient points have been organized into three major categories: first, the matter of population growth and its pressures on employment and migration; second, the problem of internal and external trade and its impact on income distribution, which automatically affects the existing class structure; and third, the issue of national and Latin American integration and the continent's relations with the industrialized nations, including the question of the multinational corporations.

The Population Factor

It is not my intention to imply that the population factor is a complete explanation for all of Latin America's socioeconomic and political problems. Far from it. It is a serious, extremely influential factor that must be not only studied but resolved, and resolved in the very near future. Some of the reasons for this urgency are presented here and in the sections that follow. It must be borne in mind that all the factors discussed are interrelated. I believe, along with many others, however, that if population growth is allowed to continue at the explosive rates that Latin America is experiencing, no amount of natural and technological resources will be able to meet even the basic needs of coming generations.

The reader is invited to analyze the statistics contained in Table 12. In addition, Table 13 makes the point clearly: the populations of most Latin American countries are growing at fantastic rates. Mexico in particular is growing so fast that population there is doubling every sixteen years (assuming of course the same rate of increase). At this rate, Mexico will have over 120 million people in 1991, and Latin America, growing at 2.9% a year, will have over 600 million just before the year 2000. This is a frightening thought.

In non-mechanized agricultural societies, children have been needed for their labor, and their consumption requirements have been relatively easy to meet from the land itself. These societies are being phased out throughout the continent. Few pockets of true rural life remain, and even in these areas the orientation is urban. Haiti, Bolivia, Guatemala, Honduras, Paraguay and El Salvador are still heavily rural. They are small countries, the largest of which is Guatemala with a population of about 6 million, 31% urban. At the other end of the scale, Argentina, Venezuela, Uruguay and Chile are highly urban. Latin America is now almost entirely urban and rapidly developing in both agricultural and rural technology. The implication of these facts for population policies is clear.

The second half of Table 13 gives urban population growth rates for each nation as a whole. As with all statistics, the table simplifies complex realities. It is well known that certain cities—capital cities in the case of Latin America—tend to grow faster than other industrial urban areas. Buenos Aires, Lima, Bogota, Caracas, Mexico City (all capital cities) and Sao Paulo and Monterrey (industrial cities) have

Table 12   Latin American Population Statistics

Country	Area, km²	Population Mid 1975	Est. Population 1980	G.N.P. 1974 $ Millions	% Of Total Government Expenditure Public Health	Housinc
Argentina	2,776,656[a]	25,036,300	26,971,100	36,551.3	4.0(1975)	3.0(1975)
Barbados	430	242,000	244,400	184.9	8.0(1974)	4.7(1974)
Bolivia	1,098,581	5,633,800	6,405,100	1,481.1	9.8(1974)	1.2(1974)
Brazil	8,511,965	107,145,200	123,013,400	79,172.3	2.6(1974)	0.3(1974)
Chile	756,945	10,253,000	11,264,700	10,910.4	6.5(1974)	6.2(1974)
Cuba	n.a.	n.a.	n.a.	n.a.	n.a.	n.a.
Colombia	1,138,338	23,415,800	26,883,700	10,325.6	7.4(1974)	0.8(1974)
Costa Rica	50,900	1,990,000	2,318,000	1,459.9	6.2(1974)	n.a.
Dominican Republic	48,442	4,725,000	5,477,700	2,793.0	9.6(1974)	3.8(1974)
Ecuador	270,670	6,690,000	7,717,600	2,791.6	7.2(1974)	n.a.
El Salvador	20,935	4,108,400	4,879,500	1,712.0	11.0(1974)	n.a.
Guatemala	108,889	5,852,000	6,718,700	3,531.0	9.3(1974)	n.a.
Haiti	27,750	4,583,800	4,986,800	696.0	15.7('72-'73)	n.a.
Honduras	112,088	2,712,000	3,024,000	989.3	9.0(1974)	1.0(1974)
Jamaica	10,962	2,014,000	2,169,700	1,992.7	11.9('74-'75)	0.8('74-75)
Mexico	1,967,183	60,094,000	71,911,000	44,823.3	3.2(1974)	n.a.
Nicaragua	139,000	2,143,400	2,460,800	1,361.3	4.3(1974)	10.2('74)
Panama	75,650	1,667,700	1,942,700	1,702.2	5.6(1974)	0.7(1974)
Paraguay	406,752	2,646,900	3,053,600	948.2	4.1(1974)	0.3(1974)
Peru	1,280,219	15,615,000	18,135,000	7,493.3	4.8(1974)	1.1(1974)
Trinidad and Tobago	5,128	1,096,400	1,204,600	1,185.1	5.5(1974)	1.1(1974)
Uruguay	186,926	2,764,000	2,862,100	2,568.7	6.6(1973)	n.a.
Venezuela	898,805	11,993,100	14,106,800	16,536.4	3.2(1974)	3.7(1974)

[a]Excludes 1,247,803 km² of land in the Antarctic, the Falkland Islands and other islands in the Southern Atlantic.

[b]Persons 15 years of age or older.

Source: Inter-American Development Bank, Annual Report, 1975, passim.

grown astronomically in the last fifteen years. Mexico City is already the largest in the world and yet was way down the list in 1960. Keeping this in mind, the reader is invited to look at the urbanization rates given in the table and at the doubling time for each urban population in each country (again assuming the same growth rates). It is not difficult to reach alarming conclusions.

Urbanization in Latin America is not to be thought of as the same as urbanization in the First World nations. Actually, urbanization in Latin America (with the exception of a few industrial centers) has meant primarily depopulation of the rural countryside. It has

Table 12 Latin American Population Statistics

% OF TOTAL GOVERNMENT EXPENDITURE EDUCATION	% OF LITERACY	% OF URBAN POPULATION	YRS. OF LIFE EXPECTANCY AT BIRTH	INFANT DEATH RATE. PER M	DEATH RATE. PER M
13.7(1975)	93.0(1970)	82.5(1975)	68.2(1970-75)	60.1(1970-75)	8.4(1970)
19.5(1974)	97.0(1974)	45.0(1975)	68.4(1974)	34.0(1974)	8.6(1974)
25.9(1974)	57.0(1974)	30.9(1975)	45.0(1970-75)	159.0(1974)	19.0(1974)
6.0(1974)	79.8^b(1974)	61.5(1975)	61.0(1970-75)	85-95(1970)	9.1(1970-75)
13.8(1974)	89.7(1974)	80.5(1975)	62.6(1970-75)	63.3(1974)	7.4(1974)
n.a.	n.a.	n.a.	n.a.	n.a.	n.a.
19.5(1974)	77.6(1974)	66.8(1975)	51.0(1972)	93.8(1974)	9.4(1974)
27.0(1974)	88.4(1973)	42.2(1975)	69.4(1970-75)	35.0(1974)	4.9(1974)
12.4(1974)	67.2(1970)	46.3(1975)	60.4(1972)	48.7(1972)	6.8(1972)
23.0(1974)	75.1(1974)	42.0(1975)	60.0(1970-75)	71.6(1974)	10.8(1974)
23.7(1974)	59.5(1974)	39.8(1975)	57.8(1970-75)	58.2(1974)	11.1(1974)
15.6(1974)	45.0(1974)	31.4(1975)	53.0(1970-75)	90.0(1974)	13.0(1974)
12.0('72-'73)	24.7(1971)	22.0(1975)	50.0(1970-75)	149.1(1973)	15.0(1973)
18.0(1974)	54.7(1974)	32.5(1975)	58.8(1970-75)	117.6(1974)	14.2(1974)
21.0('74-'75)	81.9(1960)	52.9(1975)	70.2(1970-75)	26.2(1974)	7.2(1974)
16.7(1974)	76.3(1970)	61.2(1975)	64.0(1970-75)	68.0(1974)	9.1(1974)
13.3(1974)	52.6(1974)	52.1(1975)	52.5(1970-75)	45.0(1971)	7.2(1974)
12.5(1974)	84.0(1973)	50.4(1975)	66.5(1970-75)	31.0(1974)	5.3(1974)
18.0(1974)	79.7(1972)	36.1(1974)	61.9(1970-75)	84.3(1973)	8.9(1974)
19.4(1974)	67.7(1970)	63.5(1975)	54.6(1970-75)	65.1(1970)	13.7(1970-75)
9.7(1974)	95.0(1970)	56.6(1975)	68.1(1970)	32.4(1973)	7.1(1973)
15.8(1973)	89.8(1975)	80.8(1963)	72.0(1973)	40.4(1971)	9.8(1971)
9.4(1974)	77.1(1971)	82.6(1975)	66.4(1970-75)	46.6(1974)	6.3(1974)

been more the consequence of "push" factors such as *minifundio* and *latifundio* (small and large land holdings), military recruitment and civil warfare, poor soil conservation practices, and social services and infrastructures than the actual or supposed work opportunities of the

Table 13   Latin American Population Statistics

POPULATION AVERAGE ANNUAL GROWTH RATES LATIN AMERICAN COUNTRIES 1970-75 (IN RANK ORDER)	%	WILL DOUBLE IN (YEARS)	URBAN POPULATION GROWTH RATES LATIN AMERICAN COUNTRIES 1960-75 (IN RANK ORDER)	%	WILL DOUBLE IN (YEARS)
Mexico	4.2	16.4	Jamaica	7.1	9.7
El Salvador	3.7	18.6	Dominican Republic	6.0	11.5
Paraguay	3.5	19.7	Peru	5.7	12.1
Dominican Republic	3.1	22.2	Colombia	5.1	13.5
Panama	3.1	22.2	Mexico	5.0	13.8
Venezuela	3.1	22.2	Costa Rica	4.9	14.1
Costa Rica	3.0	23.0	Nicaragua	4.9	14.1
Peru	3.0	23.0	Brazil	4.8	14.1
LATIN AMERICA	2.9	23.7	Venezuela	4.8	14.1
Ecuador	2.9	23.7	Honduras	4.6	15.0
Brazil	2.8	23.7	Panama	4.4	15.7
Guatemala	2.8	24.6	Trinidad and Tobago	4.4	15.7
Nicaragua	2.8	24.6	LATIN AMERICA	4.3	16.0
Bolivia	2.7	25.5	Ecuador	4.2	16.4
Colombia	2.7	25.5	Haiti	3.9	17.7
Honduras	2.2	31.3	El Salvador	3.8	18.1
Chile	1.8	38.3	Bolivia	3.6	19.1
Haiti	1.6	43.1	Chile	3.1	22.2
Jamaica	1.5	46.0	Paraguay	3.1	22.2
Trinidad and Tobago	1.3	53.1	Argentina	2.3	30.0
Argentina	1.2	57.5	Guatemala	2.2	31.3
Barbados	0.3	230	Barbados	1.0	69.0
Uruguay	0.3	230	Uruguay	0.7	98.5

Adapted from IDB, Economic and Social Progress in Latin America, Annual Report 1975, Tables 1 and 2, p. 373.

cities. As Prebisch (1970) has demonstrated, the demand for labor has been lagging far behind the supply, which is largely unskilled. The cold fact of Latin America is that with increasing industrialization and urbanization, unemployment and underemployment have increased precisely because the countryside has declined and even deteriorated in terms of meeting the growing population's basic needs.

As discussed next, the movement of people toward urban areas has not been evenly spread. Neither has this occurred anywhere else in the world. The pattern in Latin America has been for the urban centers to be very few and very large and to surround the continent as seaports (see map, p. xix). There are two significant exceptions to this rule—Mexico City and Bogota. Santiago, Chile could be the third exception, but Santiago is not too far from the sea. It seems that this trend is continuing through the 1970's and in the next decade, unless the forces discussed on page 199 are more rationalized.

Historically, few primary cities have tended to absorb both external and internal migrations. The sole exception to this rule used to be the cities of Colombia, whose inner-oriented economy tended to spill over from Bogota and Medellin to Cali, Bucaramanga and Cucuta, all inland, and to Barranquilla on the Caribbean. In recent years, Argentina has seen the spill-over reaching Rosario and Cordoba toward the Northwest, and Brazil has seen the development of the well-known Sao Paulo, Rio, Belo Horizonte triangle. A similar regionalization is taking place in Mexico, where the capital is stretching out toward Guadalajara in the northwest and Puebla to the south. In other words, second-order cities are beginning to absorb some of the population pressures.

Naturally, the routes of migration point in the direction of growing urban centers. With the exception of northwestern Brazil, the Amazonia of central South America and some areas of Central America which are still open to colonization, most Latin Americans move to primary cities. Argentina, Chile, Peru, Venezuela and Guatemala each have only one primary city of considerable size. Mexico City and Bogota, the latter about one fourth of the size of the former, have each attracted about half of the internal migration of their respective countries. The "pull" from the United States and Venezuela has made for rapid growth in the respective border cities of Mexico and Colombia.

In the case of Brazil, where Sao Paulo's population has more than doubled since 1960, attracting people from all parts of the country, other cities have also attracted migrants. The largest of the cities are shown in Table 14. Migrations in Brazil, in contrast with Mexico and Colombia, move toward the Atlantic; they are largely unidirectional.

Table 14   Population of Major Cities in Latin America

CITY		POPULATION
Argentina		
Buenos Aires (capital)	(1974)	8,925,000
Rosario	(1970)	810,840
Cordoba	(1970)	798,663
La Plata	(1970)	506,287
Bolivia		
La Paz (capital)	(1975)	660,700
Brazil		
Sao Paulo	(1970)	5,869,966
Rio de Janeiro	(1970)	4,252,009
Belo Horizonte	(1970)	1,228,295
Porto Alegre	(1970)	869,795
Salvador	(1970)	1,005,216
Recife	(1970)	1,046,454
Fortaleza	(1970)	828,763
Chile		
Santiago (capital)	(1975)	3,262,990
Colombia		
Bogota (capital)	(1973)	2,855,065
Cali	(1973)	923,264
Medellin	(1973)	1,417,384
Barranquilla	(1973)	726,726
Costa Rica		
San Jose (capital)	(1973)	395,401

CITY		POPULATION
Cuba		
Havana (capital)	(1970)	1,751,216
Ecuador		
Quito (capital)	(1972)	564,900
Guayaquil	(1972)	860,900
El Salvador		
San Salvador (capital)	(1971)	337,171
Guatemala		
Guatemala City (capital)	(1973)	706,920
Mexico		
Mexico City (capital)	(1975)	11,339,774
Guadalajara	(1975)	1,963,277
Monterrey	(1975)	1,637,681
Peru		
Lima (capital)	(1972)	3,302,523
Uruguay		
Montevideo (capital)	(1975)	1,229,748
Venezuela		
Caracas (capital)	(1971)	2,175,400
Maracaibo	(1971)	651,574

SOURCE. UN Statistical Yearbook, 1976, passim.

The Caracas metropolitan area now shares with the oil area of Maracaibo most of Venezuela's internal migration. Cuidad Guayana in the western portion of the country has been planned for a population of 300,000 in 1980, with a potential expansion to 500,000 (Robinson, 1969)—a relatively large size for Venezuela.

The countries so far mentioned in this connection are not the only ones affected by internal migration. Every country is so affected and will continue to be so long as the conditions of life remain so unstable.

There is both an exchange of people from country to country within Latin America and with North America. The main target of migration in the hemisphere for all nations is the United States. Venezuela is the major target for Colombians.

Since 1968, the revised U.S. Immigration Act has limited the number of immigrants admitted annually from the Western Hemisphere to 125,000. For the first time in the history of Pan-American relations the United States has fixed entry quotas for the rest of the continent. Latin Americans did not like the new policy, although the law left open avenues for people to migrate outside of the quotas in order to reunite families.

Table 8 on page 83 shows that over 700,000 Latin Americans immigrated to the United States from 1958 to 1965. Table 15 shows over 1.5 million for 1966-1975. The total number of immigrants therefore doubled, although the period is longer. From the point of view of total numbers the figures are not very telling. Migration to the United States has clearly increased beyond the statutory limitations, but not in alarming proportions. There are two aspects of the overall migration phenomenon that should be discussed.

The first is that the major occupational groups represented in Table 15 have changed in their significance in the migration stream compared with what is reflected in Table 8. The percentage distribution for housewives, children and others has increased from 57% in Table 8 to 61% in Table 15. Among the remaining categories, professionals, which occupied the second place in Table 8, now occupy fifth place. Operatives and craftsmen moved to first and second place respectively, indicating a selective migration with an emphasis on the skilled labor category. On the other hand, the so-called professional "brain drain" has evidently slowed down in proportion to other migrant groups, not in absolute figures. These have grown from 46,000 to over 71,000 in ten years.

The second aspect of the overall migration to the United States from Latin America, although not found in reliable statistical reports, is the number of illegal aliens that has by any estimate exploded in recent years. The "numbers game" puts the illegal alien population in the United States between 4 and 12 million, and the number of arrests in 1974 around 800,000 (U.S. House of Representatives, *Hearings,* 1975). Although the majority of the illegal aliens are not Latin American, it appears that the majority apprehended are; in fact, over 80% of them are Mexican and most of them are apprehended in the American Southwest.

Migration factors are multiple and complex. Population growth

Table 15 Immigrants Admitted to United States
from Latin American Countries by
Major Occupational Groups (1966-1975)

OCCUPATIONAL GROUPS	ABSOLUTE	RELATIVE
Professionals	71,651	4.6
Farmers	3,044	0.2
Managers	23,145	1.4
Clericals	60,701	3.9
Sales Workers	11,784	0.8
Craftsmen	91,249	6.0
Operatives	102,272	6.6
Private Household	84,419	5.5
Service Workers	59,929	3.8
Farm Laborers	18,126	1.2
Laborers	82,569	5.3
Housewives, children and other with no reported occupation	937,209	60.7
TOTAL	1,546,098	100.0

Adapted from Table 8 of *United States Immigration and Naturalization Service Annual Report*, 1966-1975.
See Table 8, page 83.

and pressure on natural and economic resources are two of them. Employment trends have been critical since job opportunities have not kept pace with the number of people entering the labor force. It was thought that industrialization would meet the labor supply if rural life could be improved. Neither of these has occurred. Thus the unemployment rates in both urban and rural areas have soared and the rate of economic growth has lagged behind the rising employment need (Prebisch 1970, MacEoin 1971, Oxaal et al, 1975). According to Prebisch (1970, p. 81), not even an 8% annual growth for this and the next decade will meet the employment demands of Latin America. Only Brazil has sustained a comparable rate, but the inequalities resulting have been so blatant that the military dictatorship has kept the lid down by terror and torture. Needless to add, Brazil's unemployment rate remains high.

In no Latin American country has the unemployment rate been

less than 10% of the labor force in recent years, a symptom of inadequate development. However, as Vasena and Pazos (1973) have maintained, improved consumption, not improved employment, is the objective of the social welfare resulting from the economic development process. With regard to consumption, Latin American conditions are dismal for 70% of the population, according to some estimates (Lindqvist 1972). Population control is not the sole solution but it is a good solution. Latin America has realized this and is stimulating family planning programs.

Sociological Significance of Trade Areas

After production, trade is a fundamental condition of social, economic and political relations in all societies, even those as ideologically guided as the societies of Latin America. In the mid-seventies one can easily still find large areas of the hemisphere where trade is restricted to the boundaries of the village or township. This applies to regions in central and southern Mexico, to most of Central America, to the Andean countries including Paraguay, and to the hinterlands of the remaining countries. They are not truly peasant societies but they are certainly rural or semirural. Although the contrast between these regions and the highly urbanized areas (discussed on p. 35) is sharp, the contrast becomes sharper if one excludes the marginal sectors of the large cities. The physical continuity from the commercial, industrial and upper middle-class residential areas of the Latin American city to its adjacent proletarian and lower class quarters is deceiving. The ocntrast between these urban areas and the rural region is also deceiving. The observer is dealing with different types of trade areas and different types of trade relations.

To develop this point we can conceive of four types of trade areas that interlock, often in the same region, although the first to be mentioned may not be found at all in many regions for reasons explicit in its character.

The first is the tribal-linguistic trade area characteristic of Indian regions and described on page 13. Although this trade is today part of the money economy of the various countries, neverthless it still contains cultural features of bartering and of intertribal and intra-lingual traditional interaction. When members of the tribe move to metropolitan areas, their trade traditions reappear in organized form in the peripheries of those areas. This type of trade, although pre-dominantly Indian, is not purely Indian. There are plenty of non-Indian participants who have learned to adjust their Westernized be-havior to the transactions of tribal-linguistic trade, who have also learned Indian ways and language, and who respect the personal re-lations that this type of trade implies.

The second type of trade is the local and regional commercial trade. Impersonal in character, true commercialism becomes evident and understood in this type. It is almost totally capitalistic, conducted for profit and oriented toward metropolitan and national consump-tion. It is here that the middle man functions in a clear role without any consideration to the economic conditions of the producer. It is a "free" trade. Peasants and small farmers participate in this trade net-work with the full realization that the forces of the market are heart-less and that in the face of them the small producer is powerless. No organization has ever helped him. With few exceptions, farmers co-operatives have historically failed in Latin America, although in re-cent years the Inter-American Development Bank has extended credit to all forms of cooperatives to the amount of 272 million dollars (*IDB News,* March 1977).

The third type of trade to be introduced is the con-urban peri-pheral, almost indistinguishable, considering the transactions invol-ved, from the tribal-linguistic trade. Again, it is only a mixture of barter, credit and money. The buyer can only afford small purchases at a time or has to pay when he is paid or has to actually trade things or. labor for the commodities "bought." It is a trade both institutionally and physically peripheral. It is peripheral to the commercial market just considered and to the industrial one to be discussed, and it is peripheral to rural and urban communities alike. The North Ameri-can reader must remember that most Latin American suburbias are the "marginal" areas where the unemployed and underemployed tend to dwell.

Finally there is the industrial trade, where a heavy exchange of manufactured commodities and of services takes place, physically located in the heart of small and large cities and in extensions of these "hearts" throughout the metropolitan community. This is also undertaken clearly for profit and also penetrated by secondary and tertiary activities. The first and third types of trade areas are characterized by primary products, fundamentally agricultural, whereas the second type is mixed.

The industrial type of trade is the one closely tied with foreign investment and foreign trade, although a great deal of the products exported are primary. These primary products, however, are not produced by peasants and small farmers. They normally come from the hacienda, the plantation and similar forms of extractive enterprises such as lumbering and mining companies.

These ideal types of trade make no sense unless the relationship between dependency and exploitation is fully understood. By and of themselves they make nice socioanthropological classifications, but they do not offer any insight into the processes at work. It is the relationship of economic domination and subordination between capital accumulation at the top and sheer survival and subsistence at the bottom that makes sense.

There is a suction effect running from the bottom to the top in the closely interlocked trade system that has kept Latin America underdeveloped or, more exactly, great portions of Latin America underdeveloped. Others have called this process "internal colonialism." But there is no longer any colonialism. In the colonial condition there is no free trade because the political process controls the economic process. Under present conditions the economic process is at the bottom independent of political controls, and at the top controls the political process, as may be seen more clearly next.

The internal or domestic trade systems are ultimately subordinated to external or foreign trade regardless of whether the markets abroad are located in the United States, the Soviet Union or China. Sociologically this is so because local social class structures create and are created synchronously by the trade systems. The author has observed the formation of these structures throughout the years. Unfortunately, in the original edition no attention was paid to the role of trade in the process. Most observers have concentrated on the structuration of occupations as a function of technological change. This perspective minimizes and obscures the significance of trade in class formation. It also minimizes the spatial features of both trade centers and of the social classes that grow in these centers. A look at a map indicating the location of economic activities in Latin America will convince the observer of the validity of this position. With the exception of a few secondary cities in Argentina and Colombia, all other centers of economic activity are located on the seashores of the continent, oriented toward and linked to foreign trade. And it is a deficit foreign trade (see Odell and Preston, op. cit., p. 188).

Oligarchies occupy the place they do because they have been able to control and even monopolize the foreign and domestic trade of the commodities they produce. Moreover, through their financing of their suppliers in the lower levels of the trade system described, they are also able not only to maximize their gains but to guarantee the existence of the groups with which they trade. In this way the oligarchies have been able to perpetuate and enlarge the traditional disparity of income distribution that affects Latin American societies and that other authors have discussed.

The solution to this most critical Latin American problem would be *un crecimiento hacia adentro* (an inward growth), to use the expression of Raul Prebisch, but not primarily for Latin America as postulated by Prebisch. It would be an inward growth within each country—that is, income distribution must be expanded in order to increase the purchasing power of the non-industrial trade areas so that people in these areas gain access to basic commodities. The best example of what *not* to do in this connection is Uruguay, which ran itself into bankruptcy by allowing Montevideo to grow, the price being the starvation of the rest of the nation. The best example of what to do is Cuba, which decentralized economic growth from Havana. True believers of course hate this model. For the moderate there must be a middle road. It has yet to emerge in the continent.

Latin American Integration

Efforts to integrate Latin America are as old as the political inde-. pendence of the countries themselves. Simon Bolivar dreamed of a United States of Latin America and organized La Gran Colombia, consisting of the countries that today compose the Andean

Group—Venezuela, Colombia, Ecuador, Peru and Bolivia. Bolivar's dream was never attempted, and his Gran Colombia began to disintegrate while he was still living. On his death the disintegration became total. For his model Bolivar had the United States of America. But his was a political integration with no consideration for and no foundation on economic realities. Even the brightest leader often falls victim to the prevalent zeitgeist. The 19th century saw the consolidation of the nation-state, a political reality to which economic factors were subordinated. It has taken the economic awareness of the 20th century for Latin America to move toward economic integration (and this only after World War II) and it will probably take until the 21st century for Latin America to pay attention to social inequality.

Until recently, Latin America has been basically an exporter of primary products (bananas, copper, coffee, iron, oil) to the industrialized world (the United States, Canada and Europe). Until recently, Latin American countries have focussed on internal national political integration, accompanied by some internal economic integration. The emphasis has been on counterinsurgency, assisted at one time by the US Green Berets and the CIA. Latin American economic integration has been a phenomenon of the 60's as a consequence of the foreign exchange crises of the late 50's. In other words, Latin American integration has been a byproduct of its unfavorable foreign trade relations with the First World. The increasing external debt has aggravated Latin America's dependency to alarming proportions and has awakened the continent to an inward development—that is, a development from within, both national and regional.

This is not to deny the significance of other internal forces for economic integration. Population pressures have already been analyzed and demands for employment considered. As a response, large investments in industrial development have been made, with no significant effect on income distribution. In 1970, for example, the following disparities in per capita income were observed:

INCOME PERCENTILE	AVERAGE INCOME ($ AT 1960 PRICES)
30% of the population with the lowest incomes	73
Next 50% of population	273
Next 15% of population	940
Top 5% of population	2,815
Overall average	440

Thus the level of income of the top 5% was 39 times higher than the level of income of the poorest 30% of the Latin American population (Pinto and DiFilippo, 1976, p. 96).

Equally remarkable are the disparities in per capita income from country to country. From data given in the IDB report for 1975 the following table has been derived and the countries listed in rank order.

Table 16   Gross Domestic Product Per Capita
Latin American Countries 1974
(in 1973 dollars)

COUNTRY	AMOUNT	COUNTRY	AMOUNT
Argentina	1,482.9	Nicaragua	652.9
Venezuela	1,421.6	Guatemala	620.1
Trinidad and Tobago	1,101.4	Dominican Republic	612.2
Chile	1,083.2	Peru	494.5
Panama	1,052.1	Colombia	450.6
Jamaica	1,004.1	El Salvador	434.3
Uruguay	936.1	Ecuador	429.4
Mexico	771.2	Paraguay	383.0
Barbados	770.5	Honduras	372.7
Brazil	759.5	Bolivia	270.8
Costa Rica	754.9	Haiti	154.1

SOURCE. Inter American Development Bank, Economic and Social Progress in Latin America, Annual Report 1975, passim.

Argentina (and closely behind, Venezuela) has a per capita income almost ten times higher than Haiti and five times higher than Bolivia. Argentina, by contrast, has a per capita income five times lower than the United States, whose per capita income is about 50 times that of Haiti.

These and other harsh economic realities have transformed concerns for political integration into concerns for economic integration. The first has been an attempt to keep the societies in order through discipline—military discipline. Eventually the military itself has come to realize the uselessness of institutionalized violence to keep internal peace. Thus the continent has seen an upsurge of "leftist" military regimes, clearly engaged in fundamental reforms. The cases of Peru, Bolivia and Ecuador have been outstanding.

The remainder of this section will be devoted to an overview of recent efforts made by Latin American countries to integrate their national markets, to strengthen regional international trade areas, often with the assistance of multinational corporations, and to the future of Latin American cooperation vis-a-vis the capitalist and socialist systems.

The most impressive effort for national economic integration in Latin America was the one by President Juscelino Kubitschek (1956-61) to move the capital of Brazil from the lush bay of Guanabara to the open lands of Goias, almost a thousand kilometers toward the interior. The construction of Brasilia began in 1956, the first year of Kubitschek's term in office. At the same time German steel makers were invited to locate in Belo Horizonte, about 600 kilometers southeast of Brasilia, toward the coast. Roads were to be built in all directions from the new national capital to the state capitals. The idea was to move Brazil's development west—toward Rio Branco, Porto Velho and Manaus in the Amazon's hinterlands and thus to link the west to the east. At the time, the idea was thought to be absurd. Twenty years later the dream has become reality. Brazil's well known industrial triangle stretches from Rio to Belo Horizonte to Sao Paulo. It is now possible to travel by land from Porto Alegre near Uruguay in the south to Belem on the mouth of the world's largest river in the north, passing through Brasilia. And it is also possible to go by car from Sao Paulo to Peru, again via Brasilia. In each case the distances are immense.

To be sure, the interior of the country has not yet been brought into full contact with the industrial and populated east coast. There are likewise large areas of the center still untamed. Also, the cost in both economic and human terms has been beyond belief. The fact remains that the integration process is working relatively well, rapidly and ruthlessly.

If the internal development of Brazil has been multidirectional, development in Argentina has been primarily in the northwest, toward Rosario and Cordoba. Development in Brazil has originated from the central government in Brasilia with the full assistance of Sao Paulo's captains of industry. In contrast, Rosario and Cordoba have had to fight for development against the highly centralized economy of the Buenos Aires-La Plata industrial axis.

Historically, since colonial times, Mendoza, due west from Buenos Aires on the border with Chile, has developed with its own natural resources, water, climate and soil and with European know-how into the wine and dried fruit industry center of the nation. More than three-fourths of the wine exported by Argentina, itself the fourth wine producer in the world, comes from Mendoza (Crossley 1971). Similarly, the "littoral" provinces on the Parana-Plata estuary can trace their development back in history. Thus the economic integration of Argentina is not a recent phenomenon. What is of recent vintage is integration toward the periphery or, rather, a more even economic growth from Buenos Aires toward the provincial urban centers. With political stability based on better income distribution, Argentina could easily return to the prosperity of earlier decades. the country already has the highest literacy rate and the lowest population growth rate in the continent.

The contemporary development of Venezuela, the country with the second highest per capita income in Latin America, and its attempts at economic integration, are based almost totally on oil revenues. Without them, Venezuela would probably have a negative balance of payments like the non-oil-producing countries, with the exception of Argentina. As it is, Venezuela's $6 billion plus favorable trade balance almost canceled out the $7 billion unfavorable balance of payments of Brazil in 1974 (IDB, op. cit., p. 398). The main efforts at economic integration have been centered in the northern corridor of the country running from Caracas to Maracaibo. The planned city of Guyana in the eastern part of the country is a relatively minor extension considering that most of the national territory remains out of the mainstream of integration. In a sense, Venezuela is a replica of Argentina, although their source of wealth is different—oil and cattle respectively. But the prevalence of one primary city and the extension of a development corridor from it in only one direction are similar.

For some time this was also the case in Mexico. For decades, Mexico City absorbed industry and population. Currently it is the largest city in the world in population, but industrial expansion has moved toward Puebla in the south, toward Cuernavaca in the west and toward Queretaro in the north. Moreover, Mexico City's hegemony has been challenged by Monterrey, not too far from the U.S. south-central frontier, and Guadalajara in Mexico's central region. Since 1965, with the stimulation of the northern border industrialization program, the Mexican cities of Matamoros, Reynosa, Ciudad Juarez, Nogales, Mexicali and Tijuana have successfully added industrial development and population pull. In the last two decades these border cities have grown dramatically.

Until two years ago, when huge oil deposits were found in the south, Mexico's economy was anchored primarily on tourism from the United States and agriculture. Now oil is the principal source of revenues. However, the attraction of employment in the United States remains a high incentive in the migration of Mexican population northward and in the growth of the border cities mentioned. Actually, it is the U.S. influence—among other means, through the twin plant program—that has revitalized Mexico's border frontier. Even the large irrigated agricultural areas of Nayarit and Sonora in the northwest and of Coahuila and Tamaulipas in the northeast aim their products at the U.S. markets. Thus Mexico, because of its unique geographic location bordering the United States, has been able to combine inward and outward development rather well. Its big problems have been population growth, the largest in the hemisphere, for which the United States has been an escape valve, and the heavy industrialization program, machine-based, that makes little use of the abundant labor supply.

By contrast with the countries discussed so far, the development of Colombia has been bipolar. Two centers of power have historically faced each other—Bogota, the capital of the country, and Medellin, its industrial heart. At one time the wealth of Medellin was based on mining. The rugged conditions of the Colombian geography have contributed to the split that has now been opened up by the recent growth of widely dispersed centers of commerce. South of Medellin, in the upper Cauca valley, Cali has become an industrial and agricultural metropolis. North of Medellin on the Caribbean sea, at the mouth of the Magdalena river, Barranquilla has become the largest Colombian port. On the low Andean mountains entering Venezuela, Bucaramanga, northeast of Bogota, has in turn attracted population and investment from oil, cattle and farming enterprises. Thus the mountains and valleys of Colombia, less than half of the national territory, are relatively integrated. The other regions—the east and southeast, the *llanos* (lowlands) and the jungles adjacent to the jungles of Venezuela, Brazil, Peru and Ecuador—remain marginal.

In explaining Colombian integration, the unique physiographic structure must be related to the unique social class structure. In no other Latin American country have two oligarchies been able to retain power in a true elitist fashion for so long and with so little spillover to the masses. In few other countries has foreign exchange been so generously spent on luxury goods. It is perhaps symbolic that Colombia is the only country on earth where a gallon of gasoline costs only 15 cents (U.S.).

The other Andean countries—Ecuador, Peru and Bolivia—owe their higher level of economic activity of recent years to oil, fishing (except Bolivia) and mining. More than other South American countries, these three lack the elementary infrastructure necessary for the beginning of a healthy economic integration. Bolivia, in particular, is far from developing a good transportation system linking the various parts of the country. Manufacturing, significant in the formation of a middle class and a proletariat, is strong in Ecuador, weak in Bolivia and somewhat less weak in Peru. The Marginal Highway, projected by Belaunde Terry, is under piecemeal construction but very far from its goal, which is to link Venezuela, Colombia, Ecuador, Peru and Bolivia with Brazil at various points and Paraguay and Argentina at the eastern foot of the Andes. It is intended to attract colonization and to open new lands for present-day marginal families. of the three countries, Bolivia has the most problems and the lowest per capita income; of the three, Peru carries the highest foreign debt, exceeding $800 million in 1974. However, Peru has just found (May 1977) large new oil deposits in the east and has finished building an oil pipeline to carry 30,000 barrels daily to the Pacific.

As in Colombia, economic integration is bipolar in Ecuador. Guayaquil, the industrial city and port on the Pacific, rivals Quito in power and development, attracting about equal waves of interprovincial migrations. In Peru, Lima and the coastal departments south of Lima continue to dominate the socioeconomic structure of the country, with little hope for the north and the interior. Finally Bolivia, landlocked since 1881, has barely integrated the Altiplano that runs from La Paz to Sucre and Potosi through Oruro and Cochabamba. In the meantime, the eastern two-thirds of the country remain empty and isolated.

The government of Chile has been considering the decentralization of the economy from the central area (Santiago-Concepcion-Valparaiso) toward the north and south of the country. No recent information on the results is available. Since agricultural productivity declined during the Allende regime because of rapid advances in agrarian reform, the subsequent military dictatorship restored more than 3,000 farm units to individual producers in 1975. The results are not yet known. Unemployment rates, low in the early 70's, rose again to 16.5% at the end of 1975. Results of the 1976 plan to curb unemployment remain to be seen. Thus the conditions of Chilean integration are at this moment obscure. What is clear is that, given the political consciousness of the Chilean masses, the planned decentralization will diffuse resistance to the brutalities of the regime but not without some consideration to distributive justice.

Paraguay and Uruguay close the discussion of South American countries. The contrast between the two is remarkable. They are completely different not only geographically but in the ethnic composition of the population, in the class structure and in degrees of socioeconomic integration. Paraguay is rural, has an extractive type of economy, is landlocked like Bolivia, and is ruled with iron hands that have forced one-fourth of the population into exile in Argentina and thousands of others to Brazil, Bolivia and Uruguay. Lacking, like Bolivia, the most elementary infrastructure, the little integration there is stretches from the capital Asuncion to Encarnacion on the southeastern border near the province of Misiones in Argentina and west to Puerto Iguazu on the border with Brazil. The north and northeast, over three-fourths of the country, remain terribly underdeveloped and inaccessible.

In contrast with Paraguay, the imbalance of Uruguay leans toward extreme centralization of economic activities in the capital, Montevideo, and in the rest of the coast toward Buenos Aires. While this region progresses, the rest of the country languishes. In Paraguay the burden of development is carried by the peasants, in Uruguay by farmers and the urban middle classes.

The six Central American republics may be grouped into two integration and development stages: Panama and Costa Rica, neighbors in the southeast of the region, and El Salvador, Nicaragua, Honduras and Guatemala in the northwest. Panama used to be a province of Colombia until the United States inspired and assisted its independence in 1903. When Mexico obtained its independence from Spain in 1821, the province of Chiapas joined the new confederation. Two years later the other provinces formed a short-lived Central American republic. As in the case of La Gran Colombia, the few rich families of the area, with little in common and great wealth to protect, came to cherish power. But it was a feudal power, economically extractive and exploitive, that returned to the land and its products the bare minimum through investment. It is well known that to this day one family rules in Nicaragua.

Under the impact of the economic realities of the war and post-war periods, the Central America republics did turn some of their attention to internal integration. Panama began to penetrate the interior, mostly toward Costa Rica. Costa Rica in turn began to move toward the Pacific. El Salvador, unable to introduce reforms in land tenure, began to lose population to Honduras, causing a short armed conflict in the 60's, the "Soccer War" of 1969. Guatemala has been corroded by internal warfare reflecting the imbalance in land and income distribution and by losses of people to Mexico. Honduras, concentrated in the Altiplano by history, custom, and climate, shares with Nicaragua the largest inhospitable tropical lowlands of the region extending toward and along the Caribbean Sea. Even though all of these countries depend on three crops—coffee, bananas and sugarcane. Honduras still is *the* banana republic of the area. Of all these countries only Panama has seriously planned diversification, including a decreasing dependence on the Canal's revenues. In every case, as in Paraguay and Bolivia to the south, the Indian and the peasant pay the price of urban growth, and when they migrate to the cities they become victims of urban decay.

The countries in the Caribbean islands offer a variety of models of development and of internal or national integration. Puerto Rico, an appendage to the US economy in the form of a commonwealth, has decentralized by regions, and exports huge numbers of migrants to the mainland. Cuba, in the socialist bloc, has forced out dissenters and decentralized by regions, and exports huge numbers of migrants to the mainland. Cuba, in the socialist bloc, has forced out dissenters and decentralized again by regions, creating with the help of the USSR a very healthy but dependent integration. The other three countries that (unlike Cuba) form part of the inter-American system are very badly developed. Jamaica's higher per capita income, based primarily on mining and tourism, conceals a very unequal distribution of income, thus hampering further integration and development. The Dominican republic, "characterized in the early 70's by a relatively well diversified productive structure," is also characterized by a "marked dualism between urban and rural development and a skewed income distribution" (IDB, op cit., p. 214). Haiti is the last case in the hemisphere not only of underdevelopment but of self-destruction. "Reduced to its bare bones—only the most optimistic can envisage anything but a totally Malthusian solution in an island lacking any kind of resource including soil productivity" (Niddrie, 1971, p. 105).

For years Latin American countries have realized that national integration is unattainable without the regional integration that by-passes national boundaries. An excellent example of the good resulting from international cooperation is the Pan-American Health Organization, formed at the beginning of the century. An earlier but less successful effort materialized in 1890 with the establishment of the International Union of American Republics, the predecessor of the Organization of American States (OAS) born at the Chapultepec Conference in 1945. These organizations have been political in nature, though with economic undertones. Years later, under pressure fom Latin America, the United States accepted the need for an Inter-American Development Bank, which was established in 1958. The Bank has been the real backbone of the Latin American integration crystallizing in the hemisphere presently.

As the charter of the OAS was being drawn up in 1948, the UN was organizing the Economic Commission for Latin America (ECLA) that from its inception was utilized by Raul Prebisch to stimulate the economic integration of the region. However, it took twelve years for two organizations of nations concerned with widening their trade zones to emerge. The Latin American Free Trade Association (LAFTA) and the Central American Common Market (CACM) were established in 1960. The first consisted of Mexico and the independent nations of South America—Colombia, Venezuela, Brazil, Uruguay, Argentina, Paraguay, Chile, Bolivia, Peru and Ecuador. The second consisted of five Central American republics—Guatemala, Honduras, El Salvador, Nicaragua and Costa Rica. Panama did not join either organization. From the beginning the philosophy of ECLA has been to rationalize the economic and social progress of Latin America by import substitution at the national level and by industrialization and the enlargement of trade zones for industrial production. The idea was to decrease dependency by creating local industries, and stimulating their growth by extending the markets over national frontiers. To this end, tariffs had to be lowered or removed and monetary and fiscal policies harmonized.

In organizing these common markets, Latin America could draw from extra-continental and continental experience. First, of course, was the model of the European Economic Community (EEC); more important, some Latin American countries could use their own experience. For years, Argentina, Uruguay, Brazil and Chile had had reciprocal trade agreements and had bartered their main products. Argentina, for example, had traded wheat for Brazilian coffee. Thus Argentina, Brazil and Chile spearheaded the organization of LAFTA that Mexico, Paraguay, Peru and Uruguay later joined. Their efforts were stimulated by ECLA.

Like similar organizations, LAFTA has had good and bad times. At the end of the 70's it has become an effective instrument of Latin American integration. It recently held "the Fourth Round of Collective Negotiations," which resulted in the adoption of guidelines for future formal agreements. Following those negotiating meetings, "the protocol establishing the LAFTA Council of Ministers of Foreign Affairs entered into effect with the deposit of the last instrument of ratification" (IDB, op. cit., p. 101). By 1974, intrazonal trade had increased considerably for almost all member countries, and for all except three the intrazonal balance of payments was positive. It should be remembered that all South American countries and Mexico are members of LAFTA.

Also with the purpose of promoting a balanced industrial production, the Central American Common Market (CACM) has sought to widen the small national trade areas characteristic of the isthmus countries. Costa Rica, El Salvador, Guatemala, Honduras and Nicaragua comprise the organization. Panama and the Caribbean islands, except Cuba, share freely—i.e., without membership—the trade area. The most prosperous years of CACM were the middle

60's. It appears that the late 70's may again be prosperous. This could be a result of the newly organized Economic and Social Community of Central America (EESCA) and of the ECLA Economic Coordinating Committee of the Central American Isthmus held in Tegucigalpa in May 1975.

As in the late 60's (Tancer 1976), CACM countries were still running a balance of trade deficit with the rest of the world in the middle 70's. In this respect they resemble the rest of Latin America except Argentina, Ecuador and Venezuela. As for LAFTA, the intrazonal trade has increased considerably in the last ten years for CACM. Evidently the "Soccer War" of 1969 did not have the deleterious effects that some observers predicted.

Dissatisfied with the performance of LAFTA, President Eduardo Frei of Chile had suggested in 1965 the establishment of a subregional organization to promote socioeconomic integration. In 1968 the Andean Development Corporation (CAF) was established, and in 1969 the Andean Community (ANCOM). An unusual aspect of the charter of ANCOM was the emphasis on "equitable distribution of the benefits derived from integration among the member countries so as to reduce the differences existing between them" (quoted in Tancer 1976, p. 59). ANCOM consists of Chile, Bolivia, Peru, Ecuador, Colombia and Venezuela. In 1975-76 they emphasized the production of petrochemicals, the Andean trunk highway system and agriculture. Bolivia and Ecuador, as less developed countries, were given special consideration in accordance with the founding principles of the Cartagena agreement. Intraregional trade has increased considerably among the member countries, as well as the exchange of technology and technicians.

The Caribbean Free Trade Association (CARIFTA) was created in 1968 after the failure of the West Indian Federation, whose purpose was political unity. At first it consisted of Antigua, Barbados and Guyana, and was later enlarged to include Jamaica, Montserrat, St. Vincent, Trinidad and Tobago, Dominica, Grenada, St. Kitts, Nevis-Anguilla and Santa Lucia (Bradford, 1974, p. 76). Belize (British Honduras), which is still a colony, joined the organization in 1970. The main purposes have been tariff reduction and labor exchange among member nations. CARIFTA has been the parent organization for a new Caribbean Community (CARI-COM) created by Barbados, Guyana, Jamaica and Trinidad and Tobago in 1973. In the accounting of the Inter-American Development Bank these four countries, which are the most prosperous of the group, have also been the most active. The total value of their 1974 trade passed 6 billion dollars. Less than half of this amount went for exports, a deficit again, as for most countries in the hemisphere (IDB, ibid., p. 110). The last effort at integration was made in October 1975 by 23 Latin American countries with the creation of the Latin American Economic System (SELA) to: "a) promote regional cooperation in order to achieve an integral self-sustained and independent development; b) support the integration process of the region; c) promote the preparation of economic and social programs and projects that are relevant to the members; d) operate as a consulting and coordinating mechanism in Latin America in order to formulate joint positions and strategies on economic and social topics; and e) promote measures aimed at ensuring preferential treatment for the relatively less developed countries and special actions for those countries with a limited market" (IDB, ibid., pp. 111-112).

The mind and muscle of recent Latin American integration and development has been the Inter-American Development Bank (see p. 218). No aspect of the socioeconomic life of the area has been left out of its sphere of influence. The emphasis, as could be expected, has been on developing infrastructure and on stimulating productivity. However, education in all its facets has been a significant consideration, as well as the promotion of health and culture. Other banks and similar financial mechanisms have been formed throughout the continent in recent years. In fact the last attempt at overall financial integration took place in Mexico City in March 1975 with the Conference on Financing of Latin American Development (CONFINDE). The conference was convened by Mexico's Nacional Financiera, by the Central American Bank for Economic Integration (CABEI), by the Caribbean Development Bank (CDB), by the Andean Development Corporation (CAF), and by the Latin American Association of Development Finance Institutions (ALIDE).

These efforts are were extremely relevant both for economic integration and for social progress. The most significant meaning, from the point of view of Latin American self-assertion emphasized throughout this book, is that Latin America is promoting development from within. To be sure, reliance on foreign institutions continues to be great. Non-Latin America multinationals continue to be present and their presence is felt everywhere. But Latin American integration aims not only at import substitution but at substituting foreign multinationals by native multinationals. That this could be accomplished may be seen in the commodity agreements or cartels that Latin America has organized or joined in recent years. In other words, Latin America has learned a lesson.

Although the multinationals are not just a contemporary phenomenon in the Third World—there were already land companies and water and land transportation companies operating in several countries—the size and number of such corporations has increased. Some of them are monopolies or oligopolies, such as the United Fruit Company, Grace Line, ITT, Anaconda, Kennecott, Phelps-Dodge and American Smelting, Royal Dutch-Shell, British Petroleum, Exxon, Gulf, Texaco, Chevron and Mobil, IBM, Crown Zellerbach, General Electric, RCA, N.V. Philips and in the automobile field five US corporations, two German, two Italian, three French, two Japanese and one Swedish, to cite the best known (Behrman, 1972). In practically every industrial activity from typewriters to refrigerators, shipping, railroad cars and meat packing, in some commercial activities such as department stores and supermarkets, in services such as banking, there is at least one multinational. Frequently, local companies are hidden subsidiaries of foreign multinationals.

Multinationals have been praised for all the good and blamed for all the evil in development and underdevelopment. It has been said that they have modernized the continent—although for the few, not for the masses; that they have brought capital—but taken more than they have invested; that they have contributed to technological development—but retained the well paid managerial positions; that they have spread industries—but only if local governments provide the infrastructure; that they have stimulated education—but taken away the most capable. And so on, ad infinitum. The literature from both sides is growing, as can be seen in the selected bibliography at the end of this Postscript.

It is not just in the last few years that Latin American nations have tried to face collectively the problem of unstable prices for the primary products they export. While the industrialized countries can control the prices of the machinery they sell, developing nations either deal with perishable commodities or they depend on one or few as major sources of foreign exchange. Thus for decades the developing nations have tried to negotiate commodity agreements to stabilize prices. In the 30's, for example, they reached agreements on tin, wheat, rubber, timber, tea, sugar, beef, and coffee. These agreements were short-lived. After World War II, Latin American countries began to arrive at more durable agreements. Here are some illustrations: In 1962 Latin America joined forces with African nations to induce Europe and the United States to accept a coffee commodity agreement. The International Coffee Agreement (ICA), as it is called, was renewed in 1968, 1973 and 1975. The 1977 prices are, however, not only related to the agreement but to bad weather conditions in Brazil. It should be added that the agreement is not just a price-setting mechanism. It establishes quotas for participating countries.

After ten years of continuing efforts to arrive at a cocoa commodity agreement, an association of producers was finally established in 1965. Originally from Mexico, cocoa is now produced in larger quantities by some African nations.

The petroleum cartel has been the most successful ever. It was first suggested by Venezuela in the 1940's and created in 1960, naturally disturbing the multinationals of the oil oligopoly. What had made the producing nations mobilize for final action was a sudden unilateral reduction in price decided by the companies in 1959 and again at the beginning of 1960. Immediately, Venezuela, Iran, Iraq, Saudi Arabia and Kuwait created OPEC, which had doubled its membership by 1974 when the oil embargo and price increase shook the world. For the first time the industrialized nations came to realize that the rules of the game they had set and upheld high-handedly for so many years could be used against their interests.

Since 1973 other cartels have been created with Latin American participation. The most critical have been the ones for iron ore, bauxite, copper, sugar and bananas. The last two have been most difficult to coalesce. For the sugar convention Cuba returned to the fold of Latin American collective action. And to attack the problems wholesale Jose Figueres of Costa Rica even organized a United Front of Exporters of Raw Materials (IDB-INTAL, no date, p. 16). Again, Latin America has learned a lesson.

Latin America has learned that to develop within the capitalistic system prevalent in the West, it has to establish two networks of multinationals: One network would control the prices of primary products in the world market in order to assure certain levels of stability of revenues for any planning or budgeting of development. This is the function of the cartel-like organizations. But Latin America must control the prices of industrial products. For this, a second, native network of multinationals must be created and regional markets delineated. LAFTA, CACM and the rest are meeting this need. Neither one nor the other type of multinationals can survive in a politically unstable society. Nor can the third type, the foreign multinationals. In a participatory democracy the claims of the various social classes must be heard. To allow this process in Latin America, where extreme inequalities are rampant, would disturb the required stability. The resulting choice has been centralized control by the state as the administrator or manager of development. Thus military regimes have forced stability everywhere except in Venezuela, Costa Rica and Mexico. Colombia has frequently been ruled by the military even under the present Liberal government in spite of the fact that over 500,000 Colombians, most of them without papers, work in Venezuela, where the oil wealth is building infrastructures for which labor is needed. This explains in part the temporary democracy of Venezuela. Costa Rica is a land of farmers; and Mexico's one party system, as discussed on page 124, is a conglomerate of pressure groups benefiting a labor aristocracy and the technocrats, but again forcing millions to live, mostly illegally, in the United States. No wonder that some writers have talked about the underdevelopment of development (Frank, 1967, 1969 among others).

There is another cold and tearful fact. A second cost of this imposed stability has been torture and terrorism, both documented and condemned in respectable international forums; various forms of old human exploitation such as chattel slavery, debt bondage, serfdom, sham adoption and exploitation of children, traffic in persons and even servile forms of marriage that the Anti-Slavery Society of London has helped to solve (Katz, 1977); and the conventional forms of unemployment and underemployment referred to on page 200. For some, the conditions are better than they were before; for others, the conditions have deteriorated if one considers how far other countries and the local privileged groups have gone.

The task facing Latin American nations, although not as critical as the one faced by many other nations in the developing world (Vasena and Pazos, 1973), is obviously immense. In undertaking it Latin America has used various models of development, but none of them has been purely capitalistic—i.e. fully based on the free enterprise system. On the opposite side one of them has been clearly socialistic, the Cuban model. Salvador Allende tried a Marxist democracy in Chile, with the results and the end that are well known. Of the military regimes (five in Central America and seven in South America) none is clearly on the left or clearly on the right. In fact, a political pragmatism is penetrating the Latin American political scene. By 1973 an Uruguayan economist and executive secretary of ECLA could say: "We have a socialist Latin America; we have a capitalist Latin America in the sense used by the industrialized community; we have intermediate regimes that utilize revolutionary systems to advance high intensity processes of change; we have countries advancing through the strong dynamics of the external sector; we have economies based, fundamentally, on the intensive exploration of their internal resources. We have such a number of different cases that from the start we must be cautious about any intent to generalize" (Iglesias, 1973, p. 48).

Not that ideological battles have ceased. It is when the final decision is made that the influence or fear of the group with the most clout prevails; and no group is ideologically pure. Kalman Silvert's characterization of Latin America as a conflict society is as accurate today as it ever was. Nevertheless, the process of integration, both national and regional, continues. it can be said of the trade area, "In 1975, Latin American countries purchased goods totaling $5.4 billion *within* the region, an eightfold increase over 1960" (*IDB News,* April 1977, Vol. 4, No. 3, p. 6).

Summary and Policy Implications

The preceding has been a summary of the major problems that Latin America faces in the 70's. As with all overviews they run the risk of simplifying realities that are complex in themselves and in their connections with other realities. Population has continued to grow faster than in other continents, although not at the same rate everywhere, and people continue to abandon a rural life that in many instances is worse than the urban conditions they enter. True, population growth rates have decreased a little and economic growth has increased. Nevertheless, even in those countries where the latter are higher than the former, the standard of living of the masses has not improved significantly. Thus unemployment and underemployment remain a serious problem.

By the same token large segments of population remain trapped in trade areas delineated by ethnic and linguistic boundaries, thus allowing for the coexistence of feudal, capitalist and industrial societies characterized by very distinct economic power. These societies are not adjacent; there is a hierarchy in which the benefits of trade tend to accumulate as in the past in the hands of the few, resulting in the deprivation of the majority. The middle classes, including the new technocracy, have increased. The proletariat has increased, but they continue to live beyond their means, whereas the masses have not reached decent levels of consumption and the upper class spends on undertaxed luxury goods. Thus the trade areas discussed perpetuate more or less the same general and class structures and more or less the same concentration of wealth.

Finally, Latin American integration has followed an uncertain course, but it has not collapsed. On the contrary, its prospects for the future are based now on solid facts and on clear awareness. To be sure, Latin American capital continues to move in unknown amounts to the industrial world, draining the local sources of investment as a result. In this way, however, it has added to the over-accumulation of capital already existing in the First World and it is returning, with less risk, under the aegis of the foreign multinationals. This process and the consolidation of primary commodity cartels must result in the interlocking of the three types of multinationals into a solid network.

This will expand and improve the technocracy still more and will perhaps open some opportunities to the masses. How many and how fast is the question.

Latin American has not tried to solve these problems piecemeal. It has undertaken massive programs of reconstruction and development. To meet the population problem, family planning services may be found in any barrio, town and village, and decentralization efforts have been made or are under consideration at least where the population concentration problem has become excessive. The problem is so serious is some instances that the effort, no matter how great, seems insignificant compared with the result. Mexico, for example, borrowed $120 million dollars from the World Bank in the Spring of 1976 to stimulate the family planning program. It is quite probable that the effect of this effort, a considerable one for the Mexican economy, may not be noticeable within the next five years. Venezuela's planned city might appear as a small effort in the eyes of foreign observers, but for the country it is significant. In brief, both governments and people are aware of and are acting on the population problem.

There have also been huge investments in infrastructure. An extensive network of farm-to-market and colonization roads has been planned and is gradually being constructed throughout the continent. Given the configuration of the land and the frequent and heavy rains in the tropical zones, these works are difficult and expensive. The Pan-American highway has not been connected between Panama and Colombia precisely for these reasons—the terrain is swampy here and rugged there, the climate hot and humid, the whole zone uninhabited. The "Marginal Highway" of the Andean countries mentioned on page 215 faces similar difficulties. The costs are immense and the countries poor.

Water projects for both irrigation and home use have been undertaken. Sewage lines in urban centers are always in the process of construction and reconstruction. Power plants are being built, streets paved, public buildings erected, schools opened, machinery for infrastructure works imported, seldom produced locally. Funds for all this must be raised internally and externally; thus the state debt is constantly on the increase. These projects mentioned produce little or no income.

From all of this it is not difficult to see the tremendous task of coordinating the trade areas discussed and of bringing disparate communities into physical contact. At the same time, radio and television make the masses aware of their needs and their rights, of what other countries like the United States have done. People then demand instand attention that even the most populist government cannot give unless it goes, like Cuba, all the way.

It is in this light that Latin America's movement toward integration makes perfect sense. What does not make sense is that its implementation has been lopsided. Great emphasis has been placed on industrialization and import substitution, with the virtual neglect of agriculture and rural life and of the purchasing power of the masses. The basic form of integration is integration of the industrial and agricultural sectors. Unfortunately it was thought that agriculture had to be industrialized on a large scale—i.e. developed into agribusiness. It was thought that the small farm was inefficient and low in productivity. The temporary decrease in productivity that follows every attempt at agrarian reform has been taken as permanent. The orientation has been, of course, to the foreign market, to the balance of foreign exchange. It has been, fundamentally, economic. People count as producers not as consumers. In spite of the claims, it has in fact been a feudal not a truly modern capitalistic orientation.

In this context the old conflict between town and country has not been resolved but sharpened. Schooling has been technical and industrial, with a view to the large machinery of the urban setting. Small power tools for the farmer have been an incidental, second thought. The dream has been the huge combine, the giant tractor, the field open to the horizon. In a land of abundant labor the choice has been machine-intensive production—a choice that has created a dilemma.

The forces at work are understandable. All the forms of community known to mankind coexist in Latin America: the gathering, the hunting, the agricultural feudal, the industrial. The development of Latin America has been outward, and until very recently colonial, and still is within the sphere of influence of imperialistic nations of contrasting ideological hues. The development of Latin America has been upward, in the direction of the primary cities where government and industrial leaders reside. They in turn have been oriented toward Paris, London and New York City, historically in that order. Ironically, the economic development of Latin America has been anti-economical, as the weakness or failure of internal market indicates.

Latin America has been caught, then, in a field of forces like a piece of iron pulled by magnets from all directions—from the direction of foreign demand and internal consumption; from the center and the periphery in the world economic system; from the class at the top and the classes at the bottom; from the infrastructure and the superstructure; from the metropolis and the rural village; from Christian policies and Marxist principles; from communism, socialism and capitalism; from the *oikos* and the *polis* or from the home and the collectivity; from thrift and conspicuous consumption. To find the right course has been, and will continue to be, difficult. There are no simple solutions. But free advice may be obtained from the Protestant ethic credited with the development of capitalism: stimulate thrift and cut out conspicuous consumption. Advice may also come from the older Greek posture on wisdom and social justice, easy to elucidate but difficult to practice. To bring back wisdom and social justice to the *polis* may take more forceful marches, strikes and demonstrations and even revolutions. John F. Kennedy once said that those who make social change impossible make social revolutions feasible. This fundamental dilemma still persists in Latin America.

Glossary

Foreign terms in alaphabetical order.

Abrazo   embrace
Adelantado   the representative of the Crown in early colonial times
Aggiornamento   up-dating (in latter-day Roman Catholicism)
Alianza Popular Revolucionaria Americana (APRA)   American Popu-
   lar Revolutionary Alliance
Alianzas   alliances, usually political
Alma   soul, meaning a cultural complex rather than a psychic phe-
   nomenon
Amigulsmo   the exaggerated emphasis on friendship
Animas benditas   the blessed souls (of Purgatory)
ALALC, Associacion Latino Americana de Libre Comercio   Latin
   American Free Trade Association
a la norteamericana   in the American way
Barriada   a generalizing term for the slums around the cities in most
   countries
Barrio   city quarter, sector, frequently working or lower class
Basílica   a title which is conferred upon certain churches by the Pope
   as a special honor; a church so honored
blanco   white; a member of the white race
Bogotazo   the riots of April 9, 1948 in Bogota, the capital of Colombia
   and the subsequent 3-day abortive revolution
Caballerosidad   gentlemanly behavior; male courtesy, often assumed
   false
Caboclos   in Brazil, an American Indian or Indian-white mixture
   (Freyre, *The Masters and the Slaves,* p. xv)

231

Cacique   Indian chief; county political boss
Caciquismo   the cultural characteristic of accepting *caciques*
Callampas   Chilean for *favelas*; mushrooms
Casa grande   the house, always large, where the plantation owner lived with his legitimate family; also, the home in which a man shelters his legitimate family
Casa chica   the place a man keeps his mistress
Caudillo   usually a self-made leader followed by his relatives and friends
Colegio   an often private school for children of ages 6-20; sometimes a boarding school
Colonizadores   settlers, the Iberians that colonized the new continent
Colorado   the liberal party of Uruguay
Comadre   literally co-mother. See *compadre* below
Comandos Populares   a militant political party in Chile
Compadrazgo   the socioreligious bond between *compadres* (parents and godparents)
Compadre   co-parent; the person selected to represent the parents in the baptismal ceremony by holding the child up to the baptizing minister; the child's parents in relation to the godparents
Comunas   a small political subdivision of city government; also a *barrio*
Congregación   a religious association
Congregaciones marianas   associations usually of women, dedicated to Mary
Con los tuyos con razón o sin ella   your relatives, right or wrong
Conquistador   conqueror, normally Spanish or Portuguese
Coronelismo   another expression for *generalismo*, with obvious emphasis on lower levels
Criollo   originally the child of Spaniards or Portuguese born in Latin America
Culatismo   the systematic enforcement of order and political power through the police (gun butt)
Cura   parish priest; technically the church parson; loosely, any priest
Día de difuntos   All Souls Day
Dolor   pain, suffering, in a moral, sentimental sense
Duende   sprite; goblin
Égalité   equality
El buen hijo   the good son
El santo de su devoción   the saint of his devotion, his chosen saint
Encomendero   the person or the organization to whom, or to which, the *encomienda* was granted
Encomienda   the Spanish government assignment of Indians, with the land, to a distinguished servant of the Crown, with the obligation to Christianize the Indians and the right to exact labor in return
Es lo último que se pierde   it is the last thing to lose

Estancia   a large cattle ranch on which permanent handlaborers live and work in payment for the use of the parcels they occupy

Facultad; facultades   school(s) in a university system

Familismo   the cultural trait of making nonfamilial relations familial

Favela   Brazilian expression for *barriada*

Fiesta   usually a religious celebration

Filhotismo   an expression (Brazilian) for nepotism

Fraternité   brotherhood (of man)

Fundo   Chilean for *hacienda*

Generalismo   the tendency to accept military men as rulers

Golpismo   the tendency toward coups d'etats

Hacendado   the owner of an *hacienda*

Hacienda   a relatively diversified rural enterprise for which tenants work in payment for the use of the parcels of land they occupy

Hermandad   a religious or quasi-religious association of men

Hispanidad   the cultural trait of recognizing loyalty to hispanic traditions

Indio   Indian, with a connotation of disdain

Junta   board of directors; most often applied to small military ruling groups

La carne   the flesh, implying the pleasures of the body

La dignidad de la persona   the dignity of the person, in a general, rather than an individual sense

Ladino   a Guatemalan term for *mestizo*

La raza   the race, the ethnic and cultural condition of being Latin-American

La raza cósmica   the cosmic race, the end product of the miscegenation of all ethnic groups

La Santa Madre Iglesia   the Holy Mother Church

La vida es una lucha   life is a battle

La violencia   violenco, the Colombian expression for the guerrilla warfare now 20 years old in Colombia

La Virgen del Carmen   Our Lady of Mount Carmel, often the patroness of the armed forces and of prostitues

Las relaciones patronales   labor-management relations

Leguleyismo   the tendency to create legal tangles

Liberté   freedom

Líder   Spanish spelling of leader

Lucha   struggle

Machete   big farm-laborer's knife

Machismo   the quality of manliness

Macho   male, a "real" man; also a male mule

Mana   supernatural power (a Polynesian term very popular in Latin America)

Mañana   tomorrow

Mandonismo   the tendency to tolerate powerful political figures

Matonismo   from *matón* (killer), ruling by threats of death, by the gun

Mayordomo   foreman; often the hacendado's bodyguard

Mestizaje   the quality of being *mestizo* in a sociocultural sense

Mestizo   originally the child of a Spaniard (or a Portuguese) and an Indian; later the child of a European and an Indian, or of *mestizos,* or of a *mestizo* and an Indian

Misa campal   a mass celebrated in the open air

Milagrosa   a name for Mary, who supposedly appeared to a nun in France

Nacional   the aristocratic, conservative party (Chile)

Nació de pie   was born on his feet; lucky

Novena   a formalized series of prayers said for nine consecutive days with some new prayers each day, at the end of which some miracle is anticipated

Organización Latino Americana de Solidaridad, OLAS   a Cuban-founded and housed organization to promote revolution in the hemisphere (*Olas* means waves)

Orgullo   pride, conceit, vanity

Orgulloso   proud, conceited, vain

Palabra   word; *la palabra,* the word, with the implication of firm commitments

Partido de la Revolución Mexicana   Party of the Mexican Revolution

Partido Liberal   Liberal Party

Partido Nacional Revolucionario   National Revolutionary Party

Partido Revolucionario Institucional; PRI   Institutional Revolutionary Party

Patrón   farm boss; landlord; any superior

Patroncito   diminutive of *patrón*

Perro que ladre no muerde   a barking dog does not bite

Personalismo   the attribution of power to the person rather than to the position; cultural tendency to follow persons rather than ideologies

Plaza   town square

Ponerse a la cabeza   to lead, literally to put onself at the head of a group

Presidentialismo   the attitude of expecting presidential solutions to all problems

¿Quién sabe?   who knows?

Rectores   university presidents

Romería   pilgrimage, usually to a distant shrine, to fulfill a pious promise

Salitre   saltpetre; niter; potassium nitrate

Santísimo Sacramento   the Most Holy Sacrament (the Eucharist)

Se obedece pero no se cumple   laws may be obeyed without fulfilling them; that is, laws may always be evaded

Serpentinas   long, thin, colorful paper ribbons

Simpático   charming; originally, compassionate

Tenentismo   derived from lieutenant; the emphasis on proliferation of military rank and power, with a taint of nepotism

Testamento   a verbalized will, mixed with guidance and advice, made public to gathered relatives and friends shortly before dying

Tristeza   sorrow, sadness, with cosmic implications

Tlacotli   Aztec for slave

Turco   Turk, including all who come from the Middle East, except the Jews; sometimes any foreigner

Villas miseria   Argentinian for *barriadas* or *favelas*

Zenzala   the barracks surrounding the plantation house where the slaves were sheltered

Bibliography

Aguilar Monteverde, Alonso. *Teoria y Politica del Desarrollo Latinoamericano.* Mexico: UNAM. 1967.

Amin, Samir. *Accumulation on a World Scale: A Critique of the Theory of Underdevelopment.* Trans. by Brian Pearce. New York and London: Monthly Review Press. Vols. 1 and 2. 1974.

Barnet, Richard, and Ronald Muller. *Global Reach. The Power of Multinational Corporations.* New York: Simon and Schuster. 1974.

Behrman, Jack N. *The Role of International Companies in Latin American Integration.* Lexington, Mass.: Heath. 1972.

Bernard, Jessie. *The Sociology of Community.* Glenview, Illinois: Scott, Foresman. 1973.

Blakemore, Harold, and Clifford T. Smith. *Latin America: Geographical Perspective.* London: Methuen. 1971.

Bravo, Jimenez, Manuel, et al. *El Perfil de Mexico en 1980.* Mexico: Siglo XXI Editores. 1970.

Campos, Roberto de Oliveira. *Reflections on Latin American Development.* Austin and London: University of Texas Press. 1967.

Cardoso, Fernando H. *Empresario Industrial e desenvolvimiento economico: Sao Paulo: Difusao Europeiado Livro.* 1964.

Cardoso, Fernando, H., and E. Faletto. *Dependencia y Desarrollo en America Latina,* Mexico: Siglo XXI Editores. 1970.

Carmona, Fernando, Guillermo Montano, Jorge Carrion and Alonso Monteverde. *El Milagro Mexicano.* Mexico: Editorial Nuestro Tiempo. 3rd edition. 1973.

Chilcote, Ronald H., and Joel C. Edelstein. *Latin America: The Struggle with Dependency and Beyond.* New York: John Wiley. 1974.

Cockroft, James D., Andre Gundar Frank, and Dale L. Johnson. *Dependence and Development,* Garden City, New York: Anchor. 1972.

Conde, Roberto Cortes. *The First Stages of Modernization in Latin America.* New York: Harper and Row. 1974.

Crossley, J, Culin. "The River Plata Countries." In: Blakemore and Smith, 1971. *op. cit.*

Diebold, J. "Why be scared of them." *Foreign Policy* 12 (Fall), 79-95, 1973.

Dos Santos, Theotonio. "The Structure of dependence." *American Economic Review.* May. 1970.

———"The Crisis of development theory and the problem of dependence in Latin America." In: H. Bernstein, ed., *Underdevelopment and Development.* Hammersworth: Penguin. 1973.

Ferguson, Yale H. "Trends in Inter-American Relations: 1972—Mid-1974." In: Ronald G. Hellman and Jon Rosenbaum (eds), *Latin America: The Search for a New International Role.* New York: John Wiley. 1975.

Foxley, Alejandro. *Income Distribution in Latin America.* London: Cambridge University Press. 1976.

Frank, Andre Gunder. *Capitalism and Underdevelopment in Latin America: Historical Studies of Chile and Brazil.* New York and London: Monthly Review Press. 1967.

———*Latin America: Underdevelopment or Revolution.* New York and London: Monthly Review Press. 1969.

———*Lumpenbourgeoisie: Lumpendevelopment—Dependence, Class and Politics in Latin America.* New York and London: Monthly Review Press. 1972.

Furtado, Celso. *Economic Growth of Brazil, A Survey from Colonial to Modern Times.* Berkeley: University of California Press. 1963.

——*Brazil hoy.* Mexico: Siglo XXI Editores. 1970a.

——*Obstacles to Development in Latin America.* Garden City, N.Y.: Anchor.1970b.

——*Economic Development of Latin America: A Survey from Colonial Times to Cuban Revolution.* London: Cambridge University Press. 1971. *Colonial Times to the Cuban Revolution.* London: Cambridge University Press. 1971.

Gilbert, Alan. *Latin American Development: A Geographical Perspective.* Baltimore: Penguin. 1974.

Hellman, Ronald G., and H. Jon Rosenbaum. *Latin America: The Search for a New International Role.* London, Sidney, Toronto, New York: John Wiley. 1975.

Iglesias, Enrique. "La Integracion Economica Latinoamericana en la Planificacion Nacional del Desarrollo." In: E. Wyndham-White et al, p. 48. 1973. *op. cit.*

Inter-American Development Bank, Institute for Latin American Integration. *The Latin American Integration Process in 1974.* Buenos Aires, Argentina. No date.

Jaguaribe, Helio. "Political aspects of economic development in Latin America." In: Claudio Veliz, ed., *Obstacles to Change in Latin America.* New York: Oxford University Press. 1969.

——*Political Development: A General Theory and a Latin American Case Study.* New York: Harper and Row. 1973.

Janvry, Alain de. "The Political Economy of Rural Development in Latin America: An Interpretation." *American Journal of Agricultural Economics.* Vol. 57, No. 3 (August), 493. 1975.

Janvry, Alain de. "Material Determinants of the World Food Crisis." *Berkeley Journal of Sociology.* Vol. 21: 3-26. 1976-77.

Katz, Donald. "The Slave Trade." *The New Republic,* June 4, pp. 19-21. 1977.

Krieger Vasena, Adalbert, and Javier Pazos. *Latin America: A Broader World Role.* London: Ernest Benn, 1973.

Lewis, W. Arthur, *Development Planning: The Essentials of Economic Policy.* New York: Harper and Row. 1966.

Lindqvist, Sven. *The Shadow: Latin America Faces the Seventies.* Baltimore: Penguin. 1969-72.

Liss, Sheldon, and Peggy K. *Man, State and Society in Latin American History.* New York: Praeger. 1972.

Lopez Rosado, Diego. *Problemas Economicos de Mexico.* Mexico: UNAM. 4th Edition. 1975.

Lozada, Salvador Maris. *Dependencia y Empresas Multi-Nacionales.* Buenos Aires: Edit Universitaria. 1974.

MacEoin, Gary. *Revolution Next Door: Latin America in the 1970s.* New York: Holt, Rinehart and Winston. 1971.

Niddrie, David L. "The Caribbean." In: Blakemore and Smith, 1971. *op cit.*

Odell, Peter R., and David A. Preston, *Economies and Societies in Latin America: A Geographical Interpretation.* London, New York, Sidney, Toronto: John Wiley. 1973.

Olien, Michael W. *Latin Americans: Contemporary Peoples and Their Cultural Traditions.* New York: Holt, Rinehart and Winston. 1973.

Oxaal, Ivar, Tony Barnett, and David Booth. *Beyond the Sociology of Development: Economy and Society in Latin America and Africa.* London and Boston: Routledge and Kegan Paul. 1975.

Parkinson, F. *Latin America, the Cold War and the World Powers 1945-1973: A Study in Diplomatic History*. Beverly Hills and London: Sage. 1974.

Penrose Edith. *The Large International Firm in Developing Countries: The International Petroleum Industry*. Cambridge, Mass.: MIT Press. 1968.

Petras, James, ed. *Latin America. From Dependence to Revolution*. New York: Wiley. 1973.

Pinto, Anibal. *Chile: Una Economica Dificil*. Mexico: Fondo de Cultura. 1965.

——_"Political aspects of economic development in Latin America." In: Claudio Veliz, ed., *Obstacles to Change in Latin America*. New York: Oxford University Press. p. 10. 1969.

Pinto, Anibal and Armando Di Filippo. "Notes on income distribution and redistribution strategy in Latin America." In: Foxley, 1976. *op. cit.*

Prebisch, Raul. *The Economic Development of Latin America and its Principal Problems*. New York. United Nations. 1950.

——_*Transformacion y desarrollo La Gran Tarea de America Latina*. Washington: BID (Mayo), 1970.

Quijano, Anibal, *Notas sobre el concepto de marginalidad social*. Santiago, Chile: CEPAL Division de Asuntos Sociales. 1966.

——_"Tendencies in Peruvian Development and Class Structure." In: James Petras and Maurice Zeitlin, eds., *Latin America: Reform or Revolution*. New York: Fawcett. 1968.

Quijano, Anibal with Francisco Weffort. See Weffort. 1973. *op cit.*

Robinson, D.J. "The city as a centre of change in modern Venezuela." In: *Cities in a Changing Latin America*. Latin American Publication Fund, Sussex, England. 1969.

Rostow, Walt Whitman. *The Stages of Economic Growth. A Non-Communist Manifesto*. London: Cambridge University Press. 1962.

Sunkel, Osvaldo. "National development policy and external dependence in Latin America." *Journal of Development Studies*. Vol. 6, No. 1. 1969.

——_and P. Paz, *El Subdesarrollo Latinoamericao y la Teoria del Desarrollo*. Mexico: Siglo XXI Editores. 1970.

——_"Capitalismo transnacional y desintegracion nacional." *El Trimestre Economico*, April-June. 1971.

Tancer, Shoshana B. *Economic Nationalism in Latin America; The Quest for Economic Independence*. New York, Washington, London: Praeger. 1976.

United Nations, Department of Economic and Social Affairs. *Multinational Corporations in World Development* (ST/ECA/190). 1973.

United States House of Representatives, 94th Congress. *Illegal Aliens*. Hearings, Subcommittee on Immigration. Citizenship and International Law of the Committee of the Judiciary. Washington, D.C.: U.S. Government Printing Office. 1975.

Weffort, Francisco, and Anibal Quijano. *Populismo, Marginalizacion y Dependencia*. Costa Rics: Editorial Universitaria Centroamericana, EDUCA. 1973.

Wyndham-White, Eric, Bela Balassa, et al. *La Integracion lationamericana en una etapa de decisiones*. Buenos Aires: BID/INTAL. 1973.

Winnie, William W. *Latin American Development* (Latin American Studies No. 8). Los Angeles: UCLA. 1967.

Index

Index

DUE DATE